Vassar
The Remarkable Growth
of a Man and His College
1855-1865

By Edward R. Linner

Edited by Elizabeth A. Daniels

Vassar College
Poughkeepsie, New York

Published with the generous assistance of the Lucy Maynard
Salmon Fund for Research.

Published by the Vassar College Publications Department,
Poughkeepsie, New York.

Library of Congress Cataloging in Publications Data.

Linner, Edward R.
Vassar: The Remarkable Growth of a Man and His College 1855-1865
Includes index.

84-050158

ISBN - 0-916663-00-0

Printing by Hamilton Reproductions Inc., Poughkeepsie, New York.

Binding by Hamilton Printing, Greenbush, New York.

Typography by Bauer Typography, Beacon, New York.

Book and jacket designed by Ben Rayfield, Vassar College Publications Manager.

To Celestia

CONTENTS

Author's Preface

Very little has been written of the history of Vassar College or its founder in over sixty years. James Monroe Taylor's rather comprehensive study, *Before Vassar Opened*, was published in 1914. To some extent, Taylor depended upon and quoted from the Jewett manuscript, *Origin of Vassar College* (1879). He also used excerpts from letters of the period available at the time. Elizabeth Hazelton Haight, in her edition of the autobiography and letters of Vassar, published at about the same time, edited portions of Matthew Vassar's incomplete autobiography and some of the more interesting notations from his diary. Her selection of letters, however, gives but one side of a very interesting correspondence.

The present study is intended to show how Vassar's education through early reading was enlarged in later years by contact with people whose experience had been totally different from his own. His personal library and his contact with some of the best minds of the early nineteenth century prepared him in part for the great work that lay before him in the decade 1855-1865. Meetings with his fellow townsmen in his oyster house, his visits to Wilson's bookshop, and his activity in town and county affairs were also of significant value. His education in those last years of his life, however, was undertaken in every waking hour.

The difficulty which had to be faced in the research for this book was that the Vassar letters and papers are by no means complete. Although in a great many instances only Vassar's side of a given correspondence remains, his dealings with the college's first president, Milo P. Jewett, as well as with other close advisers—Charles A. Raymond, Sarah Josepha Hale, and Elias Lyman Magoon— can be fully followed. In these cases, a more or less complete correspondence relates to major events in the early history of Vassar College and deals with important aspects of its development over the years 1855-1865.

The story told here of the decade of discussion and decision-making encompassing the development of Vassar College relies largely upon documentary evidence.

—Edward R. Linner

Editor's Note

Matthew Vassar knew that he wanted to leave a monument to posterity. Having amassed a small fortune in Poughkeepsie as a self-made man in the 1840s, he returned for a visit to England, from which his family had emigrated in 1796 when he was four years old. During his visit he traced his roots to Guy's Hospital in Southwark, London, where on a memorial tablet to Sir Thomas Guy, his ancestor, he read: "It is peculiar to this beneficent Man to have persevered during a long course of prosperous industry in pouring forth to the wants of Others all that he had earned by labour or withheld from self-indulgence." In his diary Vassar states that the idea of devoting a portion of his estate to some charitable purpose was conceived at this moment. Edward Linner's work is a study of how that general unfocused desire gave birth to the reality of Vassar College in Vassar's lifetime.

This study does not attempt to place the college precisely in a history of higher education in the United States. It has very little to say about the college after it actually opened its doors. Rather, it deals with the influences at work on Vassar, a man of great common sense but little learning, as he set out to accomplish his purposes. The book shows Vassar in the last ten years of his life as he responded to the multiple maneuverings of other individuals. Slowly and cautiously learning from his own experience, he created the college.

Edward Linner died before he had a chance to see this book through publication. After he retired from the faculty of Vassar College, where he taught chemistry from 1934 to 1965, he decided to explore the life of Matthew Vassar as it bore on the origins of the college. During the course of his research, he unearthed many materials not previously scrutinized by scholars.

He wished to acknowledge his gratitude to the Vassar College library for permission to quote extensively from archival materials in the Francis Fitz Randolph Rare Book Room of the Lockwood Library. He wished especially to thank Miss Frances Goudy, the librarian in charge of the collection at that time, and Miss Eleanor Rogers, secretary, for their generous assistance in his research. Miss Goudy found many sources of information for him and discussed problems. The Adriance Memorial Library of Poughkeepsie, New York, and the libraries of Dartmouth College and the University of Rochester furnished needed copies of letters and manuscripts. The *Vassar Quarterly* gave permission to quote from its pages. The Nantucket Press permitted quotation from Helen Wright's book, *Sweeper in the Sky, The Life of Maria Mitchell,* and the University of Chicago Press permitted quotation from *The Journal of Benjamin Moran,* edited by Sarah A. Wallace and Frances E. Gillespie (Chicago, 1948).

x

The original spellings and punctuation have been preserved in the materials drawn from manuscripts. Matthew Vassar had a fine sense of language but often misspelled words.

In its final stages, the book was edited by Elizabeth Adams Daniels, Professor of English on the Helen D. Lockwood Chair, who often discussed Vassar history with Edward Linner before he died. The book probably would not have been published without the very able assistance of Geraldine Herron, editorial assistant in the Press and Information Office of Vassar College, who copy-edited the book and also gave a great deal of valuable advice to the editor; the same is true of Ben Rayfield, publications manager at Vassar College, who designed the book and saw to its publication. Others were extremely helpful in the enterprise. Bonnie Jean Bastow '84 assisted in the selection of photographs from the college's Special Collections Library, in the compilation of the index, and in innumerable other ways. Lisa Browar, curator of rare books and manuscripts, and Nancy S. Mackechnie, assistant curator, made rechecking manuscript materials more pleasant. Sally Mills, curator of the Vassar College Art Gallery, thoughtfully read the manuscript and made some suggestions, as did Janet Linner Townsend. Dixie M. Sheridan, assistant to the president and press secretary, has been most cordial in her assistance in this project, as have been Beth Darlington, Anthony Wohl, Clyde Griffen, and Michael Murray, professors at Vassar College. Judith Appelbaum generously offered advice about publication.

The publication of this book has been subsidized by a grant from the Lucy Maynard Salmon Fund of Vassar College. President Virginia B. Smith added to the subsidy from funds at her disposal.

The publication of this book by Vassar College anticipates the approach of the one hundred and twenty-fifth anniversary, in 1986, of the founding of the college in 1861.

—Elizabeth A. Daniels

CHRONOLOGY

29 April 1792   Matthew Vassar was born in East Dereham, parish of Tuddingham, Norfolk, England, the son of Ann Bennett and James Vassar. .

October 1796   The James Vassar family emigrated to the United States for reasons of religious dissent.

1797   The family settled in Dutchess County, on a farm on Wappingers Creek near Poughkeepsie, New York.

1801   James Vassar moved to Poughkeepsie and built a brewery.

1808   The day before Matthew was to be apprenticed to a tanner when he was fifteen years old, he ran away to Balm-town near Newburgh. Three years later he returned to Poughkeepsie and took over the bookkeeping for his father's brewery.

1811   The brewery burned and Matthew's brother died of smoke inhalation. James retired, and Matthew started his own brewery.

1812   Vassar opened an oyster saloon in the basement of the County Court House. He sold his beer by day.

1813   Matthew Vassar was married to Catharine Valentine and built a brewery on Vassar and Bridge streets in Poughkeepsie.

1819   Vassar was elected a trustee of the village of Poughkeepsie.

1824   Vassar was elected recording secretary of the Dutchess County Colonization Society for "colonizing the free people of colour, of the United States, with their consent and choice."

1829   Matthew Vassar became a partner with Matthew Vassar Jr. and John Guy Vassar in Vassar & Co. Brewery.

1831   Matthew Vassar was one of the incorporators of the Poughkeepsie Savings Bank and later became president of the Farmers and Manufacturers National Bank, chartered in 1834.

1832   Matthew Vassar was one of the subscribers to the Poughkeepsie Whaling Company and also a director.

1835   Matthew Vassar was elected president of the village of Poughkeepsie.

1836   A new set of buildings now housed the Vassar Brewery on the river front.

1837   Lydia Booth, Vassar's niece by marriage, moved her female seminary from Fredericksburg, Virginia, to Poughkeepsie. The school was known as the Cottage Hill Seminary. Matthew Vassar became interested in women's education through this niece.

1842 Vassar was elected president of the Hudson River Railroad.

1844 Vassar and his wife sailed to Europe on the *Northumberland.*

1852 Matthew Vassar was president of the Poughkeepsie Lyceum of Literature, Science and the Mechanic Arts and invited Ralph Waldo Emerson to speak.

1855 Milo P. Jewett purchased the Cottage Hill Seminary from Matthew Vassar, whose niece, Lydia Booth, had died. Shortly thereafter Jewett suggested the idea of the college to Matthew Vassar.

—Based on Dorothy A. Plum and
George B. Dowell, eds.,
The Great Experiment, A Chronicle of Vassar,
Vassar College, 1961, pp. 3-6.

. . .Gentlemen, this enterprise, which I regard as the last great work of my life, I commit to you as a sacred trust, which I feel assured you will discharge with fidelity and uprightness, with wisdom and prudence, with ability and energy.

It is my fervent desire that I may live to see the Institution in successful operation; and if God shall give me life and strength, I shall gladly employ my best faculties in co-operating with you, to secure the full and perfect consummation of the work before us.

—Matthew Vassar in his speech
at the first meeting of the
board of trustees of Vassar
College, 26 February 1861

Matthew Vassar, painted by Charles L. Elliott "as the founder of a great public charity, to associate the man with the noblest labor that crowns his life."

Introduction
The Community as Academy

The only description of Matthew Vassar's appearance in the 1860s was given by Benson J. Lossing,[a] who wrote of him:

> In person he is a little less than medium height, well proportioned, and compactly built. He has a fair complexion, with lingerings of the ruddiness of good health upon his cheeks. The brown hair of his earlier days is much outmeasured by the whiter crown of age. His dark gray eyes beam with the luster of vigorous middle life and the radiance of inextinguishable good-humor. His nose is of the Roman type and firmly set, and the general expression of his face is pleasant to friends and strangers; for upon his countenance, whether in action or in repose, is seen the perpetual sunshine of a gentle, cheerful nature; while his voice, low and flexible, is always musical with kindly cadences.[1]

One may say that since the executive committee of the trustees of Vassar College had commissioned Lossing to write this book, *Vassar College and Its Founder*, he must of necessity present this favorable description with which the volume opens. But Lossing was a man of independence and would have felt no compulsion to write a description that did not represent the man.

In fact, these words in a sense might be said to characterize the face in a portrait of Vassar painted by James Henry Wright in 1861. There are many points of resemblance between them. In the portrait, the face is unsmiling, but benign; the lips denote a firmness of purpose; the nose is well shaped and "of the Roman type and firmly set." Wright seemed to have caught the essence of the man, for the critic of the *Poughkeepsie Telegraph* of 12 November 1861 wrote of this portrait: "[Mr. Wright's work] shows unusual maturity and thoughtfulness. [The portrait] is Mr. Vassar as his friends know him, and daily meet him." This reviewer proceeded to compare the Wright portrait with one by Charles L. Elliott, completed about the same time, which represents Vassar as "the founder of a great public charity—to associate the man with the noblest labor that crowns his life."[2] In other words, here in Elliott's work Matthew Vassar is pictured in a special role—a role that he was to assume in his last years, while Wright represented him as Lossing had described him—an ordinary, everyday person.

1

Matthew Vassar, in 1861, painted by James Henry Wright. "Vassar as his friends daily meet him."

Milo P. Jewett found him to be just such a person. He was easy to talk with and proved to be approachable from their very first meeting. Jewett began to expound his theories of the responsibility of the rich man to society, but Vassar hardly needed such instruction for, from 1840, the question of how to put his fortune to some worthwhile purpose was ever present with him. Any such discussion was just an extension and clarification of his ideas. How many schemes he had considered and discarded from 1840 to 1855 cannot be set down with any exactness. Actually, in reading his letters and manuscripts, one can find but two—the founding of a great community hospital and the building and endowing of a college for women. Others, such as the financing of a hospital for the insane, were not admitted by him, but were in each instance attributed to him. The idea of founding and endowing a college was not one to be entered upon impulsively and without much thought, and it cannot be known with any certainty how deeply Vassar was prepared to go into his fortune in endowing it and seeing it in operation.

He asked only for a suitable memorial to perpetuate the family name. All of Jewett's flattery and coaxing meant nothing, for the founder was seeking a use of his fortune that would make the Vassar name respected for generations to come—respected because he had established a great thing. It was to be the endowment of a college for women, and once he saw its merits clearly, nothing was to stop him. He realized that when he turned over half of his fortune to a board of trustees, in which he must have great faith, he and they would see his plan accomplished. No matter what was said of him or what others thought of him, he would be steadfast. He had put his hand to the plow and there was to be no turning back.

To one whose mind had been trained in the business of running a brewery and in the wise investment of money, it must have been pure joy to work in so alien a field. It was no surprise to him to learn that building a college was not just a matter of bricks and mortar, because his service on the board of trustees of the University of Rochester from 1853 prepared him for the interesting reports that were to come from various trustee committees of his own college. They were to reveal much of the inner workings of a college. Once started, the discussion and the planning would go on without disturbing this one central thing—Matthew Vassar's education as to what a college really was and what steps must be taken to accomplish its establishment. How conscious he was of what was happening to him is hard to estimate, but his communications with his trustees make clear that from meeting to meeting, his understanding was deepening. His letters during this period bear witness to it, too. The founding and building of Vassar College was surely a "grand enterprise" and for Matthew Vassar, a great adventure.

Milo Jewett could not have failed to recognize quite early in their friendship Vassar's strength and understanding. The qualities he pos-

OUR CRADLE

Matthew Vassar's "cradle" was a brewery on the Hudson River in Poughkeepsie. Vassar Brewery built these particular buildings in 1836.

sessed could belong only to one who had done more with life than amass a modest fortune. Vassar was one of that large body of nineteenth-century men who received few, if any, opportunities for a formal education. Yet, like others of them, he so lived his life that he became a broadly educated man. The community in which he lived was to take the place of an academy. The time he devoted to reading and to studying what he had read would shape his thinking and his reactions to life about him.

•

The local press of the day is a mine of information of everyday life in Poughkeepsie in the nineteenth century. The pages of the *Poughkeepsie Journal*, the *Poughkeepsie Journal and Eagle*, and its successor the *Poughkeepsie Eagle*, reported much of Vassar's activity in the town, beginning in March 1813 with an announcement of his marriage to Catharine Valentine of Fishkill, New York. Eleven years later at the age of thirty-two, Vassar was a village trustee,[b] a notable post. This position was of sufficient importance to give him a place with sixty-four of his townsmen at breakfast with the Marquis de Lafayette, who visited Poughkeepsie on his triumphant tour of the United States in 1824. In the 1830s, news items show that Vassar had been elected to the boards of three banks and on one of these, he served for two terms as president. His name appeared on the rolls of those concerned with the development of a fine town that was already expanding eastward. He was president of the Improvement Society—a group of worthy citizens who met to formulate plans which, when carried out, would improve the quality of life by laying sidewalks, adequately lighting the streets, planting trees, and in general making this small town a gracious and beautiful place in which to live. Very early he was in the forefront of a movement to bring the railroad through Poughkeepsie. A press notice of the opening of the Hudson River Railroad,[c] which Vassar did much to promote, and to which he subscribed $10,000, tells how he acted as chief conductor of a starting train on the new tracks along the Hudson River. He contributed half of the sum required to build the Baptist church on Lafayette Place, a block from his own residence. His gifts to the Baptist society were many, though he had no formal affiliation with it.

Even in the cultural activities of Poughkeepsie, Matthew Vassar took his place. He was on the boards of most of the educational institutions of the town, among them the Dutchess County Academy. He was appointed to the examining committee of the local grammar school. At one meeting of parents, he exhorted them to visit the school and take some active interest in the educational programs open to their sons and daughters. His involvement in the Poughkeepsie Lyceum of Literature and the Mechanical Arts began in 1847. He served as its president on numerous occasions in the years that followed, making a much-commented upon opening address for the year 1852/53. He took an interest in the cemetery movement, buying a farm south of Poughkeepsie to offer as cemetery land. It later was developed as Springside.

One can be less certain of Vassar's experience in the arts. Poughkeepsie, as the center of the cultural life of the Hudson Valley, boasted of a theater where at one time Fanny Kemble[d] appeared and received an ovation. There is no way of knowing whether Vassar enjoyed the theater or whether he had some religious scruples against it. It has been said, however, that he was the first person to improve the quality of church music in the community by furnishing funds to support a vocal quartet in the local Baptist church, the first church in the town to initiate this practice. Vassar had admired the music in churches of New York and Philadelphia and decided that the musical part of the service of the small church on Lafayette Place would benefit by the adoption of such an idea. Vassar's knowledge and critical understanding of painting, sculpture, and architecture were rudimentary; he admitted the fact freely. In this connection, Lossing related an interesting story in his history of Vassar and his college. It seemed that Vassar purchased several small statues which he saw and admired when he was traveling in Italy in the 1840s. After he had paid for them and arranged for their shipment, he had some second thoughts. He decided that his modest home in Poughkeepsie was hardly an appropriate place for displaying such works of art. He did not want his friends and neighbors to regard him as displaying his wealth ostentatiously. So wrote

Lossing, "He left them in Italy."[3] (Later, however, he had them installed at Springside, a less modest place than the house in town.)

Possibly, one of the great influences on Vassar was the reading that he did over the years. A part of his library remains, but what ideas he may have gleaned in the course of his reading cannot be ascertained. Though each book bears his signature or a facsimile of it, there are no other marginalia or underlinings in the text, which makes it impossible to know his thoughts on what he had read.

One may be sure that Matthew Vasssar did not use these books just to fill his library shelves, however, for comments in a few of his letters indicate that he had perused at least some of them. In a letter to Professor Edward Youmans in 1861, he wrote:

> Some weeks since when you were in our City and at my house I personally made my thanks to you for those books and wished to know the price &c, you earnestly replied that if I would read the first chapter in "Education" headed "What knowledge is of most worth," you would be compensated. Taking you at your word, I am entitled to withhold my thanks even, for I have read the *whole book*, thereby more the cancelling of that debt...The views and sentiments therein inculcated are plain demonstrative practical ones, such that any common sense mind might adopt, and just the ones most needed at the present time to counteract the pernicious degenerating principles that are being instilled in the minds of the rising generations of both sexes, dignified by the name of Education.[4]

The book was Herbert Spencer's *Education: Intellectual, Moral and Physical.*

John H. Raymond, the second president of Vassar College, became an intimate friend of Vassar, and a year after Vassar's death in 1868 wrote an excellent biographical sketch of him as a part of a report to the Regents of New York State. A small portion of it reads as follows:

> [Mr. Vassar] had the confidence of his fellow townsmen and received many marks of the esteem in which he was held. Though denied early advantages of education, he neglected no opportunity which subsequent life afforded him. His thirst for knowledge was insatiable. He was particularly interested in studying the practical application of science to useful arts and became familiar with the works of Pope, Young, Cowper and other poets who were the delight of his contemporaries. Throughout his life he was a devoted reader and intelligent student of the Bible. By such means he fitted himself to enjoy the society of intelligent and cultivated men, and acquired, not only a wide range of ideas but no mean power of expression both by tongue and pen.[5]

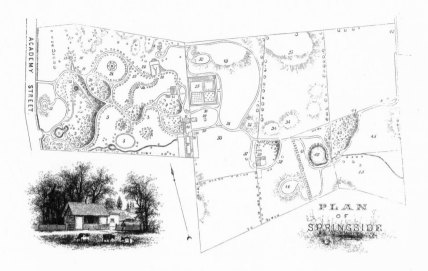

A design of Springside, Matthew Vassar's country estate, south of Poughkeepsie. The site of Springside still in 1984 shows many evidences of Downing's original design.

This is the opinion of a man who knew and enjoyed a close friendship with Vassar in the last years of his life. Raymond's reference to Vassar's wide reading is borne out by a study of the titles of books in Vassar's personal library, a portion of which is preserved in the Vassariana materials in Special Collections.

If the volumes from his library which have survived are representative, it would seem that Vassar's taste in reading was rather catholic. An early report of the librarian at Vassar College acknowledged the receipt of 405 books—possibly only a portion of Vassar's personal library—purchased from the Vassar estate in 1870. Judging from publication dates, Vassar must have started purchasing books for his library early in his career and have continued to add to it up to the time of his death. About 20 percent of the extant collection includes federal reports and documents, and reference books of one sort or another. Well over two-thirds of the remainder are in the fields of history, literature, religion, and travel, with the rest distributed among political science, domestic architecture and gardening, and natural science—in that order. Any classification leaves much to be desired. Where, for instance, does one put a directory of a cemetery or books on temperance, like the *Drunkard's Doom*? Yet these are important, for they had a bearing on Vassar's interests at some point in his career. This is true of many of the books that found their way into the collection. A number of them on travel, architecture, the planning of gardens on rather a grand scale, and the care of horses and cattle were added in the 1840s, the years of the Vassars' European travel. At the end of that decade, Vassar acquired and began to develop his beautiful estate, Springside.

•

Even this brief review of the nature of Vassar's collection would not be complete without recognizing some of the local writers whose books were included in it. At the same time, it is necessary to draw attention to the bookshop located on Main Street in Poughkeepsie. It was in many ways a center of the intellectual life of the village and but a short distance from Vassar's town house.

In the period roughly between 1820 and 1860 when Vassar was interested in it, the shop had two proprietors. The first, Paraclete Potter, was an energetic man involved in practically every aspect of Poughkeepsie life. He played a part in many civic projects. His business enterprises were widespread and included among them a partnership with Vassar in the Poughkeepsie Whaling Company. He was the editor of the local paper and, of course, was the proprietor of the Potter Book Store until 1841 when he sold it along with his other interests and migrated to Wisconsin, where he lived for the rest of his life.

William Wilson, his successor in the book business, was a Scotsman, born in the village of Crieff. He was a man of parts. He loved music and did some composing. His early poetry and essays appeared in reviews and journals in Scotland. In Edinburgh where he lived just before coming to America, he had a literary reputation and had many friends with interests like his own. Among them were the encyclopedists, Robert and William Chambers. William Wilson migrated to the United States in 1830 where he continued his literary endeavors by editing and writing. He acquired the bookshop in 1841 and was actively associated with it until his retirement in 1860.

The shop was a popular gathering place, a village institution and "a sort of club where all those fond of literature and of discussion were wont to gather." In early records, the location of other places of business was made with reference to it—for instance, "Adriance & Co., clock and watch makers five doors east of Potter's book store."[6] One can imagine Vassar walking those few blocks from his house to the shop for an evening of discussion of local and national politics and the economic conditions of the day, topics that were of interest to him. While there he met the town worthies and any interesting visitors who happened to be in town at the time. William Chambers, Wilson's friend of Edinburgh days, was one of these. Vassar met Chambers in the Wilson bookstore for he claimed "the honor of a short acquaintance as well as of some correspondence" with him.[7]

Of local men of letters, Benson J. Lossing, who was to edit Wilson's poetry after the latter's death in 1869, Rufus Babcock,[e] and Samuel F. B. Morse[f]—all of whom were members of Vassar's first board of trustees—would have been among those who had a part in the sessions at the Wilson

Main Street, Poughkeepsie, in 1850

shop. Certainly, such interesting characters as Andrew Jackson Davis, "the seer of Poughkeepsie" and Andrew Jackson Downing from Newburgh, across the river, joined in the discussions there. Even Henry Wheeler Shaw, the creator of *Josh Billings* and another resident of the town, would hardly have missed such an evening's entertainment.

Of the literary visitors, perhaps the most interesting was Andrew Jackson Davis, who wrote *The Great Harmonia* in 1851. Davis added to the title "being a philosophical revelation of the natural, spiritual and celestial universe." In the town, Davis had a reputation as a clairvoyant and spiritualist. He was supposed to have written his book while in a trance. During his residence in Poughkeepsie, he became the chief proponent for spiritualism and drew about him some prominent citizens. He left Poughkeepsie as a relatively young man.

The native Lossing was a prolific writer, particularly on historical subjects. His studies of the Revolution were illustrated with his own woodcuts. In the sixties and later, he turned his attention to the Civil War. Perhaps his most enduring work is *The Hudson from the Wilderness to the Sea*, a fine study of the river, charmingly illustrated with his original sketches. Babcock, who lived in Poughkeepsie at two different times, was responsible for a *Memoir of John Mason Peck, D.D., Forty Years of Pioneer Life*, a history of John Peck, who lived in nearby Amenia and in later life was a missionary to the frontier country, which at mid-century included Illinois and Missouri. Of course, there are those charming books of Andrew Jackson Downing,

Matthew Vassar, leading citizen of the village of Poughkeepsie; founder of Vassar College; a product of his age

who did so much for the domestic architecture and the art of estate planning in the Hudson Valley in the 1840s and 1850s. His early death in 1852 was a tragedy.[g]

It is surprising to find that so many of the men who wrote the books represented in Matthew Vassar's collection were like him in that they had little formal education. Their ideas, developed over years of observation, reading, study, and contemplation, were well stated, for they had an uncanny ability to write about their findings and the conclusions reached from them. There is plenty of evidence, too, that these men were adaptable, that they could do more than one thing well. In many ways, Vassar resembled them. He was a product of his age. Books written by such men formed the backbone of Vassar's library and over the years, formed the basis of his education. His active business life, his part in community affairs of both town and county did not entirely fill his days, for the books in his library indicate that he still had time to consider the controversies of his day, to enjoy the study of history and science, to read poems, to make Springside the place of beauty that it became, to prepare for days of relaxation and travel and, last but not least, to enable him to hold his own with people that he approached with some diffidence in explaining, putting forward, and perfecting such an important project as his college.

Chapter I

Vassar and Jewett

Without Milo P. Jewett, there would have been no Vassar College.

Chapter I

In the *New York World Record* of the spring of 1855, there appeared an advertisement for the sale of the Cottage Hill Seminary in Poughkeepsie, New York. It attracted the attention of Milo P. Jewett, who wished to purchase a school for young ladies. This seminary was the property of Matthew Vassar. He did not supervise the education of the young women who attended it, but left that to his niece, Lydia Booth. Some years later, he explained how he had become involved in this project: "About this period [1845]," he wrote, "took quite an interest in a Niece of mine Lydia Booth who was then engaged in a small way in the tuition of Children resulting in after years in the opening of a female Seminary in Po'keepsie, being the first of its kind excepting one other Mrs. Conger in the Village. The force of circumstances brought me occasionaly in buisiness entercourse with my Niece."[1]

Vassar was interested in Lydia Booth and what she was doing, but at her death in November 1854 his personal concern with the seminary was gone and he decided to sell it. Jewett became interested and prudently inquired about the general situation of Rufus Babcock, who had been the minister of the Baptist church in Poughkeepsie in the mid-1820s and knew Vassar. Babcock advised him that the seminary was of the "Baptist School of Poughkeepsie." Later Jewett wrote some details of the transaction: "When I opened negotiations for purchasing Cottage Hill, Dr Babcock urged on Mr. Vassar the advantages that would accrue to the Baptist Cause in Po'keepsie and in the State, should I become the purchaser. The property was held at $10,000—but influenced by the representations alluded to, Mr. Vassar offered a bonus of $2000. The result was, on the 12th day of July 1855, I left Alabama with my family for Po'keepsie.... Such were the circumstances under which I first met Mr Vassar."[2]

This new owner of the Cottage Hill Seminary was no ordinary schoolmaster. A New Englander, born in 1808, he had a broad education. After attending the academy in Bradford, Vermont, he entered Dartmouth College and graduated with a Bachelor of Arts degree in 1828. A year spent in teaching in an academy at Plymouth, New Hampshire, gave him an opportunity to read law in the office of Josiah Quincy. In 1829, he entered Andover Theological Seminary to prepare for the Congregational ministry. But, because of his appointment in 1833 to the first faculty of Marietta College in Ohio, an institution sponsored by the Presbyterian church, he thought it best to go there as a Presbyterian. So he proceeded to receive his license to preach from the presbytery of Newburyport, Massachusetts.

Jewett spent four happy years at Marietta and his resignation of his chair at the end of this period shows how fine the lines of sectarianism were drawn. "After a year and a half of painful conflict between the prejudices of early education," he wrote, "the attractions of an honorable position and of the happiest associations with my colleagues on the one hand, and my convictions of truth and duty on the other, I yielded all and in June 1838 was baptized into the fellowship of the Baptist Church. . . . Having been appointed to my Professorship as a Presbyterian, I felt bound in honor to resign my place."[3]

Within six months, he was in Marion, Alabama, where he opened a school for young ladies. This institution was adopted by the southern Baptists and it was assigned the name Judson Female Institution in honor of a famous Baptist missionary to Burma in the early years of the century. (It still exists today as a college for young women.) During his years at Judson Institution, Jewett wrote many religious pamphlets and papers, and traveled extensively through the South, publicizing his institution. The sixteen years that he spent in Marion were happy and successful, but in 1854 he decided for some undisclosed reason to abandon it all and to return north. And so he came to Poughkeepsie, met Matthew Vassar, and soon became his close, intimate friend and adviser for the next ten years.

Vassar was sixty-three at the time of their first meeting. Though he had retired from active participation in business, there were still details requiring his attention and he was, as he always had been, active in local and state affairs. His health was not good, he suffered days of indisposition when he complained of his "poor head." Apparently, he was subject to slight strokes which never completely incapacitated him but distressed him and, more often than not, demanded his complete rest for several days. This state of affairs did not seem to worry him unduly, but it made him quite aware of his frailty. How often he prefaced his remarks to the trustees in later years with some reference to the passing of time and the "gracious providence" that permitted him and them to meet together once more. So it was that more often than before his thoughts turned to the consideration of plans "to apply a large portion of [his] estate to some benevolent object."[4]

Yet as early as 1840, as a relatively young man, Vassar had been considering fitting ways of spending his ever accumulating fortune. He had no children and apparently felt no obligations to his nephews whom he had started on successful careers in the brewing business. Ideas of possible philanthropic causes were considered and discarded. Surely one of them was suggested tentatively by Lydia Booth—the possibility of doing something for the higher education of women. Vassar himself in addressing the board of trustees on 23 February 1864 admitted that his

> interest on the subject of female education was awakened not less than twenty years ago by an intimate female friend and relative, now deceased, who conducted a seminary of long standing and character in this City. That close intimacy and interest continued many years, until just before the institution passed into the hands of our President [Jewett]. It was this fact, more than any other, and more than all others, that awakened me early to the *possibility* and *necessity* of an institution like the one we now propose.[5]

There was no grand design, however, and no questions were raised as to what must be done and how to proceed to meet the needs of such an institution. The idea was relegated to the back of his mind from which it was brought back by Jewett and developed into a magnificent reality.

Between the years 1840 and 1855, there undoubtedly were other plans and designs too for using his entire fortune. Vassar concluded, after his trip abroad, that of them all, the one that would be of the most use to mankind and perpetuate the Vassar name was a hospital, endowed and built to serve the larger community of which Poughkeepsie was the center. It was to be financed by the combined resources of himself and his two nephews, Matthew Vassar Jr. and John Guy Vassar. The project had great appeal and had been suggested by a visit to Sir Thomas Guy's hospital in London. It went back to 1845 when he and his wife, Catharine, with Cyrus Swan, his lawyer and secretary, were on a grand tour of the European continent and the British Isles. During their stay in London, he inspected the great hospital on the south bank of the Thames and was impressed by the magnitude of the gift that had made it possible. He was so highly pleased with the general plan and arrangement of the hospital that he had drawings made of the structure. But what was of great appeal in this philanthropic endeavor of Sir Thomas Guy, with whom Vassar claimed a distant family connection, was that he built it during his lifetime. Vassar was struck by the fact that his British relative had watched the progress of the building of his hospital and that he had lived long enough to see it ready to receive patients. So Vassar conferred with his nephews and laid plans for the use of his considerable fortune. In all their discussions about building a hospital, one wish was forgotten—he would not see the hospital completed in his lifetime for it was to be begun at the death of the last survivor of the three Vassars.

It was at this point that Jewett entered Vassar's life, and it was he who changed everything and brought Vassar College into being. There grew between these two men a friendship that developed into an intimacy which made possible a free exchange of ideas and confidences. Jewett admired Vassar, although his deliberateness and caution sometimes irked him exceedingly. Twenty-five years later, he wrote of him:

These transactions [involving the purchase of the Cottage Hill School] brought me into intimate social and personal relations with him. . . . He was regarded as the wealthiest man in Po'keepsie, and was well known in that part of the Empire State as a shrewd, energetic, and successful business man. Without the advantages of early education, he had learned much by contact with others who had enjoyed greater advantages, and had a breadth of view seldom found among persons whose early life imposed so many disabilities. Possessing a genial, kindly nature he enjoyed the society of his friends, and talked fluently and sensibly upon the topics of the times.[6]

Within a year, Vassar thought highly enough of Jewett to try him out on some of his special friends. There are two letters among the Vassar correspondence of the mid-1850s that bear on the subject, both of them to Martin B. Anderson,[a] president of the University of Rochester. Matthew Vassar, as a trustee of this institution, planned to attend the university commencement exercises there. On 2 July 1856, quite early in his friendship with Jewett, he wrote to Anderson: "I will be there on Monday evening next, accompanied with my friend Prof^r M P Jewett of the 'Cottage Hill Seminary.' " The second letter dated a week later stated: "Prof^r Jewett unites in bearing testimony to the very interesting & credible exercises."[7]

When these two new friends were together, their conversations centered on religious and ethical questions and as the friendship ripened, Jewett began to sound out Vassar on his opinions about the proper use to which his wealth might be applied. Vassar made clear that, since he had no direct heir, he was seeking a worthy benefaction to which he might apply his entire fortune. One day in a burst of confidence, he expounded his favorite plan to his friend and explained his wish to create some institution that would be of lasting value to mankind. He told how moved he was by Sir Thomas Guy's impressive gift to the City of London and how intrigued he was that the great philanthropist had lived to watch the construction of the hospital and had seen it ready to receive its first patients. He confided in Jewett the plan that he and his nephews had made to build and endow a great hospital in Poughkeepsie.

According to Jewett's account of the incident, Vassar ended the exposition of this plan by saying, "In making this disposition of my property, I desire to build a monument for myself, to perpetuate my own name, to do something for Po'keepsie where I have made all my money, and to do good to my fellowmen. . . . And now what do you think of my plan?"[8]

Jewett's bluntly expressed response was deflating to say the least. It was given in an uncompromising statement: "It does not strike me favorably. Great Hospitals are for great cities; like London and Paris, New York and New Orleans. To spend two or three millions of dollars in establishing a Hospital in Po'keepsie, not a seaport and a town which can never have over forty or fifty thousand inhabitants, seems to me a very unwise use of money. Indeed, I think you might as well throw it into the Hudson River."[9]

Vassar must have been somewhat taken aback by this attack but, apparently, he took it for what it was worth, though no immediate change of plan was undertaken. The subject of how he might make some other disposition of his property in a way that suited him went on in these sessions in his office. A point was eventually reached when the would-be founder was unhappy and confused with the whole issue. In his dilemma, he gave vent to his feelings and exclaimed with some exasperation and impatience: "I wish somebody would tell me what to do with my money.

It's the plague of my life—keeps me awake o nights—stocks going down, banks breaking, insurance companies failing!"[10]

At last the time had arrived for which Jewett had been waiting. According to his account of the incident, he quickly replied: "Well, Mr. Vassar, for several years past, I have had a scheme in my mind which I am unable to carry out, but it is one which you are abundantly able to execute and which I think will meet all your wishes in the disposal of your property. . . . It is *to build and endow a College for Young Women which shall be to them, what Yale and Harvard are to young men.* There is not an *endowed* College for Young Women in the world. We have plenty of Female Colleges (so called) in this country but they are Colleges only in name—they have no funds, no libraries, cabinets, museums, or apparatus worth mentioning. If you will establish a real College for girls and endow it, you will build a monument for yourself more lasting than the Pyramids; you will perpetuate your name to the latest generations; it will be the pride and glory of Po'keepsie, an honor to the State and a blessing to the world."[11]

This proposal met with some astonishment on Vassar's part, but with enough interest and approval that Jewett added in his history: "*Then and there Vassar College was born.*"[12]

Now these are the reflections and recollections of an older man, for Jewett was seventy-one when he composed the document *Origin of Vassar College* (1879) and set down his remembrances of his dealings with Vassar, a decade or more after these events had taken place. The implication in the reported conversations in the manuscript is that this idea was placed before Vassar without any earlier suggestion or preparation. But Vassar was a keen businessman, not ordinarily given to impulsive action and usually reserving time for the careful consideration of any plan, particularly one that involved the expenditure of large sums of money. To sink his entire fortune in a venture, no matter how grand it seemed, called for serious contemplation. It must be remembered, too, that he had already been gently indoctrinated by his niece. As Maria Mitchell[b] so aptly put it in her diary at the time of Vassar's death in 1868: "The bent in the direction he took was given by a woman. . . . A niece, a teacher in a common school, said to him 'Uncle Matthew, do something for women,' and this chance deed grew into Vassar College."[13]

It wasn't quite this simple, but the astronomer later came to realize, as she grew to know Vassar from his almost daily visits with her and her father in the Observatory, that he was influenced in his thinking by Lydia Booth. She said of him further that his mind was not a decided one and that he took his time to receive an idea, to develop it, and to make it his own. Then and only then did he begin to plan its realization. Vassar's niece planted the seed of an idea, a fact that he conceded often enough, but Jewett fed and watered it. Without him, there would have been no Vassar College. Vassar had a keen mind for details and he was to show Jewett and his associates in carrying out the scheme that he could learn, that he would receive and study plans carefully and knowingly. He adopted acceptable suggestions and adapted them to his grand purpose. He acknowledged readily enough his ignorance of educational planning, but in the years that followed, no man with his keenness of intellect could fail to pick up and enlarge upon those germinating ideas.

Jewett made remarkable progress in these talks with Vassar during the first few months of their acquaintance. Though they became intimate friends in a short time, it still is surprising that Vassar discussed his affairs so openly with Jewett. Vassar had had a large experience with men and affairs, not only in his business dealings, but in his many activities in town and county affairs. Jewett must have impressed him from the beginning, and it is difficult to see just why. A picture of Jewett taken in the late 1850s is not prepossessing. There is little indication in it that here was a man who could move mountains if he so willed. A description of a contemporary gave a first impression of this man that is hardly favorable. In his personal journal, an entry of 23 April 1862, Benjamin Moran[c] recorded: "A tall, stout man. . .whose manners indicated a very slight knowledge of the world, but a very high opinion of himself, has been honoring us and boring us today. His name is M. P. Jewett and his real profession is that of a school master, he being the 'President' not of a republic, but of a young Ladies' seminary at Poughkeepsie, N.Y. President Jewett is about five feet 10 inches high, has a meaningless face and is about fifty years of age."[14] Moran was hardly impressed nor is one who attempts to judge this man's character from his photograph. It is impossible to imagine his face lighting up with enthusiasm for any cause. One can only wonder how he could have moved anyone to do great things. Yet, he did just that! Vassar gave him his confidence and as the months went on, he was to lean upon him more and more.

As these two friends were discussing a variety of religious topics, Jewett was able to bring up the subject which he, as a devotedly religious man, wanted to impress upon Vassar—his responsibility as a man of wealth. This was a problem that had troubled Vassar for at least a decade and that is why his mind was so receptive to a plan of worth that fired his imagination. He believed that he had it solved in the decision to build a hospital, but his behavior betrayed his uncertainty.

In the longer 1879 version of his *Origin of Vassar College*, Jewett claimed that at the time of those discussions he had for several years been nursing a great scheme and took upon himself all the credit for the idea of an endowed woman's college. Yet in an earlier version of the *Origin*, he wrote:

> Discussion respecting the hospital continued for some weeks. . .until I determined to make a suggestion which, in justice to my dear wife, I will here record, originated with her—her kind heart always beating with benevolent impulses. . . .Mr Vassar I think I can suggest a

method of disposing of your property, by which you will confer signal benefits on Poughkeepsie; build a monument for your self more lasting than the Pyramids; become a benefactor of your country & of the world, & greatly honor & glorify God. "What is your plan?" It is that you shall erect and endow a College for the education of young ladies.[15]

Fifteen years separated these two versions. Though the latter did not specify any time limits, it would seem that the idea of a college for women was somewhat new to the Jewetts in 1855, assuming, of course, that they had been recently discussing it together.

Jewett recognized that Vassar as an experienced businessman would proceed with caution in any project involving large expenditures of money. He must see for himself—convince himself that so fine a dream could become a reality. In turn Vassar recognized that, large as his fortune was, the enterprise would be costly. The question was whether his thousands would be enough to build and equip a great college and leave a sum sufficient to endow it adequately. Available funds must be spent with caution,

Milo P. Jewett, the first president of the college

always bearing in mind that they must serve the two purposes. His college must not only be a great one, but it must be a lasting memorial to the Vassar name and benefit coming generations of young women. His imagination ranged far into the future.

Jewett was aware of all these considerations. He agreed with his wealthy friend, but he showed, from time to time, a veiled impatience whenever Vassar hesitated or refused to act until he had assured himself that each step to be taken was sound and moving in the direction he wished. Jewett was in a hurry to realize his dream and refused to understand Vassar's hesitancy and his changes of mind.

This was a venture unlike any Vassar had contemplated in his life. He would build big, but he would build well or not at all. But Jewett's spirits never flagged, his purpose never varied. Though he was busy with the affairs of his Cottage Hill Seminary, he seemed to have plenty of time in the two years, 1855 and 1856, to answer Vassar's questions, to allay his fears and encourage him to embark on a course that would help him to realize his "grand enterprise."

After the two men had talked together, they often wrote notes to one another which help in understanding Vassar's perplexities and Jewett's faith in the rightness of this ambitious project and the feasibility of accomplishing it. The first of such letters, written by Jewett in late October or early November of 1856, was a lengthy summary of arguments that might have been used in one of their meetings. Beginning with a florid statement, "*Mind* is a glorious endowment, and there is no reason why the mind of a female should not be cultivated with unwearied assiduity," it continued in this vein for eleven pages of manuscript.[16] The primary purpose of a college education for women would be to enable them to direct the mental development of the young, either at home or in school. He drove home each point with a fitting example, or learned reference. Jewett estimated that two million children in the United States were without the benefits of an education in their homes or in the grammar schools of this country. "Uneducated," he predicted, "these children will grow up to fill our Jails & penitentiaries, & to burden the honest & industrious with the expense of their pauperism & crime." From these statements, he easily moved on to recognize the increasing role that women as teachers would play in the coming years. He explained:

Altho' these [women] are not to be lawyers, divines & legislators; yet *they are to be* the *wives* & *mothers* of lawyers & ministers, legislators & statesmen; or if never wives & mothers, thousands of them must be the Teachers of our future public men, as well as, of the masses of the people.[17]

What followed was in a similar vein and included existing educational opportunities open to women, a study of trends in women's education, and a recounting of the contributions of those who recognized this need and who were doing something about it. He ended with a fine flourish:

> ...And, now, my dear Mr. Vassar, I will add but a word more. I do not doubt but you will be able to secure the cordial cooperation of your nephews, so far as the incorporation of the necessary provisions into their wills is concerned; but, even if you should not secure, at the present time, the desired pledges, have you not ample resources within your own control, which will enable you, independently of all others, to inaugurate a new era in literature & science, by founding Vassar College? I feel assured you would enjoy a high degree of happiness in directing so blessed a work. Assisted by the grace of God, you have but to *resolve*, and the commencement of this splendid enterprise is secured."[18]

There is no indication in this long letter of what woman's role in the world could be other than that of an educated mother or teacher. He did not picture her as a professor in such a college or as its president, studying its weaknesses and limitations of curriculum and doing something to remedy any existing shortcomings. He made no mention of women in any other role—that of a doctor or missionary, professions which were quite acceptable for women in the mid-nineteenth century. Would he have frowned upon Vassar's graduates of the next ten years, who did not fit into this pattern—such as one who became a prominent psychologist, a second who became the first woman instructor at Massachusetts Institute of Technology, a third who became a chemist in a large drug firm, and a fourth who became the head statistician of an oil company?[19d]

Vassar might have remarked on the severe limitations that Jewett would impose on the activities of women, but the chances are that he missed these references. His mind was occupied with problems associated with the financing of the college. He was to learn later that his friend did not think the educated woman quite capable of accepting a professorship at Vassar College—something that Vassar himself not only desired but much later pleaded for with great eloquence.

Throughout the year 1856, conferences dealt with the practicality of the plan and the approximate initial cost it might involve if it were to be carried out adequately. Jewett indicated that he had corresponded with many eminent educators, making his letters perfectly general, in an attempt to keep the name of the possible donor of such a college quite secret. Most replies yielded enthusiastic comment and acclaim. Vassar had little part in these inquiries, yet he did make independent surveys of his own. As a trustee of a young university, he knew men whom he could count on to be discreet in keeping his secret, among them Anderson, its president.

There were adverse opinions, too, like those of William Chambers. In a letter dated 29 March 1858 he addressed his friend, William Wilson, the Poughkeepsie book dealer. Chambers intended it for Vassar's personal attention. It showed open disapproval of the establishment of so large a college as was envisaged. Four years later in a letter to his friend, S. Austin Allibone,[20] an author, bibliographer, and librarian, Vassar referred to this letter in a sardonic, amused tone. At any rate, the results of all such correspondence were helpful and gave both gentlemen renewed confidence in the soundness of the proposal. Vassar was particularly reassured in spite of negative opinions like those of Chambers.

It is interesting that Vassar agreed to such a program of letter-writing even though there was no statement that revealed his intentions. Jewett claimed that Vassar wished to keep the matter from public knowledge in those early months of planning and study until a comprehensive, workable scheme had been evolved. "He conferred with no one but myself respecting it," Jewett wrote years later.[21] Vassar, however, was not to be pushed into making any fast commitments; he would preserve his freedom of action. After all, this was not an ordinary business transaction that one could settle in a few days or weeks. It was a large project that eventually was to absorb his entire fortune. He had to be sure that in founding a college, he was accomplishing something of lasting benefit to women and through them to his country and the world. It must be something that would continue to grow and add luster to the Vassar name in years to come. Under such circumstances , it was difficult to imagine him conferring with only one adviser on a plan that involved so much, particularly since he had known this man for such a short time. How unnatural it would have been had he not turned to tried and true friends to whom he had often gone for advice. As a matter of course, he would have conferred with his nephews and close business associates: Matthew Vassar Jr. and his brother, John Guy Vassar; Cyrus Swan; Cornelius DuBois, his banker and financial adviser; Charles W. Swift, a business associate. Then there was Anderson, who had a fund of firsthand knowledge about building and financing a college. He could hardly have failed to seek the advice of these men at such a crucial time.

Why Jewett thought he was the sole counselor is difficult to understand for he admitted readily enough "How quickly [Vassar] brought forward the popular objections against higher education for women: objections, some of which originated in his own mind accustomed carefully to weigh considerations on both sides of questions involving the expenditure of money. Other objections were suggested to him by his heirs and their confidential adviser, with the view of diverting him from his purpose."[22] Jewett was to become increasingly impatient with those who were in Vassar 's confidence, particularly those who did not support him in every detail. Most of his anger was directed against the two nephews, especially Matthew Vassar Jr. So strong was his feeling against them that he devoted considerable space in his *Origin of Vassar College* (1879) to explaining their perfidy. Even in the earlier version, he mentioned no names but complained: "The efforts made to deter Mr. V. from his purpose—by argument, persuasion, flattery, ridicule & abuse—will never be known in this world. To *God only* be the glory of Mr. V's persistence in his generous design."[23]

Jewett in his later life reserved most of his scorn for the nephews. Quite wrongly, he accused them of a miserly concern for their uncle's fortune. How could either of them covet his fortune? They were bound by their uncle's will of early 1850 eventually to use the funds from his estate for the endowment of a hospital. Each of them in the mid-nineteenth century had independent fortunes of three or four hundred thousand dollars. John Guy had retired from the business quite early in his career and was often away from Poughkeepsie for long periods of time. He traveled extensively in Europe, Africa, and the Far East absorbing the culture of the Old World and investigating the wonders of far-off places. His letters formed the basis of a description of his experiences and appeared in a book of travel published about 1861.[24]

Matthew Vassar Jr. on the other hand, devoting his time to extensive business and financial affairs, was a fitting successor to his uncle in the brewing business. Both of these nephews, by wise investment, increased their holdings immensely. Jewett's accusation of their greed and parsimony, consequently, is not convincing. Both of them, one a confirmed bachelor, were like many of their contemporaries in that they could not understand all the concern about women's right to an education. They could hardly have been expected to be enthusiastic about their uncle's plans and Jewett's part in advancing them. Yet, when the die was finally cast, both of them bowed to the inevitable and became members of the first board of trustees. Matthew Jr. became the first treasurer of the college, a post to which he gave unstintingly of his time until his death in 1881. He proved an able protector of the college funds. The Vassar Brothers Laboratory of Science was the gift of both brothers in later years, and both remembered the needs of the college in their respective wills. Yet the early distrust of Jewett's motives is understandable. They resented his influence over their uncle.

On his part, Jewett recognized his ascendancy over all of Vassar's advisers at this time. He seemed oblivious to the fact that his influence and, therefore, his motives were suspected to the same extent as he suspected theirs. Though he had Vassar's trust and confidence, he wanted more. Even in 1861, after Jewett had won his objective, he could not free himself from a feeling of irritation at any interference with his plans for the college. He could only assign ignoble motives to those who did not go along with him completely. Slowly, his suspicion turned on others, until finally the whole situation became intolerable.

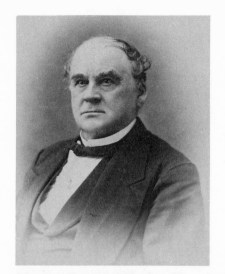

John Guy Vassar and Matthew Vassar Jr., Matthew Vassar's two nephews, who were much involved in the plans for the college.

But this was all a part of the future. For the present , Jewett saw that his immediate problem was to convince Vassar to begin the construction of the college at once, with all that it involved. This should not have required much persuasion on Jewett's part for one of the attractions of Sir Thomas Guy's great benefaction was that the erection of the hospital had been in his lifetime. The involvement with his nephews in the endowment of a hospital in Poughkeepsie had temporarily relegated the matter of timing to the back of Vassar's mind. Yet it required very little effort to revive it, even though he still had some doubts and vexing questions about procedure. He saw that the time had come to draw up some concrete plans and put them on paper where one might study them. Then, these uncertainties might be resolved and the whole project become a reasonable, workable possibility.

From his years of experience in the administration of a seminary for young women, Jewett had a fund of knowledge which he could impart to Vassar concerning the planning of the college. He made valuable suggestions and resolved questions as they arose. The period from June 1857 to June 1858 saw an unfolding of general plans and solutions to some of the problems. For the present, a very general educational program was discussed in enough detail to permit the drawing of some conclusions about the size of the college population, the number of teachers and buildings required to deal effectively with a student body of fair size.

The decision finally reached was to plan the construction of one huge college building, large enough to house four hundred students and the faculty with their families and to contain all lecture rooms, laboratories, and administrative offices. It had also to provide room for a library of

A view of Main, looking down the long driveway from The Lodge and Gate-House on Raymond Avenue. On the right can be seen the Riding School and Calisthenium, designed by J.A. Wood and completed in 1866. Matthew Vassar saw to it that students could take their exercise in Main by having Renwick provide wide, airy corridors.

10,000 volumes and a chapel for daily and Sunday worship. It was to serve all purposes except for instruction in astronomy, the nature of which required a separate building. This at least gave some focus to their lengthy conversations. Jewett, ever-present answering questions and making suggestions, was to find Vassar quick to grasp details and to bring to their conferences valuable ideas of his own .

The time soon came to submit their combined ideas for the college structure to an achitect. Jewett was sent to consult with Thomas A. Tefft,[25] a young architect in Providence, Rhode Island, and one who had successfully used brick as a building material. He submitted interesting plans. The college building now seemed a reality even though it was only on paper. It was possible to estimate what funds would have to be available immediately to proceed with the project. A business letter written by Vassar to Jewett indicated the point reached in these meetings. It was down-to-earth and summarized what had been accomplished thus far, posed some questions, and confronted the magnitude of the enterprise directly. It gently warned Jewett that they must face the practicalities of the situation together. The letter was dated Monday, 29 December 1856:

My dear Friend:

Miss Smith handed me (yesterday) your able and copious Essay upon the value of a high standard of Female Education in this Country, and closing with the importance (if not immediate action in the contemplated enterprise at least) in the *Testamentary* arrangements for the future &c.

I can readily my dear Sir appreciate & perceive how a mind like yours, cast in the mould of Female Government and long trained in directing the mental & moral faculties of the gentler sex, can be so animated & warmed by a prospective realization of such a Colossal, and glorious a scheme, but my dear friend there are always *two sides* to all human plans, and a wise and disinterested projector will carefully consider and examine both. Understand me I wish not to raise questions & doubts to *our* enterprise that are not *improbable* to *occur*, but to my mind there are reasonable probabilities that may *occur* which would interpose at least some serious objections to our Plans...First from a rough estimate I have made as to the cost of a group of buildings, I think we may safely add to Mr. Tefft's estimate 30 pr cent which would no more than cover the *usual* difficulties in this department of artistic Science, say in round numbers for

College Buildings as per Plans &c		$300,000	
land 60 acres		30,000	
Embellishments with		10,000	
Furniture		15,000	
Library		10,000	
Philosophical Apparatus	$5,000		
Cabinet, Paintings, Sculpture	15,000		
Endowments			$385,000
Presidents Salary	$5,000-$75,000		
10 Professorships	1,500-225,000		300,000
10 Lady Teachers)			
Incidental Expenses)			
		Total	$685,000

Thus $685,000 will be required to see in motion all this complete machinery according to the designs Plans, &c before any pecuniary returns can be realized.—Suppose the figures *all right* and the whole work to be commenced & accomplished within the ensuing 5 years, who is to take the charge and bear the great burden of labor, Building & appendages with all its multifarious ramifications—should a large proportionable degree of it fall upon my shoulders with the intermediate labors to convert much of my Estate into available means to meet the forthcoming disbursements. I fear it would soon make my old bones rattle in the graves.

I wish my dear Friend to look at this matter from a strict business point of view, as my heart & soul with a clear head, honest purpose & tolerable fair fortune (although not princely as many suppose) I do intend (thank God for the *will*) shall be devoted in the main for the good of man.

Now leaving for the present the matter of the *Endowment* would it be wise in me to begin such a *gigantic* scheme without my Nephews assurance to aid the enterprise.—I think not—

Again, can you be reasonably certain that a literary Institution of such a magnitude will not excite the envy & prejudice of all engaged in lesser instrumentalities of Female Education & especially is it small in the least degree with a Religious denominational Character. Are there not constant rivalships springing up in bordering cities & towns throughout our Country more quiet and select that would divide the patronage. Is there not an ungrounded prejudice in the American mind to colassal Establishments of all kinds. Do not common people regard them as *aristocratic*—something in the same light as in a few of our Colleges & Universities—and altho we propose to make it accessable [to] indigent females, would not that be *construed* to our disadvantage by the more wealthy portion of the community, would they not say, why take a gang of poor girls to make ladies of them in feelings and claims, when we cant make them such in fact? Is it not better to qualify a person to be *first* rate in their line of life than to try to *hoist* them out of it, and leave them in the great majority of cases fit for neither earth nor sea.

Do we know or can we find any stupendous employment of capital that has been economically disbursed by agents or that usually succeeds upon the first trial. Are not almost all corporated individual enterprises of *gigantic* magnitude signal failures in our Country? I throw out these enquiries not for discouragement, but for the purpose of information, as I well know that you would no more engage in the enterprise without assurance of a successful issue than myself—

I have penned the foregoing with some considerable haste altho' they are reflections which have engaged my mind for the week past as opportunity would permit. But expecting to leave home again tomorrow, I thought to place them before you for your consideration.

I remain truly yours, &c

M. Vassar[26]

This letter reveals the conclusions that had been reached in the many meetings, and it also reveals Vassar's concern about a complete plan. His rough calculation of funds needed to insure the realization of a splendid, complete, new college included a provision for endowed salaries, but did not provide for any operating expenses for the first year. It was generally realistic, and the total, $685,000, was about $285,000 above the amount finally presented to the trustees at their first meeting. That despairing cry "Who is to take charge and bear the great burden" was an expression of real concern. He had not yet realized that the college was going to be his preoccupation for the rest of his life and that he would take great joy in the labor involved. Those "old bones" would survive the stress and strain. They never faltered and they did not "rattle in the graves" before September 1865, when Vassar saw his young ladies and the faculty arrive to make his college a living thing.

The questions pressed are those any cautious businessman would have raised in 1860, particularly if he had been warned of the perils of embarking on a plan of such wide scope by his advisers. Jewett recognized that some of the problems suggested did not necessarily originate with Vassar himself, and the implication was clear that Vassar was not at all certain of the degree of cooperation he might expect from the two younger Vassars. Within a day, Vassar had Jewett's reply, a long-winded epistle showing just a shade of forbearance in setting matters straight. Jewett pointed out that any man embarking on such a unique enterprise would require great patience and fortitude in the face of his critics. "The ignorant, the timid, the covetous, the envious, have always joined in condemning the plans of those who were nobler, more generous, more courageous than themselves.... Columbus was denounced as an enthusiast for dreaming of a New World....The wise man, planting himself on fixed principles, calmly surveying the whole ground covered by these principles, unterrified by obstacles, unmoved by sneers goes serenely onward, treading firmly & resolutely in the path to which God may call him."[27] It was thus that Jewett dismissed any detractors of the grand enterprise.

He asked Vassar to put two questions to himself: the first, is the enterprise judicious? the second, it is practicable? The rest of the letter was devoted to answers to these questions and to points raised by Vassar. He left no stone unturned. Again he was preaching a sermon that must have been familiar to Vassar, and it was one that Vassar had heard preached many times in recent months—with some omissions and some needed additions. At its end, he revealed that Vassar had fired off two letters in succession. One wonders what problems the second set forth. At any rate, Jewett recalculated the funds needed for a college of half the enrollment used by Vassar and made this the basis for new calculations. His total was two-thirds of that submitted by Vassar and included no endowment for salaries. In planning for a student body of half the size originally considered, he allotted but $150,000 for buildings compared to the $300,000 used by Vassar from Tefft's estimates, and included some items that had been omitted by Vassar. It is amusing to notice that Jewett halved the sum put aside for buildings, for he actually believed that he could adapt the Tefft plans for a smaller number of students himself.[28]

Although there is no record of Vassar's reaction to this letter, his great worry at that time was the value of his investments, a great portion of which were in railroad bonds. Their value had fallen in the uncertain market of the late fifties when talk of the secession of some southern states was in the air. There was doubt in his mind about whether this was an opportune time to embark on such an ambitious program, but shortly thereafter the market recovered and he was reassured. In spite of any remaining doubts, he seemed more at ease with the general idea even though he was unsure of his nephews' willingness to join with him or at least to give him some support.

Jewett, however, was very positive in his statements of his part in all deliberations that went on before this period, during it, and for the years after it up to the point of his resignation and retirement from all Vassar affairs. He was quite smug about his role. He seemed increasingly unable to understand Vassar's deliberately cautious approach to each new problem that had to be faced. Yet he claimed that he did. In writing the *Origin of Vassar College* (1879), he impressed on the reader the extent of his role, his great labors for the college and his forbearance during his active years with Vassar. He leads one to believe that the plans approved and adopted by Vassar were his—a statement all too inclusive and too self-centered to be taken literally, for Vassar was not without convictions and ideas of his own. Yet to some extent, Jewett was justified in these feelings, because without him, there would have been no Vassar College.

Vassar was very fortunate to have at his right hand a man who knew so many of the details involved in getting the project under way. Of some of these things, his other advisers were aware, but in many details such as the drawing up of a charter that would safeguard the institution, the selection of fitting and able trustees, and the proper occasion for turning over the funds to the trustees, there was really no one in Poughkeepsie who could advise so knowingly as Jewett. To be sure, Anderson in Rochester was always available, but Vassar needed someone close to him to aid him in many of these situations. As the next few years went by, Vassar was to delegate more and more affairs to Jewett, until the poor man got the idea that he was indispensable and often involved himself unwittingly in things that properly were not within his jurisdiction.

The matter of a will drawn up by Vassar in 1857 is a case in point. According to Jewett's account, it was he who suggested and drew up the document in which Vassar committed his fortune to the building and endowment of the college. Jewett recorded it as follows:

[Vassar] then wrote out a new will with his own hand in which he copied word for word my outlined Scheme and devised, bequeathed, and gave the sum of four hundred thousand dollars for the Erection, equipment and endowment of Vassar Female College said institution to be founded and conducted in accordance with the principles, plans and suggestions contained in the foregoing outlined plan. . . . I preserved no Copy of the plan but its general features are indicated in the Address to the Trustees at their first meeting in February 1861.[29]

Such an action on the part of Jewett could not help but alienate the nephews and Vassar's other local advisers, particularly since the will was drawn up without their knowledge and nullified an earlier one leaving large sums to the two nephews for the future development of the hospital. It hardly seems possible that Vassar would have drawn up such a document without the legal advice of his Poughkeepsie consultants. No copies of this will or a subsequent one,[e] which in the opinion of Jewett was simpler and more satisfactory, remain, but neither of them could have resembled—nor should they have—his final last will and testament dated February 1868. This is a masterpiece in its concise and unambiguous direction as to the disposition of his estate. He drew this one up himself.

By March 1859, the grand enterprise had assumed definite shape. The architect Tefft had died in Rome that year, so new plans and specifications for a college building were drawn by James Renwick, an architect of fine reputation for the successful planning and construction of notable buildings in New York and Washington. Jewett claimed no part in his selection, though he credited himself with the rough sketch of the interior submitted to Renwick. He gave Vassar credit for the "broad halls adjacent to the outer walls which was Mr. Vassar's own Pet idea."[30]

With the Renwick plans in Vassar's hands, the choice of a spacious parcel of land large enough to meet their individual expectations was the next order of business. In April 1859 Jewett set to work compiling a lengthy list of specifications for a suitable site, entitled, "Hints in regard to the proper location of a College for Young Ladies."[31] It was an interesting study which could serve as a model today. The only trouble was that Vassar had already been considering possible sites. His nephew, Matthew Jr., had recorded in his diary a month before Jewett had prepared his memorandum, "Engaged with M.V. and Swift out at Mill Cove Farm looking at a sight for Female College ."[32] Mill Cove Farm, the spot that the founder finally chose to be most appropriate, had some sentimental attachments for him because as a small boy, he and his sister had roamed the hills above the great meadow of the farm—just a few miles from his boyhood home. Fortunately, this place met Jewett's specifications admirably. One wonders if he was on the tour of inspection with Vassar, Swift, and Matthew Jr., who for reasons of his own chose to ignore the presence of Jewett.

The college was now an assured thing, but it was still only a set of plans, the most complete of which were Renwick's sketches and specifications for the college building. With these in his possession, Vassar was eager to press on with the realization of his project. He recognized that before any business could be transacted, members must be chosen and appointed to a board of trustees, and that this group could act only as a corporate body under the laws of New York State.

The problem of choosing the men who were to be members of this first board took several conferences. Vassar had some definite ideas of those who might serve in this capacity. His feeling that the institution was to be nonsectarian was reflected in the men he chose. Jewett, on the other hand, wished to have a majority of Baptists on the board and urged Vassar to have at least two-thirds of the membership of this denomination. He suggested also that the number be small, with a maximum of thirteen members as the ideal, and urged that the body be self-perpetuating, thereby keeping a majority of Baptists on the board. But Vassar chose several of his personal friends, business associates, and educational leaders, all of whom represented a variety of religious opinion. Yet Vassar was willing to increase the total number of trustees to twenty-nine, seventeen of whom were Baptists.

The composition of this first board is interesting. Four of the men chosen were serving with Vassar on the board of the University of Rochester; one-third were residents of Poughkeepsie; four were Baptist ministers. Five were college presidents; three had at one time been college presidents; seven had had no formal education; five were editors and publishers; three were writers. There were two lawyers on the board, but no physicians or women. Jewett seemed little concerned about the qualifications of those who were to control the destinies of the young college in the early years of its development as long as they were Baptists. He did not remark on Vassar's choices, and he seemed but little troubled by the choice of the two nephews and of his antagonist Swift. He only hoped that they would not be given positions on committees of great responsibility and power. He had won his point about having the majority of the trustees of the Baptist persuasion and in having the body self-perpetuating. In this way, he assured Vassar that the college would always be in the hands of responsible Baptist men.

At the same time, the college charter was in a state of preparation; knotty problems arose which were to lead to much controversy. Jewett, in his usual way, treated the matter as though it were important solely to Vassar and himself. In recalling the situation, he had this to say:

> In the summer and autumn of 1860 so much time was spent in preparing a Charter for the College, Mr. Vassar was deeply solicitous to have the instrument contain such provisions as would protect the Institution for all time from any perversion of its funds and from any departure from the broadly catholic spirit in which he desired it should be conducted. After a careful examination of the Charters of the chief Universities, Colleges, and female Seminaries of the United States I became

satisfied that no conditions could be introduced into the Charter which would secure absolute immunity from perversion. I cited notorious disregard of the terms of the bequest made by the eminent London merchant Thomas Hollis a Baptist for the purpose of founding a Professorship of Theology in Harvard University. I also referred Mr. Vassar to the Creed subscribed to by the professors of Andover Mass Theological Seminary which is now considered to bind them only to the substance of doctrine.

I urged that the Strongest guarantee he could possibly have that his views would be carried out in all the future, was to make the Trustees a closed Corporation, filling their own vacancies, with power of perpetual succession.

The men you would now place upon the Board, are your personal friends, and others eminent for their virtues as well as for learning and ability. These Trustees will faithfully execute your plans and will take good care that their successors shall be men of like character and spirit. This view prevailed and resulted in the Charter now before the world.[33]

Even though Jewett might have been a moving spirit in getting information as to the proper form and content of the charter, Vassar did his part within the limits of his own knowledge and experience. He was curious about all aspects of the founding of his college. He, too, studied the content of charters of other institutions, and he had friends like Anderson to whom he could turn for information and advice. He gave much thought to what such a document should contain, as is indicated by Jewett's reflection.

It was in this matter of a charter that the first serious evidence of conflict between Jewett and Vassar's advisers was displayed. Matthew Jr. had worked closely with his uncle in many activities and had proved a very dependable young man. Swan had Vassar's confidence over the years, as did Swift and DuBois.[f] Of these men, Matthew Jr. and Swift apparently sharply resented Jewett's influence over Vassar. With almost total recall of conversations, attitudes, and behavior of the people involved, Jewett gave quite a dramatic account of what resulted from this in the *Origin* (1879).

This important incident took place in March 1860. Matthew Jr. made the following entry in his diary in early February: "With M.V. & Swift in office this day talking over matter pertaining to College, &c, reducing the extent &c."[34] A month later, the following notation appeared: "Engaged this day with M.V. & Swift preparing papers for act incorporation from Legislature for Vassar high school girls and also Boys high school and Vassar Library. C. Swift goes up this day to Albany."[35] This was on Friday and on the following Tuesday, this record appeared: "(Mar 13 1860) The application for charter for 'Vassar' Colledge was favorable before Legislature but further passage or action checked by order of M.V. for Telegraph

Cyrus Swan, trustee (1861-1900) and legal adviser to Matthew Vassar. He was secretary of the board of trustees from 1861 to 1869 and secretary of the executive committee from 1865 to 1869.

from Swift on a/c of some discrepancies in Bill & phraseology of the name &c—calling it Vassar high School for Bys and one of same for girls, where as it (intended) as Female Colldge and other articles requiring adding &c &c."[36]

Jewett's account filled in the events between these two recorded incidents and explained what two high schools and a library had to do with Matthew Vassar. His narration of the events of these days in March began with:

In the winter and spring of 1860 (Matthew Vassar Jr. and his cohorts) devised a scheme by which they hoped to divert their uncles attention from the subject...they were careful to keep me in ignorance of their movements. The plot was discovered and defeated in the following manner. I was superintendant of the Sabbath School connected with our church and Matthew Vassar Jr was one of the teachers. On a Sabbath morning early in March as I entered the Sunday School room this gentleman met me gleefully rubbing his hands, his full orbed face beaming with smiles and said, Did you see yesterdays Telegraph?...I replied, Yes, what of it? He continued, Did you notice anything of special interest in the doings of the legislature at Albany? I answered No. Well he says Uncle Matthew is going to build a free City Library for Pokeepsie—erect a free high school for boys and another for Girls, and last Friday Mr Palmer member of the assembly from this district introduced a bill incorporating these institutions; and the Bill was passed to its second reading. . . . Returning home from church at noon I found my paper and sure enough, the records of Fridays legislative proceedings read as above. I was filled with astonishment and grief.[37]

That very Sunday afternoon, Jewett wrote a letter to Vassar, full of sorrow and surprise at the news that he had received. It was a long letter, but parts of it are worth recording here:

My dear Mr. Vassar

It is more than three years ago, that you were pleased to honor me with your confidence, by conferring with me respecting such disposition of your estate as would result in the greatest good to your fellow men and redound to the highest glory of God. You expressed a desire *not* to divide up your property into inconsiderable portions; but so use the aggregate as to perpetuate a name which otherwise might pass away from among men, you dying without issue. . . .

To meet those broad & benevolent views, a *College for the education of American Females* was suggested. This was shown to be an enterprise worthy of your generous aspirations, adapted to do incalculable good to our country & to the world—fitted to perpetuate your name and memory to the latest generations, a monument of your beneficence & wisdom which would be as enduring as the everlasting hills. . . .

Thus encouraged by the opinions of many of our wisest men & most experienced educators, you proceeded to make the necessary testamentary arrangements. In this, did you not act inteligently, judiciously and wisely? I think you did. Great, then was my surprise to learn, that *you have abandoned the College altogether*—have substituted for it a High School for Girls—another for Boys, and probably, a Public Library. "O what a fall is there my Countrymen!" Your advisors have razed your magnificent 120 gun ship down to a barge! You give up your *coach and six* for a *wheelbarrow*. Your monument which would have been more durable than the pyramids, is given up for a Pine Slab, placed at the head of your grave.

Your high school will be a petty *local* concern, never heard of out of Pokeepsie—certainly not beyond the limits of Dutchess County.

From the very nature & constitution, it must be local. These Schools are always *designed* to be so—to benefit the place where they are established and no other. . . . Your [high] school will be a good thing for this place it is true, but it will never meet your large & liberal views. . . .

Now my dear Mr. Vassar, I know the arguments which have been presented in order to induce you to sacrifice the College. It is said, that the undertaking is too vast—"too many eggs in one basket" &c. This is the only argument they advance, and in my humble judgement it is not any argument at all. I might answer it playfully by [a] similar analogy, but it would be unworthy of so important a theme. . . .

Do not, then, I beseech you, strip yourself of the immortal honor which God invites you to gain for yourself by establishing an Institution which shall be a name and a praise to you throughout our whole country, and down to the latest generations. [L]eave these insignificant Schools to men of smaller means & smaller hearts. Do something, I beg you, worthy of yourself, worthy of the ample fortune Providence has given you, & worthy of Him who gave it. . . .

But my heart is heavy & my hand trembles.[38]

The next morning, Jewett was summoned to Vassar's office where he faced the conspirators. His account of Vassar's reaction is strange. He was very angry and maintained that he had not seen the charter before it was taken to Albany, that this was all Swift's doing. Vassar felt that he had been deliberately misled and that he had been kept in ignorance of the intentions of the bill by strange devices. His fury was directed primarily against Swift. According to Jewett's account, the session concluded with a demand from Vassar that all further action on this bill be stopped. Jewett went further in explaining Vassar's reaction to the men behind this high school—"colledge" bill by maintaining that Vassar gave up all hope of aid or encouragement from his nephews and their advisers and that he did not mention the college again to any of them. If this were so, how does one explain Matthew Jr.'s remark in his diary dated one month later: "April 23, 1860 M.V. had Mr. Renwick Architect here last week looking over Grounds Mill Cove preparatory to buildg Female College";[39] and that of 30 August 1860: "M.V. M.V. Jr. C.W. Swift and T.L. Davies out at Mill Cove looking at lands of T.L. Davies and purchased from him 66 acres at $200 per acre for addition to present lands M.V. for Female College."[40]

At any rate, this ended Jewett's story, but there was a sequel to the whole affair. Each of the Poughkeepsie papers published a correction of the earlier account about the high school, within a week or ten days. The *Telegraph* began its editorial: "The name of our respected fellow-citizen, Matthew Vassar, having recently appeared in public journals in such connection as to give a vague and inadequate idea of his designs, we are pleased to inform our readers that we have his permission to present to our columns a brief statement of his plans in relation to the cause of education."[41] There followed a very accurate history of the origins of the idea of a college for women and its development to that date.

Vassar's interpretation of these events adds evidence to the correctness of Jewett's later interpretation. He wrote to a trusted friend a few weeks after all of these events:

It is an old adage that we cannot tell what a man is worth untill after he is dead, and we may add further, that, we cannot tell how many *friends* he will *have* untill he is near dying. They then cluster round him as close as the vine to its supporting trunk. I make these prefacetory remarks because you have doubtless seen in the late Journals of the day a "Bill" reported under our legislature proceedings, *posting* up my *generosity*, which was quite as *startling* to me as to my friends with whom I had made *confidents* in certain matters pertaining to the future disposition of portion of my Estate after my discease and which publicity was so at variance with my previous *expressed* views and intentions that they (some at least) have thought me either *beside* myself or had strangely changed my plans & purposes. Not so, however, neither the one or the other have occurred, and I trust that God in his good Providence will permit me to live, and see the "Vassar Female College" loom up with its Towers and Domes within a short few years. It was verry natural to find numerous influences at work to change my purposes, and suggestions were audibly encaught, *distinct* to understand the motives which prompted them, but discovering that my *purposes* were the result of able and distinguished advises, and to my own cool deliberations of years of close thought and study, with a fund of sound reasoning to substantiate & means to carry them out, an ebb current of opinion began to set in, and now those which seemed to be the most *alarmed* at my *"gigantic folly"* are gradualy becoming willing converts to my plans!

It is our purpose as soon as the fine weather sets in to have our Committee locate the grounds then to invite artists to make drafts & plans of the College Buildings, and at as early day as possible thereafter to break ground.[42]

This episode pointed up certain difficulties that Vassar encountered either because he would not or could not bring opposing factions together to work toward a common goal. He knew what he wanted at last, but only the deliberate action of Jewett prevented a move from which it would have been difficult to extricate himself. Now, of course, work on a proper charter moved on apace, and the final result was a concise contract the intention of which was clear.[g] It had nine sections setting up a corporation which should have "all such powers, and be subject to such duties and liabilities as are applicable to colleges."[43] Jewett accompanied Swan to Albany where on 18 January 1861 it was enacted into law by the state assembly. Jewett enjoyed himself that day. He wrote to Professor Samuel S. Sherman[h] ten days later: "The rapidity with which I pushed our Charter through, gave me quite a reputation at Albany. There was considerable difficulty in as much as the 8th section exempts Mr. Vassar from the operation of a law passed just at the close of the last winter's session. I liked the fun right well—pleasant time, & expenses paid!"[44]

Newspapers throughout the United States took up the story and made this incident the subject of articles and editorials. The praise of Vassar was general. Sarah Josepha Hale, the enthusiastic editor of *Godey's Lady's Book*, lauded the news as the one bright spot in the clouds and darkness of the approaching conflict between the States. The Poughkeepsie press was cordial and welcomed the new college heartily. *Vanity Fair* and the *New York Times* treated the idea lightly but gave it some serious words. The *Times* said:

> What do you think of a women's college? And, why not? After Allopathic and Homeopathic, and Hydropathic and patent pill Colleges and universities, and all that sort of thing, why not let the girls have one? Sure enough, Why not? For the life of me, I don't discover any valid objection. But, objections or no objections, the thing is to be. By a bill introduced this morning, Matthew Vassar, Ira Harris, William Kelly, E. L. Magoon, James Harper, B. J. Lossing, S. F. B. Morse, and a dozen more other gentlemen among them the knowing, and the known are authorized to be a body corporate of a Female College. The said College to have full powers to educate feminines and to grant sheep-skins, the same as any other College is authorized and wont to do.[45]

There were critics and skeptics, too, from whom the announcement brought questions as to the real value and probable success of the college. Some of Vassar's friends and fellow townsmen were its severest critics. Yet Vassar was greatly pleased and gratified by the generous reception of the press, while Jewett was in seventh heaven and was determined to carry plans forward as rapidly as possible. His general attitude was summed up in a letter to a friend:

> I have devoted *all* my time & thoughts to Vassar College, since my School closed—visiting Albany twice, and New York many times—further the interests of the institution besides writing 100 letters. Were it not for my presence and vigilance, I think Mr V's greedy relatives (rich too) would have defeated the enterprise, long ago. By recent Codicils, added to the will at my suggestion and known to no human being but myself, the success of the undertaking is now placed beyond all contingency.[46]

Certainly, Jewett was not the soul of discretion to have penned such a letter.

This indictment was written in September 1860, some time after Jewett had given up the Cottage Hill Seminary. For several weeks in the latter half of 1860, Jewett had come to some decisions about the amount of time he could give to Vassar and the college and still maintain the quality of his school. He had come to realize that he could not do two such demanding things—running the seminary properly and giving to Vassar the time and attention he needed. In October, he wrote to his friend Sherman: "If *I* am to have the Presidency [of Vassar College] as Mr. V. says, let the appointment be made immediately on the organization of the trustees, say 1st February, & let the Pres. be instructed to prepare a Plan of Organization, Course of Study, Discipline, &c, to be submitted to the Board in the spring 1862."[47]

It would seem from this that Vassar had committed himself to back Jewett's nomination as president and that Jewett felt safe in giving up his school to devote all of his time to helping Vassar in the busy weeks before the first trustee meeting in February 1861. He made this move knowing that he would not receive any remuneration. The promise of the presidency was enough for the present.

Not much more than a month remained in which to finish preparations for that great day, Tuesday, 26 February 1861—the day appointed for the first meeting of the board of trustees. It was to be given over to the presentation of the gift of $408,000 to carry out the enterprise, to the organization of the board into an effective instrument for meeting the manifold problems that lay ahead and to transacting any other business that might need immediate attention. The preliminary preparations took some days of meetings. Decisions of all sorts had to be made. Vassar's opening address had to be written. Members of committees had to be nominated to be presented on that day so that the business of the college could go on without delay.

On that morning in February, the meeting moved with dispatch. It was opened with prayer for the success of the great venture. Vassar addressed his friends in a very simple way, outlining for them reasons for his philanthropy, how he hoped that they would administer his generous gift, and what he hoped the general design of the project might be. Though the speech bears the imprint of Jewett, the last two paragraphs were distinctly Vassar's own. They were a simple statement of his commitment and his hopes for the college:

In conclusion, gentlemen, this enterprise, which I regard as the last, great work of my life, I commit to you as a sacred trust, which I feel assured you will discharge with fidelity and uprightness, with wisdom and prudence, with ability and energy.

It is my fervent desire that I may live to see the Institution in successful operation; and if God shall give me life and strength, I shall gladly employ my best facilities in co-operating with you to secure the full and perfect consummation of the work before us.[48]

After the election of the Honorable William Kelly[i] of nearby Rhinebeck as chairman, Vassar presented his gift in its tin box, and the day's work proceeded, broken only by a large dinner at noon in the Gregory House, where

Tuesday, 26 February 1861. The presentation of the tin box, with its gift of $408,000 to carry out the enterprise and a deed of conveyance for two hundred acres for the college site and farm. The meeting was held at the Hotel Gregory in Poughkeepsie.

the meeting was held. Jewett was satisfied with the day's work though he did not hail the election of Matthew Jr. and Swift as two of the five members of the executive committee. Vassar wrote in his diary of this date, "After Meeting the Members came to my home and examined *Elliots* Picture I then made them a present each of John G Vassar 20 Years around the world."[j]

Vassar was very busy and preoccupied in those days, but he did not forget Jewett, for whom he felt a great warmth. He acknowledged his debt to him in the following note:

My very dear friend

I feel on this national day set apart by the highest civil authority for prayer and humiliation &cc, that I cannot allow the occasion to pass without expressing to you my sincere and devout thanks, and that from the very depths of my heart, for the kind and earnest interest you manifest in my spiritual and temporal welfare, and would to God that my strength of mind and body did permit my giving you a more deep and vivid expression of them, but this morning's sun found me struggling under my old difficulties, so much so that I had to dismiss Mr. Daniels rather unceremoniously after a short interview in my office, and on returning to my domicile was obliged to rest my brain, then took up my pen to address you these brief lines.

Referring again to your note before me, if I could doubt for a moment your sincere and ingenious friendship, I should be very unhappy, because I am fully sensible that I have lost friendship with many since I commenced the great enterprise—and my heart ached and my spirits were troubled, especially the past week, from what I have heard and know to be the feelings of some of the family friends in consequence of what I am doing. But I trust in God and my Saviour to sustain me and justify me, and approve the work of my head and hands, the V. F. C. enterprise, and if I lose this friendship and favor I cannot now help it. In this enterprise I look higher than man. I am my dear friend yours most truly &c

M. Vassar[49]

Jewett regarded this first meeting of the board of trustees as a personal triumph—a triumph over all who opposed the enterprise. Looking back over these days in early 1861, he wrote with some satisfaction of his success in routing his opponents. He told of conferences before the inaugural meeting of the trustees and how he prevented a takeover by them with his strong opposition. He claimed the responsibility for the vetoing of a three-man executive committee composed of Vassar, Matthew Jr., and Swift, and saw to it that a five-member committee was substituted for it. In a letter to Anderson after the meeting of the board of trustees, he wrote:

Our friends who were so exultant before the meeting of the Board, at the idea of having everything in their own way, and who were so deeply chagrined, so utterly confounded, on finding their arrangements quietly but most effectively ignored; are engaging in their new duties with a kindly spirit, and with the fear of the next meeting of the Trustees continually before their eyes! The *moral power* of their defeat will ensure a careful walk for years to come. The whole Pedo-baptist portion of the Board was also most favorably impressed with the learning, the ability, the sound judgment, the business tact and the liberal spirit of the *Baptist* members.[50]

And so the first obstacles were overcome and the first battles won. The new president was exultant and sure that he could, with persistence and vigilance, win through to the end.

Chapter II

Vacillation and Change: 1861-1865

A page of Harper's Weekly, *30 March 1861, pictorially announces the opening of Vassar Female College.*

The times were not auspicious for any great financial project. Over the years 1855 to 1861, when the grand enterprise was in its planning stages, the growing tensions between North and South were reflected in the financial instability of the country. Matthew Vassar watched the fluctuations in the value of stocks and bonds on the exchange with alarm. News of bank failures and bankruptcies was not reassuring. Yet he was ever hopeful while drawing up plans and going through the procedures that made possible the incorporation of the college, the appointment of the trustees, and the presentation of his gift to that body. He was more concerned each day lest the dream of a college in full operation during his lifetime might not be realized. He wanted to be present when the first young Vassar students arrived on the campus.

Letters summoning those twenty-nine trustees to their first corporate meeting were dated 23 January 1861, two weeks before an event which changed a great many things—the day when six southern states banded together to form the Confederacy with Jefferson Davis their first provisional president. Four other states joined the movement, and on 12 April 1861 the attack on Fort Sumter by Confederate forces and its fall a few days later was a declaration of war. Predictions in the North were that the rebellion would be short-lived and that sanity would be restored in short order. The North was soon taught differently by the disasters at Bull Run in July 1861.

The trustees of Vassar Female College had turned over the day-to-day business and decisions to their executive committee, composed of Matthew Vassar, Matthew Jr., Cyrus Swan, Cornelius DuBois, and Charles Swift. The difficult situation challenged their business ingenuity; the five men faced the baffling question of whether to push forward with the building of the college or to postpone it to that indefinite time when peace should have been restored. They were well aware of the founder's wishes and, like him, each of them was a realistic businessman. The serious setbacks suffered by the army of the North in the early months of the war forced upon them an awareness of how insecure the times were for any straightforward financial business. Already the four other members of the committee had considered the problems associated with the immediate implementation of Vassar's plans. They discussed with him and gave him their best advice. If any one of them had been totally against the enterprise, here was a perfect opportunity to delay the building of the college for the duration of the conflict and thereby discourage the founder. On the contrary, early in May 1861 the decision was reached to start the construction of Main Building at once.

Vassar explained what the plan involved in a letter to Anderson as follows:

We are taking all the preliminary steps to commence the College buildings, have enclosed by fencing in an area of some 6 acres of grounds for the Cite, made our contract with the Builder [Mr. Harloe], and the architect, [Mr. Renwick], the former in the sum of $178,200 and the latter $5300, the last includes all plans & drawings and superintendence of the work untill completed. We propose to carry up the foundation walls to the first tier of beams this season, the following to enclose the building, the third season finish ready for occupancy in the fall of 64. Some delays have occurred on account [of] our national troubles, imparing seriously the market value of our assetts. The most depressed of these we propose to lay aside, and use only such as will result in the least sacrifice. Were it not that our expenses for salaried officers &c has been incurred amounting to some $5000 per annum and our Contracts for the Buildings made (altho' the time of commencing them is *discretionally* at the option of the Committee) we might reasonably halt. I think according to the present market value of our assetts we may place to profit & loss account up to the present time $75,000.[1]

He then used some calculations to show that a deficit of $4,000 for the year was probable if they did not proceed with caution.

The unanimous feeling of the members of the executive committee was that "[a] crisis is now upon us whether to halt until the issues of our national troubles are settled, or to proceed, in one respect the turn of public affairs will be to the advantage of the Contractor, enabling him to buy his materials at reduced prices, also labour will be cheaper, and we may also avail ourselves of a cheap rate of interest by hypothecating our Securities (instead of selling) to the amount sufficient to put up the buildings...these and other considerations final[ly] resulted in our determination to proceed [with] the work."[1]

Vassar had expressed the same view to William Kelly, the chairman of the board of trustees, a few days earlier:

At our last figuring of our assetts, we passed to Profit & loss account some $60,000, mostly Southern State Stocks, of course we would not think of disposing of them just now, nor in fact any of our securitys at the present market value. Our policy is to hypothecate so much as we may require from time to time with N. York Life & Trust Co.[2]

Hence, there seemed to have been a sincere attempt made by the members of the executive committee to see that the college buildings would be constructed with the least financial loss in a world of shifting money values and market fluctuations.

On Wednesday 3 June 1861 ground was broken for Main Building. The ceremonies of that day were simple. No great crowd was at hand; in fact, Frances Swan, who attended the ceremony, recalled years later that other than Matthew Vassar and her father, Cyrus Swan, the only persons present were Cornelius DuBois, Mrs. Swan and the two small Swan daughters, one an infant in arms; Emma Sedgwick, a cousin of Swan, and farmer Cypher. The Swan account was not quite accurate. Matthew Jr. was a bit more explicit in his diary:

> June 3. The ground was broken this day for foundation of Vassar Female College by Mr. Vassar in presence of part of Trustees of College viz. M. Vassar Jr. Cornelius DuBois, C. Swan, M. V. also Revd H Malcolm and the Farmer A. Cypher and workmen or laborers also Valkenburgh & builder Mr. Harloe—few remarks by M. V. and Malcolm. . . Revd Mr. M. asked Gods blessing on the undertaking.[3]

The *Daily Express* of Poughkeepsie added the information that Vassar himself "raised the first spade full of soil, with brief and well-chosen remarks, and with all the vigor of full manhood."[4] One of the papers reported that the Rev. H. Malcolm[a] "happened to be incidentally present and. . . spoke at the occasion."[5]

A year later on 16 May 1862, Matthew Vassar wrote to Malcolm, the following note:

> This is truly an age of *wonders* and you have contributed to the Stock. I had almost given up ever hearing from you direct, *indirectly* I have several times since we last met some year or thereabout ago, when you officiated so conspicuously with me in the Breaking of Ground for our College, were you present with me now, you would scarcely realize the amount of materials piled up upon the spot. We are about ready for the 3d tier of beams, but I decline saying more on this point for I want you to come & see for yourself. . .
>
> I send you by this day mail March Number of the American Journal of Education, where you will find a steel plate engraving Likeness of your humble Servant, with a brief Outline of his early history with a short statement made by me on the occasion of the endowment by the V.F. College in February 1861.[6]

At the second meeting of the board on 25 June 1861 Benson Lossing presented the following resolution:

> Resolved. That a Committee of five, of which the Chairman shall be one be appointed by the chair, whose duty it shall be to make arrangements for laying the corner stone of the College with appropriate ceremonies and to procure an orator for that occasion.

The following gentlemen were appointed such a Committee, Messrs Kelly, Morse, Jewett, Anderson, Lossing.[7]

Vassar, in preparation for his part in the ceremonies, applied in late August to his friend, Professor Edward L. Youmans[b] for some ideas that he might use in an informal talk on the occasion:

The time is near at hand when we shall be ready for the imposing Ceremony of laying the Corner Stone of the V. F. College 1 Oct[r] proximo, and as our views of Female Education are so much in harmony and my health and time are both unfavorable to devote myself in making suitable preparations for that occasion, I have a desire to avail myself of your thought on that Subject,—and to request the favor of soliciting the *outline* of an address to be read by me on that interesting and important crisis in the Colleges history. . . .

Notwithstanding the financial crisis, we have so managed our funds as be enabled to carry forward the College building to the Commencement of the second story and will with part of the second tier of beams completed by the 15th of Novbr. The first tier is now being placed thereon. We leave a space open in the Centre ingress or main front door of the building for to place the Corner Stone which on closing up leaves the Edifice Walls completed to the 2[d] Story. I shall be happy to have you honor us with your presence on the occasion of the Ceremony of which you will have proper notice hereafter. My purpose in addressing you this morning was as above stated to afford you time to throw together a few thoughts upon the subject referred and I will add such of mine as time and Circumstances will suggest and permit.

P.S. I do not expect to trespass upon your time without some consideration, therefore please to allow me the privilege to bear that in mind.[8]

Within a week, he wrote to Youmans again:

Your kind note of yesterday is before me, and hasten to reply in the midst of very pressing College engagements. The Committee on the Ceremonies of laying the Corner Stone of the V. F. College have been confering with Professor Raymond of Brooklyn, Dr Adams and Dr Chapin of N. Y. City to take part in the addresses on that occasion, they had written them without my knowledge. The Honbl. Edward Everett was invited & expected to deliver the address, but other pressing engagements. . . now prevents him accepting the invitations.

With reference to the preparatory remarks intimated in my last which I wanted you to supply, they must be confined chiefly to the main Subject, "The Female" "her Education" her sphere and availability for the greatest usefulness in life, and the best process to impart it &c. I suppose the whole of the entire Ceremonies ought not to occupy over 3 hours, addresses therefore must be short, but comprehensive &c &c. With these hasty remarks, I part with you untill your proposed visit to Pokeepsie.[9]

His final note was a hasty one and referred to the suggestions that the professor had offered as a basis for Vassar's speech on the occasion:

I am just in receipt of your favor of the 4th current, but ill health has not permitted an earlier reply, I now would beg to remark that the paper you left with me last month for perusal has been received since you read it over to me, at which time my mind was quite occupied with recent family afflictions and other exciting interests which rather disqualified me to judge of its merits at that time.

Upon a further examination I do not think it a suitable document for the "Laying of the Corner Stone of the College" it is too elaborate and lacks pithiness & points for such a ceremony, it would be more suitable for the Opening of the Institution. By refering to my letter of the 31st August you will notice that I merely asked you to throw together a few thoughts as an *Outline* on Female Education, which would perhaps be suggestive of interest, in my opening address on that occasion adding by P.S. "that I would award you some consideration therefore"

However without further preamble I desire to do what is right in the premises, and now ask whether you could reduce this charge within the Compass of the Circumstances which called for the same.[10]

No copy of Youmans's document is in the archives. Would that it were! After all of this preparation, no ceremony was held and so Main Building of Vassar College has no cornerstone. As the *Poughkeepsie Eagle* reported:

It was designed to have the corner stone of the College laid in October, with appropriate public exercises, but the activity of the Builder having outrun the tardier movements of the Committee of Arrangements, the design is abandoned.[11]

From these few reports, it does not appear that Jewett was at the ground-breaking ceremonies, or that he had much to do with arrangements for the laying of the cornerstone. He was, in fact, touring the northeastern states on college business. As he explained to one of his friends, he intended to spend this year after the formal incorporation of the college in "brain work, at home & in visiting the best Colleges & Fem Sem of the country—looking up a Faculty—conferring with the Committee on Faculty

& Studies, the Library, Art Gallery, Cabinets & App., &c. corresponding with our best practical educators."[12] He was not a member of the executive committee and only met with its members by invitation. His knowledge of its deliberations and decisions came largely secondhand through Vassar, who must have given him quite accurate reports of the committee's opinions and actions. Jewett, in turn, was never timid in expressing his own opinion with regard to them, so Vassar had his considered advice. With Vassar, he was anxious to see the building progress with dispatch. In those days, though he realized the magnitude of the problems that plagued the committee, he optimistically looked for the completion of the work and the opening of the college by September 1863.

Visits to institutions took Jewett mostly to colleges, universities, and libraries in New England. There is no report extant of his findings, but he wrote to his friend Sherman at this time:

My visit to Dartmouth, Amherst, Harvard, Brown & Yale was most delightful. It would have done *you* good, to see the Cabinets, Apparatus & Observatories. It interested even myself, ignorant & stupid as I am in these matters. Agassiz's, Dr. Hitchcock's, Pro. Shepard's. Elias Loomis's—splendid. Prof. Bond Jr. explained everything & showed me the workings thereof, in the Observatory.—I spent a day & night at Mt. Holyoke. Much pleased—250 girls, one of Eliza Denison's sisters is there.[13]

The idea of making these studies seemed to have been his own, for he, as president of a new college, was seeking all sorts of information that might be useful to him in his plans for its organization.

One interesting result to emerge from these tours came from his meeting with William F. Poole[c] of the Boston Athenaeum. Poole, an enthusiastic young librarian there, already had quite a reputation as the organizer and planner of institutional and research libraries. His views were comprehensive and already in 1861 his suggestions were treated with respect. How much Jewett and he discussed the needs of a library for Vassar College cannot be known with any exactness, but at a meeting of the trustees on 25 February 1862 a proposal was made and adopted "that the President and Matthew Vassar or either of them are hereby authorized to expend in their discretion from time to time as opportunity may offer a sum not exceeding twenty-five hundred dollars the whole in the purchase of books for the College Library."[14] This motion could have been inspired in part by the president's conference with Poole. The move was unfortunate for it ignored the established committee on the library, a group that had recognized the tremendous job ahead of it and had presented a thoughtful, workable scheme of procedure to the board. Vassar was open to censure for ignoring the workings of this committee, and Jewett, who must have known better, can hardly be excused for going along with it. He must have persuaded Vassar to agree to the plan, for they had already composed a catalogue of four thousand books derived mostly from Jewett's experience. Sadly, this list has been lost, as has the catalogue prepared by Poole. The latter was superior for it listed some ten thousand titles with suggestions for yearly additions to the collection. This compilation should have met the requirements of Vassar who had hoped for a library of at least ten thousand titles at the opening of the college. The successful move to ignore the library committee was particularly untimely since it was made on the eve of Jewett's departure for Europe. Of necessity, it placed an added burden upon Vassar's shoulders, one which he was hardly prepared to carry during an extended absence of his president.

These are the evidences of Jewett's "brain work" carried on during the year after the incorporation of the college. Between visits to colleges and libraries, his special duty for the year, one can assume, was to take care of letters that came to him inquiring about faculty appointments and college admissions. There were also acknowledgements of the numerous laudatory messages that continued to come and which required individual answers. The results of his various letters to educators for general information about the college organization he reported to the board of trustees early in 1862, indicating that he had responses that might be useful to him and the committee on faculty and studies. One such letter was a series of questions divided into three sections regarding the objectives and scope of the college, the character and nature of its faculty, and the nature of the curriculum to be pursued. These letters called for most comprehensive answers and should have been of great value to the president and the trustee committee on faculty and studies in planning college organization. Had he used these data effectively, his report to the trustees would have been one of substance and great interest; however, the minutes of the meeting at which the report was made on 25 February 1862 gave no useful summary of what Jewett said about these letters and what conclusions could be drawn from them.

Vassar during this period did not shirk any responsibility. If he shifted any of his burdens to the shoulders of the president, it was only because they were too heavy for him to bear when his "poor head" was feeling the strain of overwork. His letters are pleasant and delightful to read. Almost daily he made visits to the campus to show visitors the progress of the construction of the college, and his own tours of inspection were a great joy to him. He watched the progress of the construction and wrote to Renwick whenever he had doubts as to the quality of workmanship and materials.

As early as February 1861 Jewett had written Sherman: "Next year (in the spring) the Pres. will, probably, be sent to Europe—but we shall see."[15] The next reference to such a trip was in a letter from Vassar to Jewett dated a year later:

Since our last interview I have been considering the matter of your visit to Europe and how far the College interest could be promoted thereby, and how far our Bord of Trustees would be willing to bear a part of your expenses. Without any further capacity to judge of the advantages to be derived by such a visit than I now possess, and especially in view of the Bord of Trustees willingness to extend its aid to Professor Fisher[d16] for a similar object, is there not some fear that both might be defeated. All such incidental benefits as above referred, would be of little advantage unless the Corporation have funds sufficient to erect their College buildings & complete its internal arrangements,—failing in these would result in much greater damage to the Institution than the failure of any one institutional department, and had I not already suffered so much in my own pecuniary affairs, and my health was sufficiently good to give to it the most perfect supervision, I would not only advise the trip but be willing to defray all extra expenses. My maxim in all human policys is viz: whatever you do, do well—I am perfectly willing to afford you the opportunity to make the visit and for keeping up your Salary during your absence and I cannot but think that it would redound greatly to your advantage if you would thus signify to the Bord your willingness to avail yourself of so noble expression of your generosity by bearing your own expenses—if they would continue your Salary.[17]

This is a strange letter not given to any great enthusiasm but still indicating to the president that Vassar would back his endeavor if it meant no added expense to the college. In his *Origins of Vassar College* (1879), Jewett wrote in retrospect his views of the proposal:

I was well aware that the plans for the higher education of young ladies in the old world, are so unlike those prevailing in our own country, that we could not expect to gain much useful practical information from the inspection of their schools. . . . [Mr. Vassar] also thought it would give *eclat* to the College to have it announced to the public that the Trustees had sent the President to Europe to examine the institutions of Great Britain and the Continent, visit the most famous Art Galleries, Libraries Museums and Astronomical Observatories, purchase paintings and Statuary for Vassar College &c.[18]

The question arises as to which of these men wanted this study. Vassar cannot be said to have been wildly enthusiastic about the idea. Jewett in later years claimed never to have seen very much of value in it. Yet at the board meeting of 24 February, shortly after the receipt of Vassar's letter, Jewett presented the idea for the consideration and approval of that body. Matthew Jr. and Swift were the only trustees who did not support the move. Matthew Jr. recorded his feelings in his diary after the meeting:

Feby 25 Meeting of Board of Trustees of College...reports of Committees and acceptances of same—nomination of Professor of Chemistry, Mr. R.A. Fisher also resolution to purchase cabinet, (Geological) and Library of Books in part...proposition to loan Mr Fisher $1000 for travelling in Europe to improve himself and examine new Laboratorys and chemical apparatus &c....Mr. Jewett also asking permission to visit Europe for obtaining information in any new school and considered it would be acquisition to him & College—also that his salary may be continued $2000 per annum—to be absent to June 1863—M. V. Jr. opposed it on the ground that his services required at home in replying to Letters from sundry institutions—applicats for office & students also large number coming to the City on College information sight seeing &c and [in] his absence it would fall or devolve on M. V. who ought not & can not have mind more taxed than as present—C. Swift obliged to leave meeting on a/c business left his written protest to above—and the only two who opposed it, M. V. the donor having spoken in favour [of] it—none other of the board said aught against & was carried without opposition, Swift and M. V. Jr. saying aught further about the same...I cannot see that any benefit be granted or received in anything in Eng. visit—this country is far in advance [of] anything in Europe in Female Education.[19]

Considering Vassar's health and the constant demands made of him, these two trustees had a point. They saw that the burden of college business and all of Jewett's correspondence and other duties would fall on the older man's shoulders. Yet Vassar never complained and in the months of Jewett's leave when he almost single-handedly took on the double burden, he thoroughly enjoyed himself. In his correspondence of those days, he was apt to toss a phrase or two into his letters about the absence of the president. On one occasion, he was quite carried away in explaining it to the Rev. E. J. Goodspeed, who had inquired about the admission of his daughter Fanny to the college. The letter was dated 23 July 1862:

Our President M. P. Jewett is on a professional tour thro' Europe. We have letters from him weekly. I have just finished reading one from him this morning. Among other things, he speaks of being the guest at a Dinner given by Geo Peabody Esqre of London the Amn Banker to some 60 Ladies & Gentlemen at the Star & Garter Hotell Richmond Hill, among whom were present Mr Adams our Minister and several consuls, son of the Hon Ex Minister Ed[w]ard Everett—Sir Wm Gore Ousley & Lady Mrs. Van Renseller of Troy from his discription of the Dinner & Party it was a most splendid affair. I must add also that Mr. Brackett our pastor was one of the Guests.[20]

The president had sailed for Europe on 5 April 1862. He took with him "an excellent photograph of the Founder of our college, handsomely framed" which was presented to the Kensington Museum. He also took "twenty catalogues of prominent female seminaries in this State and New England. . . bound in a handsome octavo volume, and lettered, 'Female Seminaries, U.S.A.,' " which was placed in the exhibition of that year in London . "A copy of the proceedings of [the] Trustees at their first meeting was presented to the library of the British Museum, and its receipt handsomely acknowledged."[21] He traveled for several months, principally in the British Isles, Germany, France, and Italy.

The report of his experiences did not show that he had carried out the directive of the board of trustees embodied in their resolution at the February meeting of 1862 "that the President be requested during his visit to Europe to prepare a *general* and statistical report on the systems of female instruction prevailing abroad, comparing them with those adopted here and suggesting to the Board for their adoption such results as seem to be worthy of their attention to guide them in their preparation of a course of instruction."[22]

He read his report at the meeting of 20 June 1863, six months after his return. The minutes of the day reveal that trustee Swift offered a resolution to the effect that "the Board appreciate the valuable and interesting report of the President's visit to Europe and that he be requested to furnish a copy to be placed on file for future reference." Fifteen years later Jewett referred to the incident as follows:

The moment the president finished the reading of his Report, Mr. Swift sprang to his feet and read a resolution which he had previously prepared, complimenting the President and moving that the Report be accepted and placed on file to be preserved in the Archives of the College, the motion was promptly seconded by M. Vassar Jr. but before the Chairman had time to put the motion, several members arose and expressed the hope that a document so instructive and interesting, would be printed for general circulation, and it was so ordered.[23]

The minutes of the meeting show that only Lossing moved to publish the document.[24]

The present-day reader of the report is not startled by its originality. After a long preamble, it devoted itself in a general way to seven or eight aspects of educational programs of schools for young women in the British Isles and on the Continent. The most interesting section had to do with what Jewett called "Oral Instruction,"[25] a system which Vassar College was to adopt. The principal aim of this type of instruction was to replace the deadly method of rote memorization, so prevalent in the seminaries of those days, with lecture and discussion such as is carried on today. He was especially impressed by the ability of students under this system to discuss intelligently an assigned topic. Other than this, the report was meager and uninspiring, It offered little that could be of value to the committee on faculty and studies to prepare them in planning the curriculum of the new college.

Jewett recognized this for he wrote in his *Origin* (1879):

The President was absent from Po'keepsie exactly eight months, and though he had not time to secure materials for such a general and Statistical report as was contemplated in the resolution under which he was acting, yet his mission was not without valuable results. His own views of the matter appear in the last paragraph of the published report which he presented to the Trustees at their meeting in June 1863:

In conclusion it may be stated that besides examining into the systems of Education for woman which prevail in the old world I visited the libraries of the universities of Oxford and Cambridge, the Bodlean library of London, the imperial Libraries of Paris and Vienna, the Royal Libraries of Berlin, Dresden, Munich, Milan, Venice Florence and Naples; the library of the Vatican Studying their systems of Cataloguing, their shelving and arrangement of the Books on the shelves, all with the view of obtaining useful hints for our embryo Library. In all my visits to the Art galaries of Europe, the same practical object was constantly before me, the Philosophical Apparatus shown in the International Exhibition London from the most celebrated makers of Great Britain, France and Germany was also examined and catalogues of prices were obtained. At Munich I visited the famous Telescope Manufactory of Messrs Frauenhofer & Son, from which Professor Mitchell obtained the celebrated 12 inch refractor for the Cincinnati observatory, nor did the character of the specimens and the manner in which they were prepared and mounted, in the vast collections of Minerals, Birds, Beasts, Fishes, Reptiles, Insects &c &c in the British Museum, the Garden of Plants in Paris and other places, escape notice.

No little interest was felt in examining the most recent and approved School buildings for young Ladies. Of these the best that fell under my notice, is one just completed as a training College, by the British & Foreign School Society. They have introduced into it all the latest improvements known in England. I made notes of such details as I thought might be useful to us in finishing our edifice, but as a whole our building is, not only, far more extensive, grand and imposing, but contains ample provision for the health and comfort of the pupils, and for the development and culture of taste and refinment.[26]

Jewett explained the nature of his report to Anderson in a letter of 27 August 1863 in which he said:

I have sent you a copy of my Report on Organization, & of my visit to Europe. As you will perceive, the latter is designed to be entirely practical—giving results and such only as will be directly useful to Vassar College. I might easily have swelled the Report into a volume by inserting statistical details, but these are already in the hands of American educators in the works of Profs Stowe & Sachs, and of Horace Mann, et al.[27]

This was his reason for a report that gave so little information that might have had some bearing on the questions and special problems that he would face with his committee. The observations of Horace Mann and Calvin Stowe[28] were made from studies carried out almost a quarter of a century earlier and concerned themselves with elementary and secondary education in England and on the Continent; they could hardly lend themselves to the problems of planning a college for women in 1863.

His eight-month absence from Vassar College—from early April to mid-December—was a mistake. Jewett left all the decisions of these months to Vassar and the executive committee and he had little respect for or faith in two of the members of this committee. Feeling as he did about the situation, he should not have agreed to the European study. His reasons for not going would have been acceptable to Vassar. He could have pleaded the expense of so long a stay on his small salary of $2,000 during a period of declining dollar values in Europe. He could have pointed out the urgency of attacking the problems of securing a faculty and of devoting his time and energies during these months to matters of college organization and the development of a new and interesting curriculum at home. Vassar would have been quick to respond to these arguments but, apparently, in spite of Jewett's protestations voiced many years later, he felt at the time that such a project would add to his stature as an educator. The long stay so far from Poughkeepsie paved the way for future disaster.

As the principal adviser to Vassar between 1855 and 1861, Jewett had witnessed the vacillation and changeable character of Vassar as he wrestled with an idea. In the year following the first meeting of the board of trustees (February 1861), he seemed not to be aware that Vassar had moved from uncertainty of decision in the final acceptance of the idea of Vassar College to a state of intense activity with the business of building it. He had a large and diverse correspondence about this developing enterprise and he wrote of it with assurance and in glowing terms. In spite of all that Jewett might say, a profound change had taken place. Vassar was in his element. He was at the helm. He and his four advisers on the executive committee had a great deal of power. The president recognized this but he failed to realize that his almost total influence over the founder no longer existed. He no longer held first place. Certain duties might be turned over to him, but his primary role must be in the realm of curriculum and college organization.

Had he not been in Europe during these months, two incidents that developed at that time could have been resolved and trouble avoided. The one centered about the case of the Rev. Dr. Babcock. The other was the beginning of the short friendship between Vassar and Charles A. Raymond, a young man not to be confused with Dr. John H. Raymond, who became president of Vassar College after Jewett's resignation of that post.

At the age of twenty-five, Babcock had been ordained by the Hudson River Baptist Association and remained in Poughkeepsie until 1826. During his three years as minister of the Baptist church of Poughkeepsie, he had come to know Vassar and a pleasant, lasting friendship had developed between the two men. In 1862, Babcock was in his mid-sixties and looked somewhat older than his sixty-four years. His picture, taken at about that time, shows a man of determination. He was heavy-jowled, and his full mouth was turned down at the corners. He looked as though he were an uncompromising, forceful man.

Because of his experience in education, he was appointed to the committee on faculty and studies and to the committee on the library at the initial meeting of the Vassar board. He took both assignments seriously. Vassar, in letters to him in 1861 and early 1862, commended him for the thoughts he had expressed on the subject of the internal organization of the college and on the responsibility of the institution as parent *in absentia*. One paragraph of a letter to him expressed Vassar's general philosophy in this respect: "I do not believe with the majority of Parents that the more *hours* their children study at school the faster *they learn* no more than . . . that every hour taken from sleep is *one gained*. Such are *not* my views, nor would I contend [that] because the dirtiest children in the Street, are the most hearty and healthy, therefore cleanliness is a Superfluity—but I do go for *mental stimulus* of some sort and for daily exposure to the pure air in joyous unrestrained activity in spite of rags & filth."[29] Vassar noted with pleasure Babcock's intention to interview Maria Mitchell and to visit some institutions as a member of the committee on faculty and studies, for it showed his interest in the enterprise.

The first rumblings of discord between Babcock and Jewett came in a strongly expressed letter to Vassar written by Jewett from London, dated 31 May 1862. He intended it to be in Vassar's hands before the regular meeting of the board on 24 June, but there was barely enough time between these two dates for the letter to be delivered to Vassar prior to the meeting. It is evident from the letter that Jewett knew that Babcock was angling for some position of power in the organization of the new college. The really distressing part of the disclosures is the implication that Jewett knew of some of them before his departure for Europe. It would seem logical that he might have discussed them openly with Vassar earlier. But he apparently failed to do this and the tone of the letter is such that one surmises that Vassar had been kept in ignorance of these accusations until Jewett thought it well to bring them before him. It was certainly questionable behavior on the part of a trusted colleague.

The many pages of this communication are a mixture of fact, hearsay, and innuendo. It distresses one to read it and leaves the reader ill at ease with the president.

(Private and Confidential.)

May 31, 1862. London, Eng.

My dear Mr. Vassar,

In regard to every thing connected with Vassar College, I always open my heart to you freely and first of all. I do this, both because you have the best right to all facts & considerations relating to its welfare, & because my love for you & for the College prompts me to do it.

. . . It has been well understood in the Board, that no election for any Chair would be had, in the absence of the President; because such election would be an act of discourtesy towards him in a double sense —both as President, & as Chairman of the Committee on Faculty & Studies.

[I]n my anxious hours about the success of the College, it has occurred to me that you may be solicited to make a certain nomination. For some time past, I have known what you are ignorant of; namely, that Dr Babcock's stay at Paterson, has been very precarious, for a considerable time past; that the church has been persuaded to keep him up to the present moment, only because, as he assured them, he was to have a place at Vassar College; & he would leave them quietly, at an early day, if they would allow him to remain till the College should provide a home for him. Therefore, knowing our good brother is in danger of being thrown out of employment, and knowing also *he's a wise man in his generation*, I have thought he might press on you his immediate nomination to the Chaplaincy, or to some Professorship. He may also urge the opening of a school under the sanction of the Trustees, as a Preparatory Department (or School) for V.F. College, according to a Plan which he suggested to me last winter.

Now, as the opening of any such Department, or of any School under the patronage, recommendation, or sanction of the Trustees, by Dr Babcock, or by any other man, I here enter my decided Protest against it. In my judgment, formed after months of reflection , such a step, taken at this time, or at any time before the College is opened, would be most unwise & most hurtful to our interests. . . .

I have now a more painful duty to perform. You are well aware of the sincere respect, the warm regard, I have cherished for Dr B. ever since I came to Po'keepsie. In addition to the claims on my esteem which his talents & virtues gave him, he was very kind in securing pupils for Cottage Hill Sem'y. He has, also, from the first, manifested a deep interest in the College; and if his views have not always commended themselves to my judgment, I have uniformly conceded to him a sincere desire to advance the great cause. All our personal intercourse has been of the most fraternal & pleasing character; and in it I have ever found additional arguments for loving venerating a truly excellent friend & brother.

Entertaining these kind & affectionate sentiments towards Dr Babcock, it deeply grieves me that I am constrained to lay before you certain matters which it is your right to know, before you consent to present his name to the Board for any position in the Faculty of V.F. College.

For more than a year past, D^r B has stated to his friends in Po'keepsie, Paterson, New York, Boston, &c, his expectation of the Chaplaincy in Vassar College. This statement of his, circulated through the community, has been received, in many quarters, with surprise & disapprobation. Some months before the last meeting of the Board, I became apprised that some of our most active and influential Trustees would vote against him, whenever his name should be brought forward. I have never mentioned the subject to you, because I was not willing, unnecessarily, to give you pain; and because there was no occasion, at that time, to speak. But, now thinking the matter may be urged on you, I dare not be silent: my duty to the College, as, next to yourself, its earliest & best friend; and my official responsibility as its President, compel me to sacrifice my personal feelings and to put the facts in my possession into your hands.

I repeat, then, if Dr Babcock should be nominated for the chaplaincy at the coming meeting of the Board, several of our most able & widely known Trustees will feel bound by their consciences... to cast votes against him.

You will ask, as I demanded, to know the grounds of this opposition to a dear friend & brother; who, as you & I verily believed, two years ago, would be both acceptable to the College & popular in the community. You will not be more surprised and grieved than I have been, to learn that the objections are, substantially, as follows:

1. His age. When the College opens, he will be 66—a time of life at which a man should retire, even from an old, well-established institution: much more should he not seek to connect himself with a young college that needs all the vigor and energy of men under forty, instead of the failing powers of a man over sixty.

2. Dr Babcock is not, now, a popular preacher. No congregation in Po'keepsie, the objectors affirm, would accept him as their pastor, at his present age. Much less would he be endured they say, by a congregation composed of Professors' families & the young lady students.

3. There would be little prospect of any harmony of feeling or action, between Dr Babcock and his colleagues.

The disparity of age between the Doctor & most of the other members of the Faculty would forbid any cordial sympathy with him, and that would always be an element of discord. Again, it is alleged, by associates knowing his unpopularity in the community, [that the community] would be prejudiced against him from the start, & that would be a source of immediate trouble.—Once more, Dr B. *loves power,* his opponents insist, *and power he will have, at all hazards.* He has always been known as a *sharp, shrewd manager,* & they assert he would aim to control the whole Faculty & the whole institution, and so divisions, & dissensions, & ruin would be the result.

4. It is of vital importance that the Chaplain should live in the College, but D^r B's family will never permit him to reside there.

5. If Dr B. were not disqualified by age, unpopularity, & love of supreme control, there are still two other grounds of disqualification which, I am grieved to say, are strongly urged—not by Trustees only, but by many of the most judicious & warmest friends of the institution.

One of these is this: Dr Babcock's *domestic relations* have been the subject of public criticism, for several years past. . . . His opponents contend that it is unwise & inexpedient to place such an example before the inmates of a young ladies' college— . . .

The other ground of objection above referred to is the following: In D^r B's intercourse with young ladies, his manner towards them is often displeasing & disgusting. You and I know that manner is intended to be merely kind & fatherly, but his female friends do not understand this, & it is highly offensive to many. The young ladies of Vassar College would indignantly repel his *"attempts to put religion into them,"* & there would be little hope of usefulness from his labors for their spiritual good.

6. Finally, I am assured that the sentiments of a large number of the friends & future patrons of the College are expressed in the remark of a distinguished Minister of our own denomination, not a member of our Board, who spoke thus: "A Professorship for Dr Babcock in Vassar College *is just an easy stall for a worn out old horse to die in."*

I know, my dear Sir, this communication will greatly distress you; but, I feel I should be unworthy of the confidence you repose in me, and of the responsible position in which you have placed me, if I did not lay this subject before you.

You will appreciate my motives when I request you to treat this letter as *strictly confidential*—as between our consciences & our God; written, received & acted on purely from a sense of duty; from a paramount regard to the interests of the College—a regard which will permit no private partialities, no personal preferences, to destroy or injure your great public enterprise.

Yet I do not object to your showing this letter to Swan, under an injunction of secresy, if you wish to confer with him on the subject.

Should it become necessary, you can inform Dr B. that I have written, formally objecting to any action of the Trustees at their approaching meeting, in reference to the constitution of the Faculty, or the opening of a Preparatory Department, or School.

In conclusion, let me add, I sincerely trust that at a future day, some eligible situation in connection with the College will be found for the Doctor, which he can occupy with satisfaction to himself, and with the warm approval of our whole Board and of the entire community.

My wife knows nothing of the contents of this letter.

Trusting that God will preserve, direct & bless you, I remain, as always,

> Very truly & respectfully,
> Yours
> M. P. Jewett.[30]

This letter did not settle the Babcock situation nor was it intended to do so. At the annual meeting of the board of trustees a little over three weeks after the date of this letter, Babcock made the attempt that Jewett had predicted. The minutes of 24 June 1862 read:

> Dr Babcock addressed the Board in reference to completing say one third of the College Building. . . for the purpose of opening something in the nature of a preparatory department, and that it might be used to gather a corps of teachers in advance of the opening. . . Mr. Vassar followed in general approval of the remarks of Dr. Babcock in many of their aspects, that it seemed hardly possible while work was going on, but in some parts of the building and that it might be best not to disappoint public expectation by a gradual opening of the College in preference to the usual public ceremony. Dr. Babcock thereupon submitted the following resolution: "Resolved, that the propriety and wisdom of securing a preparatory department for a year or two, of the Vassar Female College be refered for consideration to the Committee on College Faculty & Studies with instructions to report at the next meeting of the Board.[31]

Jewett gave his version of the settlement of the question of the appointment of a chaplain. He wrote: "On my return Home I found Mr Vassar had adopted the idea of having the Pulpit of the College supplied from Sabbath to Sabbath by ministers of various denominations, thus at once relieving himself from his obligations to his old friend and gaining credit for his liberal sentiments."[32] How unfair these insinuations were Matthew Vassar, not a member of any church, stated plainly in his remarks at the first trustees' meeting in 1861—"All sectarian influences should be carefully avoided."[f] His decision about the office of chaplain simply carried out this intention.

The matter rested there apparently until May 1863. That Babcock had been rebuffed by Jewett and that he appealed to Vassar for sympathy and support is apparent in four letters written by Vassar to this disgruntled trustee. On 9 May 1863 Vassar observed:

> I received your very polite note of the 7th with enclosure. The latter I handed at once over to our President to reply as it is not my purpose nor wish to have anything to do in matters of the College appointments for I am persuaded that I am neither competent nor am I *inclined* to assume responsibility [where] nothing can be gained for myself or the Institution. Already have there been conflicts in its working thus far, and I am sure therefore there will be in the future. My business is to build, endow and outfit the College, and I shall have nothing to do with its internal organization. Your number *One* and *two* Statements by Mrs Babcock is entirely misapprehended. I merely remarkd this to her under the first head That at the last June Meeting you suggested the propriety and did bring forward a "Resolution" to make a few official appointments, but when it was remarked that such appointments in the absence of our President might not seem Courteous to him you at once concurred, withdrew the Suggestion and the matter was dropd . . . . Your visit to Nantucket to see Miss Mitchell was at your own suggestion and approved by our Ex. Committee who authorized me to pay or the Treasurer to pay your Expenses so that *no blame* whatever rested on you or on me in that matter. The truth is as I believe that neither anything you have *done* or left *undone* in connection with our College Matters have altered Prof. Jewetts feelings *towards you* as I *know* of, but that *Somebody* has prejudiced his mind against you I believe.
>
> You will excuse me if I rest my pen here as my head is beginning to get dizzy.[33]

Three days later Vassar resumed his correspondence with Babcock and attempted to allay his suspicions and fears.

Since my last of the 9th Current scarcely an hour has passed without my mind reverting to our College matters and bringing you in the Connection. In my last I briefly adverted to some incidents which may have changed Prof. Jewetts mind in relation to you, Altho' they were far from being satisfactory even to myself yet whatever they may be, have had their influence, I am sorry, very sorry indeed that such should be the circumstances as to lead to such results, but I Know not what to do, and would only advise patience & forebearance on your part perhaps something may "turn up" to remove them before the June Meeting, should this not be the case then I have in my mind another Scheme for your co-operation in promoting our Enterprise which I think will be honorable & gratifying to you and all concerned. . . . Do not let the development of the past few days dishearten or discourage you,—time works wonderful changes in mens minds—perhaps the Causes which led to change Jewetts, may be removed whatsoever they may be.[34]

Poor Matthew Vassar! he disliked the whole situation in which he found himself. It seems evident that he had made no headway in any attempts to placate Babcock. The following note is in answer to something Babcock had written to him. It clearly showed that Vassar was becoming exasperated with the situation:

I am this morning in receipt of yours of yesterday and allow me to repeat that I deeply deplore and most sincerely regret the position of the private affairs between you and Prof. Jewett and would to God I could enterpose some paliatives, but I know not how or where to begin, if I did I *certainly would* for a *Knowledge* of a *disease* is said to be *half its cure.* From my inmost heart I believe Prof. Jewetts prejudices against you are *candid* and *honest* and will never be changed unless the circumstances which induced them and led his mind to the present stand point are removed, whatever these may be he says he is willing and ready to disclose at the proper time. I would prefer to observe *entire silence* on what I suggested in my last letter until our next private interview or a little while before the June Meeting. . . at any rate it must be made at a *private interview.*[35]

Babcock addressed Vassar again on the matter on 1 June 1863. The impasse became too much for Vassar, and his reply to Babcock was clearly intended to close the matter. Vassar could not go further without breaking the confidence the president had imposed on him. He therefore wrote on 2 June:

Revd Rufus Babcock

My dear friend. Yours of yesterday the 1st is before me and which I have read with much interest as I do anything from your pen. In answer to your first enquiry whether "I had seen his two letters to you and your answer to his first" I reply *substantially* I have altho' not perhaps the identical or original ones send you, they were both mailed I believe before he read the Copies (if Copies) to me. When Prof Jewett spoke to me of these letters (I believe it was the first) that I reluctantly wish to be a party to the controversy but if I was drawn into it should keep back nothing from you or him, would be frankly just between you both. He then remark^d that he took the responsibility entirely on himself and would by no means draw me into the contraversy. As matters now stand it is impossible for you to fill *any chair* in the College of which Prof Jewett is President. I speak this from a knowledge of facts, because I do believe that if I was to make a point and insist on your Chaplainship or any other office in the College, Prof Jewett would at once resign. I cannot go into an argument or take part in one between you and him because I know it would be useless so far as to reconcile his feelings and it was for this reason that I stated in my last that I thought it best in you to remain entirely silent till a private interview with you either before or after the June Meeting. I do not Know which his purposes are in regard to calling the Committee on Faculty & Studies together earlier than the June Meeting, but will enquire when I next see him. He has been absent a day or two and is now very busy in his own study at home.[36]

Jewett's version of all of this as set down in his *Origin* (1879) was somewhat at variance with the impression created by these letters.

In the winter and Spring before I went to Europe, I was informed by several prominent Trustees and by other influential friends of the College that the proposed nomination of Dr Babcock would not be satisfactory. Indeed it was confidentially affirmed by persons whose views I was bound to respect, that the appointment of the D^r to any position in the College would be very unpopular and prejudicial to the interest of the new enterprise. While I was abroad the D^r urged his favorite plan of a partial opening but Mr Vassar silenced him by saying, "Nothing would be done in the matter till the return of the President." Reflecting on these matters during my absence, I was forced to the conclusion that neither Mr. Vassar nor myself, were at liberty to allow personal friendship to put at hazard the success of the College. . . I wrote to Mr. Vassar . . . giving my views and stating my reasons. As Mr. Vassar afterwards informed me, he received this letter and read it in the presence of several of his confidential advisors. After reading the letter Mr Vassar remarked to them, The President has come to the same conclusion with regard to Dr Babcock which we had arrived at some time before he wrote.

. . .Dr Babcock urged me to present his name to the Trustees at their expected meeting in February, 1863. I evaded the subject. . .He had noticed since my return, I had maintained a singular reticence, and reserve regarding this matter, and he desired me to state explicitly whether I would, or would not comply with his wishes. I replied I understood Mr Vassar has decided not to have any chaplain. . . .With much excitement he exclaimed, "He has, has he? I will see him about it." The next day I called at Mr Vassar's office when he laughingly informed me, Dr Babcock had been to see him about the Chaplaincy. Whereupon Mr. Vassar said to him, "You can never have any place in the College while Mr Jewett is President." Commenting on this startling piece of information, I said to Mr Vassar, You have done me great injustice in that statement. You know that you yourself had arrived at this conclusion before you ever heard a word from me on the subject, and it is a cruel wrong to me to place the responsibility of the D^{r}s disappointment to my account. But, I added my shoulders are broad. . . .

D^r B now entered into an alliance with the heirs, and from this time forward continuously and warily joined his efforts with theirs in a determined purpose to undermine my influence with the Founder.[37]

Careful reading of the manuscript of the *Origin* (1879) fills in the story, but one is led to suspect that there was much that Jewett chose to forget over the years or that his reporting had shown some lapses of memory. If he had been home during the crucial months of 1862 and had settled this problem between himself and Babcock, this unpleasantness might have been less intense. If he knew so much about Vassar's feeling about Babcock, why did he find it necessary to write so explicit a letter to Vassar, a letter which could have served as evidence in a rousing libel suit?

In effect, Jewett placed much of the unpleasantness at Vassar's door. Babcock soon learned that he was involved in an argument that Vassar refused to arbitrate. Vassar's candid statement in his last letter of June 1863 that "it is impossible for you to fill *any chair* in the College while Prof Jewett is President" removed any doubt from Babcock's mind that Vassar had any intention of interfering in a matter plainly within the jurisdiction of the president and the committee on faculty and studies.

The Babcock-Jewett dispute was an indication of the existence of political factions within the board. Vassar seemed only partially aware of this, for much of it must have been carried on behind his back. It went on to a point at which it could no longer be concealed. Babcock came out of this situation an unhappy man. As far as Jewett was concerned, the Babcock affair was closed, Babcock was unable to let the matter rest. Though he may not have bothered Jewett further, he continued to importune Vassar. Two records from Matthew Vassar's diary dated 13 October and 15 December (1863) tell of these:

> Rode to College with Dr Babcock had much talk about his future employment did not complain or talk hard about *Jewett* but was quite anxious to have some place in College—and tho' he could find a travelling Agency of some other sort, and as a cover for a college Professorship. viz, To solicit donation for Scholarships Endowments, and collect many valuable books as gifts from his numerous friends and acquaintances—In this occupation he would begin his labours next Spring—take leave of Patterson this fall—All this however would be done in a way without appearing as the employd or paid Agent of the College All of which I told him I would reflect upon Report &c.[38]

On 15 December he wrote:

> Doct Babcock calld at my office this P.M. when he again opened the subject of "Appointments" in the College and observd that he had been considering over the matter of the Lybrarian and Genl Agent for the collection & buying of Books and he tho' he could fill that plan to *sattisfaction* and would accept the appointment as Lybrian for *one half* the salleries we paid our Professors—To all of which *being* a *new* Suggestion I said I would reflect upon and when the proper time came would give him an answer. He remarked that he thot' probably the First B Church would give him a call to the Pastorship.[39]

As far as the records show, Babcock never served Vassar College in any capacity, other than as a trustee.

Jewett gave little space in his history of the college to discussing the development of an organizational plan. To be sure, he included a copy of his report in the *Origin* (1879) with this short preamble:

> Though for years, I had given much thought to some of the questions involved, yet there remained difficult problems to be solved and practical details were to be worked out, which required profound Study and the most careful elaboration. The distinguished gentlemen associated with me on the Committee, several of them among the foremost educators in the country, were too much occupied with the labors and responsibilities of their respective positions to be able to assist me, except by their invaluable suggestions and counsels.[40]

It would seem from this statement that Jewett had worked quite alone on this problem, since there was no mention of consultation with Vassar about any of the phases of the development of this important issue. Yet Vassar in his opening remarks to the trustees at their meeting of 23 February 1863 pointed to the progress that had been made in the construction of the building and stated that the opening of the college might have to be postponed to September 1865, a year later than had been anticipated. Then he came to the real business for which the meeting had been called— the study of the report on college organization. He continued his remarks:

> In respect to the general system of the organization proposed by your President, I heartily approve it. My attention was very much occupied during the summer, and indeed the whole year of 1862, with what is here spoken of as the University System. It was my great advantage to have had near me, and to have corresponded during that period, at very great length, with a gentleman quite familiar with not only the theory, but, to a great extent, with the practice of that system, so that when our President returned from Europe, I was already prepared to advocate and urge its introduction here. While, therefore, I regard this system as by no means a novelty, even in this country, I am not aware of its application to any such numbers of young women as we hope to gather here. However, it is not easy to discover why a system already proven in its applicability to young men, upon a large scale, and to young women only upon a smaller one, is not capable of almost indefinite expansion. For myself, I have no fears as to the success of the main features of this system.[41]

Vassar seemed to be well versed in the merits of the university system—well enough, indeed, that he suggested its adoption to Jewett as a possible model for the organization of the college. The president went along with him and eventually presented a modified form of the plan to the trustees.

But who was this gentleman who so thoroughly indoctrinated Vassar and educated him in the intricacies of the system before the February meeting of 1863? He was Charles A. Raymond. His name never appeared in the Jewett manuscript of 1879, which was extremely odd for Raymond played such a decided role in the proposed plans of organization. He helped Jewett, who related some of his difficulties to him—particularly those early experiences when Vassar was so uncertain about committing himself to the idea of a college for women.

The family of Charles Raymond's mother came from Poughkeepsie originally though she lived in New Haven in the 1860s. He attended Yale College and spent some time as a student at the Yale Theological Seminary. Like many young men trained in the North, Raymond went South to teach in the schools there for fifteen years before coming to Newburgh, New York, in 1861 or 1862. There he ran a "parlor school" for young ladies in the area. It was not a thriving concern, and he was barely able to make ends meet and support his rather large family. During the summer of 1862, he preached in the Baptist church in Poughkeepsie and there met Vassar. Shortly thereafter, he went to Hamilton, New York, where he attempted to make a success of a seminary for young ladies. He carried on a lively correspondence with Vassar from that place. Though Vassar supported him financially to some degree, the venture was not a success. Late in 1863 or early in 1864, he went to Washington, D.C., where he had obtained a position in the office of the paymaster general. His correspondence was continued from Washington through half of 1864, but most of these letters were addressed to Swan.

Jewett also knew Raymond from his days in the South as a fellow school master. He spoke of him in a letter to Sherman, as early as 1859:

I intend to go to the Convention, at Richmond, (May 6) and I want to meet you there. What say? Possibly, you might there arrange with Manly; or if not with Raymond; or some body else. Raymond is invited to Richmond Fem. Institute, since I declined. He writes me, he expects to go; but seems not, as yet, to have formally responded. He would *jump* at Judson, & I suppose, has the *tin*. Chesapeake College is to be sold under the hammer, & all is gone to smash.[42]

Raymond had been associated with Chesapeake College. Since he was already Jewett's acquaintance and since he later proved to be of some service in the matter of college organization, it is strange that no reference had been made to him in the *Origin* (1879).

Vassar welcomed anyone who was enthusiastic about his scheme for the higher education of women. Furthermore, he cultivated anyone who had suggestions to offer about carrying out such a project. Then, too, during Jewett's eight months' absence, Vassar had no adviser with whom he could speculate about the solution of the problems that vexed him. Raymond was on the scene. He had a forceful character and was certainly watchful for the promotion of his own interests. He was willing, even eager, to instruct Vassar in the elements of a plausible plan for the operation of the college.

Two years later, in 1864, Raymond wrote to Swan, then secretary of the college and still one of Vassar's trusted friends, giving his impression of Vassar's character when he first met him. Some of his remarks may have been intended to flatter, but many were true. Undoubtedly meant sincerely, the letter was dated 21 January 1864 and read as follows:

You know the nature of my relation to Mr. V. during the summer which I spent in P. preaching. I mean that of 1862. I had really never known Mr V. before, my impressions of him had been so erroneous, for I had been led to think of him only as a shrewd money-making man, that when I found him a man of cultivation and generous impulses: and withal, with broad views of educational matters and however of a generousity, able, and willing to do a grand thing in the world, by a kind reaction in which I suppose human nature sometimes indulges, I became as warmly interested in him, as in his enterprise. I saw clearly that he wanted something in the way of a System, which was new, comprehensive, and ahead of his age; and by a singular coincidence in personal history, my own specialty enabled me, perhaps better than any other living man, to give just what he wanted. It was astonishing how quickly he grasped the ideas upon which were based the plan of organization, which Mr. J. has published and which Mr. J. came to understand far more slowly than Mr. V. And as Mr. V. really made these views his own by feeling the need of them, and desiring to incorporate them into and identify them with his College, I soon had it in my heart, as a kind of pet plan of my own, to give Mr V. the credit of initiative in [the] whole thing, that he might stand before the world not only as a liberal founder, who had given a fortune, which indeed anybody who had it, could have done, but also as an *intelligent man* who had given a princely sum for a *definite, intelligent,* and *noble purpose.*[43]

Many of the letters that passed back and forth between these two men are missing, including most of those that had to do with instruction in the history and practice of the university system. Vassar may have enclosed some of them with the almost weekly letters that he addressed to Jewett during his stay in Europe. Indeed, in one of his last letters to Raymond dated 6 February 1864, long after Jewett had returned, Vassar wrote explaining his disappointment at not having those letters for reference. He wrote of them:

I am very busy just now in writing out what I want to say to our Board of Trustees at the annual meeting of the 23rd proximo and in so doing I shall try to embody such thoughts and ideas as will best convey my *original idea* on the education of woman, and for which I especially gave the endowment of $408,000 for the building of the College, ignoring as much of the old Systems of instruction as I deemed *wrong* and introducing such *new ones* as I believed to be *right* and the plan is substantially akin to the one which we often talk^d over and which you wrote me so copiously about while Professor Jewett was in Europe in 1862, and which I stated more or less in my correspondence with him in his absence abroad. Some time after Prof. Jewett returned home he requested the use of these (his letters to me) letters a little while to refresh his memory & I loaned them to him which together with mine to him he says he burnt up, therefore I have not a scrap of my correspondence with Prof. J. during his professional tour to Europe in 1862. I have since much regretted this Circumstance as I want them occasionally for reference.[44]

One wonders what motive lay behind the destruction of these papers, an action quite unlike the behavior that could be expected in the nineteenth century, when letters were saved and treasured. The papers were of no small value to Vassar, and Jewett could not have helped knowing it, since they contained a description of the university system and how it might be applied to the organization of Vassar College. They must have been quite comprehensive, for from them Vassar learned and understood the theory and its possible adaptation to Vassar College.

Raymond used his friendship with Vassar for his own advancement as well as for that of the college. His letters had a sense of easy familiarity, but at the same time, they showed a respect and a deference for Vassar. They were long, exceedingly verbose and so repetitive as to be tiresome and monotonous. Yet they often presented ideas with variations so that when the letter had been read, there was little doubt of its object. They were quite acceptable to Vassar, and all of them thought-provoking in one way or another.

In the first letter of this series, Vassar addressed his new friend in a rather surprising way—one that showed quite clearly the state of affairs existing between these two men. It was dated 30 July 1862:

My dear friend. I thank you very kindly for your valued favor of the 15th Current. Your suggestions concerning the plan of organization of officials in the V. F. College are deserving much attention and the more I have reflected and studied them the more they have commended themselves to my judgment and approbation &c.

I now specially allude to the Office of Vice President, but hope that the discussion of this question or any other between you and me on the subject of the organization of the College or its discipline, may be examined and freely discussed independent of any sinister motives, and *candor* impels me to say and acknowledge that thus far you have evinced the utmost impartiality and unselfishness. It is now however a proper time for me to express my *private thoughts,* therefore I assume the authority to *express them* that I know of no man whom in my judgment could fill the place of V. P. better than yourself nor one in whom I could most cheerfully concur in that appointment and after writing out my views somewhat in detail on this Subject to our President Prof. Jewett in my last letter, I thus signified my *opinion* and my *wishes.* However this matter must now remain open for further reflection and action untill Prof. Jewett's return when we shall take it up again, and within the present year may be able to make a proposition that will meet your entire approbation—my reasons I shall assign for advocating your appointment to *that* Department in the College that the "Suggestion" of such an office *first* came from you, *Secondly,* that your large experience in Female Education entitles your opinion and judgment to more than ordinary consideration.[45]

Now this may be one of those occasions to which Jewett referred, when he accused Vassar of taking things into his own hands. Vassar seemed positive enough at this point in his desire to have Raymond involved rather closely in college organization, but he qualified his approval by making it quite clear that no action would be taken until the president had returned home. Ultimately the appointment of Raymond to the post of vice-president was not made and no place was offered to him in the college organization.

The answer to this letter came within the week. Raymond replied:

...Your good opinion of me is certainly very kindly expressed & very comforting to myself. I don't know that you can *flatter as* well as our good friend the Doctor, but you certainly can say a kind thing in a way that is pleasing, because manifestly honestly thought, and well & sincerely expressed.

As for the future, never mind that, "we shall see what we shall see."

I have come home (from my mother's in N. Haven) sick with cold, head aching, throat as if scraped . . . I can't talk, and so I have spent two days in writing for your consideration the accompanying. Prof. Jewett has often heard me express the same opinions, and he agrees with me in sentiment. Most Teachers, especially those who have seen only the system of our American Colleges, would be afraid to try to make such an innovation. I shouldn't wonder if all your Trustees especially the "Rochester" & "Brown" men, however, would adopt it almost with acclamation. Especially if they thought it would work well *with girls.* Jewett, I am sure, after returning from Europe, where the University System prevails, will see how it can be applied to Girls and commend it. So you need have no fear that what commends itself to your practical sense is not also orthodox with College Professors. The system was introduced into this country from Europe by Thos Jefferson, when he fathered the Univy of Virginia, and I am told that Doct Wayland has published a book also defending it. Mr. Abbott of the Spingler Institute N. Y. after having some explanation of the system in vogue in the Chesapeake Coll. [had] said, "I have been trying all my life to get up such a system as that in N. Y. but I don't know how to do it." "I feel the want of it, but I can't accomplish it." And he is not alone.

I think it gives a great opening for Vassar College to make itself

felt at once, and I hope you will feel, how expedient it will be to stand at
once so high, as to make competition & even comparison impossible.
However, don't say anything on the subject to any one but bro Jewett.
Some one else may "steal our Thunder" before we are ready."[46]

Within a few days, he was expressing more concisely his ideas concerning the need for completing plans of the organization at least six
months before the opening date. He also briefly outlined how he might
make himself useful during this period in publicizing the college in much
the same way as he had his "female" seminaries in the South:

> . . .unless you will be ready to open your College, say a year from
> next month. If it were possible to have the building completed by that
> time, then it would be of the highest importance to have everything
> pertaining to your organization given to the world as soon after Jan'y
> next as possible: your organization perfected, your details all embodied
> in the form of a printed circular, which after bro. Jewetts return could
> be done, say, in *two* months. I could render you an untold amount of
> service, by canvassing the field from whence your pupils will be drawn,
> preaching and thus introducing myself to the public on Sunday & visit-
> ing through the week, explaining and urging upon parents the sure ad-
> vantages of Vassar College. While Prof. Jewett & yourself were at
> home attending to the important work of furnishing & completing
> building grounds, &c. &c., keeping up correspondence, & directing
> affairs generally. But if *two years are* to elapse as I think you informed
> me, before doing these things, then I do not see how I can aid you very
> materially. And I might in the mean time be establishing another
> seminary, which would prove one of the *feeders* of Vassar College.[47]

In the next few letters, he drew attention to the more immediate problems which he faced—those of financing the young ladies seminary at
Hamilton, New York, which he had contracted to run. He was quite free in
airing his financial affairs which seemed to be in a sorry state. He explained:

> The prospect in a business way looks dark. I certainly am caught,
> where I least expected it. Can your experience & tact tell me what to
> do? I shall leave Saturday to Preach in Phild. at the first chh, Sunday.
> Let me find a letter when I come back. I believe your nephew makes
> advantageous loans, sometimes. What must I offer to make him think
> it safe, & an object.[48]

Though he did receive some funds from his mother finally, there is no
doubt that he also received financial assistance from Vassar. In a later

letter, there is an acknowledgement of the receipt of a check for $250.

By late September 1862, Raymond's personal problems were under control, and he was ready again to take up another facet of college organization. On 22 September he wrote:

I have thought a good deal about your uneasiness concerning the pecuniary future of your College, as effected by the depression of securities. And my views, which are based upon what I have seen and experienced, are not of yesterday, would have been given to you long ago, had I not felt, as if, I *might possibly* be running counter to some of bro. Jewett's ideas upon the same subject, and I felt a delicacy in unnecessarily broaching them. When I saw that you were really annoyed however, I determined that as soon as I felt like myself, I would advance my suggestions letting them pass for what they were intrinsically worth. If you approve of them, and they seem to you sound, they will at least very much alleviate any future apprehension.

Candidly then, I am of the decided conviction that you could not do a more unfortunate thing tha[n] to leave Vassar College so liberally endowed that the teachers would be independent of their own exertions for a support. Could you so endow your Professorships, as to make them wholly independent of patronage, you would furnish positions for a class of men, who would perhaps in time become mere sinecures for lazy incumbents. I know that the best of men, need incentive, need a spur to exertion, or they will not half put forth their strength. There is no incentive like self interest, and you must make their support even, depend largely upon their effort, or you will never bring out and sustain half their energies.

If you give your magnificent building, furnished, free of rent, and endow *the building* with a sum sufficient to preserve it, with its grounds and furniture in perfect repair forever, with an additional amount to renew library & apparatus, And absolutely refuse to endow *Professorships* making your teachers earn by their success their salaries, and giving them all they can earn, to be divided among them according to a certain distribution the proportions of which shall be fixed by Law, you will have done more to keep up a lively and successful institution than if you endowed your Professorships with a million dollars.

You do not want lazy men, who will simply live and fatten on your bounty. You want energy, talent, success, and men who have such traits will make their own fortunes, with the opportunities you can give them.[49]

Vassar waited a week before answering. As he said in his reply, he had had plenty of experience in "the philosophy of adjusting remuneration for labour." He emphasized the importance that he attached to an equitable scale of salaries and showed that he had given some thought to a salary scale. This letter from Vassar was dated 2 October and read in part:

> I am perfectly aware of my ignorance to lead, and perhaps my folly even to suggest any thing new—yet relying upon a long life observation and experience in the Common business affairs of the world I may have gathered up some Knowledge that may have escaped thro' their apparent insignificancy, the minds of the more learned. Not wishing or expecting to anticipate your views intimated in your letter before me I will merely remark that the more I have reflected upon the employment of an organized salaried Corpse of Teachers the more decided and conclusive have my mind been convinced that it will be the identical shoal our College bark will strike and if not opening a seam wide enough to sink her, will at least so much impair her seaworthiness as to demand frequent repairs—with this nautical illustration (which please to excuse) I proceed to say that in my judgment every Employee from the highest to the lowest grade should in some way or other be dependent for stipend more or less upon their own exertions, and the only complexity of the Case is the mode of its arrangements. Without something of this Kind is *done* the V. F. C. begins and ends just where all its educational predecessors have and that very frequently disastrously. The first instinct of our race is *Self* make the promotory of that the chief object and there is no difficulty of finding Energy & Talent. Now then, who have we amongst us to draw up a programme on an just equitable Sliding Scale, so that every labourer get the equitable reward of his toil, thats the Problem to be solved, can Mr Raymond effect this? if so, I should like to secure his services.[50]

At the end of the month, came his opinion on the question of salaries, sandwiched in between a brief account of a fire at the brewery and plans for heating and ventilating the college building which were of great concern to him. He wrote in this letter dated 25 October as follows:

> I have taken the earliest opportunity to look over and examine your letter setting forth your plan of the working process of our College Institution and while in the main I highly approve of it, yet it admits of some modification on the Sliding Scale upon which the respective compensations are based. As it now stands it possibly might carry the Salaries of President and Profs entirely too high—take for instance the first officer y^r President at 200 pupils his share would be *$4,166.66*, suppose there is 400 pupils then his portion would be $8333.33; now

while I grant that the operation of the plan is an incentive to *industry* yet the *self interest* principle should not all inure to the employees benefit but rather to be reciprocal or divided between them and the College. But I have not time this morning to suggest a better plan if I *could,* shall therefore leave the subject for further reflection. Allow me to thank you for the present very kindly for your valuable suggestions, long before our College goes into operation I hope to have the pleasure of seeing you when we can talk over more fully all matters connected with the working of the Institution.[51]

Raymond answered this point briefly in a long letter devoted primarily to the more trivial doings of his everyday life:

I believe we left off in the midst of the subject of "paying Professors". I was trying to show you that an endowment was not necessary in order that they might be paid. That the right men would pay themselves. It seems that I proved too much, and you see that they might receive too high salaries. Practically I think they would not be excessively paid for the risk they would run, & the stimulus they would have. But you could modify the plan beyond a certain point. Though it is a question whether any diminishing of the stimulus would as effectually aid the Institution. All that you could ask of them ought to be to pay their own way, and take their own risks, letting them have what they could make. First rate talent, would thus be repaid, and such cannot be had without paying for it.[52]

Raymond decided to draw these discussions to a close by summarizing the different plans for Vassar's study. They are instructive and show that both gentlemen had given much thought to the problem. The summary of the letter will be sufficient to quote here:

... plans to be considered:
1. That of an *Endowment of Professorships.* This you do not approve, and we set it aside.
2. The Teachers partnership System, by which the profits are divided among the Teachers. This you have under consideration, but don't altogether like. It is however better than the endowment plan, for your purposes, and you have a complete schedule if you wish to adopt it. It won't however suit you as a working plan as well as this.
3. Which makes the College a sharer in the profits, and the principal sharer, but for the benefit after all of the Teachers....
—You pay the Professors a fixed salary.
—You do not make the College property liable for this, but on the contrary—you fix it so that it cannot be made liable, but you pay out of

the net profit of the concern, i.e. you make these liable 1st for teachers' salaries.

—You hold the accruing profits sacred, to be invested as a fund for guaranteeing teaching salaries,—i.e. supplying deficiencies *in the future.* And after the fund shall have reached a certain amount say $15,000, the future accretions to be divided pro rata among the teachers, in addition to stated guaranteed salaries.

—For the first five years, you, i.e. the Founder make a special provision against deficiencies, so that the teachers' salaries may be sure. This gives all the certainty of an endowment, involves the coll. property in no risks—disarms objectors—and places your coll. upon an elevated financial platform. It also makes it right that you should give somewhat less to your teachers, to whom the guarantee serves in place of a "margin" for larger income.

I think you will like this as a working arrangement. Your quick insight into practical details will enable you to grasp its advantages at once, and it meets by its originality, your unexpressed wishes.[53]

Certainly, of the plans the last would have been the easiest to administer. The final reference to a salary scale made by Vassar was in a letter to Anderson about some questions that were apt to arise at the February meeting in 1864. Of professors' salaries, he wrote, "I am not so sure but some other system can be adopted whereby fixed *emoluments* to Professors & others may be substituted for working sliding scale, it is more easy to follow in the wake of old customs, than to strike out new ones. The present age has unfolded if *not new things,* a new way of doing *old* ones."[54] One wonders whether Vassar had a clear idea of what he did consider an appropriate scale of salaries. In fact, one rather suspects that he would have professors paid on some modification of the method of paying salesmen in his brewery—but it must be something new. The whole problem was solved without much fanfare before the college opened in 1865, with a salary scale that was adequate for the times. It was complicated by the fact that the president with his family and all members of the teaching staff with theirs lived in Main Building, and subsidies were given them in terms of housing and meals. All of the members of the faculty also lived in Main Building, except Maria Mitchell, the professor of astronomy. She had an apartment in the Observatory. She and Alida Avery, the college physician and the professor of physiology, moreover, quite early discovered that they were not receiving compensation equal to that of the men and were quick to bring this fact to the attention of the trustees. In closing the subject of salaries and a salary scale, it is of interest to note that Vassar made some provisions for funds to cover the payment of salaries in the opening years of the college. When his will was read, it was discovered that no part of the funds left to Vassar College had been set aside to endow salaries.

Dr. Alida Avery, the college physician and professor of physiology, 1865-74

Surely Raymond thought of everything pertaining to the college and reported these thoughts to his correspondent. He was quick to point out to him that there might be some difficulty in securing students who were prepared for the rigors of such an education as Vassar College was to offer. Raymond seemed to have a very mixed opinion about the worth of the training that the average seminary gave its women students in those days. Jewett, who must have been aware of this and must have discussed it either with Vassar or the members of the committee on faculty and studies, however, made no specific reference to the problem in his plan of organization.

What brought this matter to Raymond's attention was the reading of a pamphlet that Vassar had sent to him for an opinion. Now Vassar was very proud of this independent evaluation of his scheme made by Moses Coit Tyler in the *New Englander*[55] of October 1862; in fact, he had reprints made of it and sent them to many friends and interested parents. Raymond's letter, largely critical as many of his opinions were, was a typical Victorian response, one that even then was on its way out. He wrote emphatically:

You may regard it as a fixed fact. You *must have a preparatory department,* blended with your College. You can only avoid it in one way & that is death to your Institution—viz: by making your College of so low a grade as to burlesque the very title of college. Your great success will be with pupils who enter at about fourteen years of age. And such will alone *graduate*. Girls are manifestly not boys; let us not forget this. Boys study for a profession; girls cannot. More than half the students in our male colleges, have passed that period of life, which leave girls in the honorable but not envied class of old maids. Love is a stronger sentiment with girls than ambition—not with boys. Men crave distinction —wealth—influence. Women crave affection—a husband—a home. You can't change nature: And if you depend upon girls who have passed eighteen years, to enter and stay four years, you will find the number who graduate very few—and these are all ugly. The good looking girls will all have lovers & be in a hurry to marry. Your only chance for securing graduates will be to so arrange your system of studies that the pupils may enter from thirteen to fourteen—one year preparatory— graduate at nineteen or twenty. You can't hold them any longer, unless they are bound to be old-maids & professional teachers. This is the practical plain truth. The idea of a College such as Tyler alludes to, is so intangible, that I suppose he couldn't help the intimation that it might fail. . . .

The last few pages about the depression of women are true of the past, but not of the present, & among us. *Per contra* the very fact that women really govern us, not through our intellects, but through our sensibilities, and that they are the ruling power, is the true ground for advocating their education.[56]

Unfortunately, there is no extant answer to this effusion, for Vassar's response would have been most interesting to read. He was rapidly being educated about the role of women in the world, and he was coming to see that it could and should be broader and more constructive than it had been. He was beginning to see, too, that the role need not only be limited to influencing men by mothers, wives, or teachers. His grand defense of his point of view, given quietly and forcefully in his talk to the trustees at their meeting of February 1864 was proof of how far he had progressed in his belief that women should receive a liberal and liberating education at the hands of devoted, well-trained women for an active role in the world.

What Raymond wrote to Vassar about the application of the university system to the college organization and curriculum cannot be known. That Jewett and Raymond worked together is certain: the correspondence between Raymond and Swan makes this clear. Such a cooperative effort was carried on largely by mail, but there is evidence that, at one point, Jewett went to Hamilton and conferred with Raymond. Raymond wrote to Vassar on 13 March 1863 of that occasion:

Jewett and I have been butting our heads together in the dark for sometime, he not getting hold of my ideas very clearly, and I wholly ignorant of his. . . . I proposed to him to make some arrangements by which we could be together during the work of organization, thinking that if my help was needed, the College could afford to pay my expenses while doing this work; and if I was not needed, I was spending so much time very unprofitably to others & to myself.

The result of my proposal to Jewett has been the development of his proposed method of completing the College organization, and which is so different from what I imagined it would be; and so different are our views of what is demanded by the occasion, that it makes all my anxieties and writings in the College behalf appear simply ridiculous, because not understood, or not wanted. However it is very clear that the time had arrived for such a discovery on my part, and that I did well in seeking to force it by my proposal. . . .

But Jewett's ideas are very different from mine. In fact his notions and mine are opposites. His idea, as I understand it, amounts practically, to the having [of] just such a school as the others have, i.e. Crittenden, Abbott, &c, only *bigger.* His general idea is this, to elect the teachers, and let each in his department arrange his subjects, and matter of instruction. This is of course *orthodox,* i.e. it is what any man who had no special object to accomplish would do. It is what has been done for forty years & to a great extent by Lady teachers, and the result is a piece of *patchwork;* no leading purpose to accomplish; no leading mind bending all the instruments of instruction to that purpose;—& guiding and assimilating the whole. In fact no object, no system at all, only a certain quantity of education furnished by each of yr men. Of course, when compared with others, it is only more of the same stuff, that is now so plentiful in Po'k & other places. The patch work is in bigger pieces because worked upon the larger framework of a great establishment.

Here you see how great a difference there is in our ideas of what is needed and how to carry out the *organization,* so as to accomplish the need. I would have *for my purpose,* a radical reform in the whole system of Fem. Studies (and I have shown Jewett how this can be done), when I speak of the need of it, & possibility of it. I have facts to refer to introduced to the world in connection with the Founding of V.F.C. and giving the founder the honor of rearing this edifice to accomplish such definite purpose. . . . I would have all my working plans & course of Studies each subject to be taught specified, and how to be taught &c prepared & adjusted in every department *before electing teachers:* (and not wait for them to teach me what should be taught, & how taught) and I would have the teachers elected to carry out the Founder's wishes, in a *fixed specified way.* . . . Jewett elects the teachers first, &

they *make out their own work.* Of course, as they are elected to do nothing in any special manner, they are not accountable to any one for their manner of teaching, and may do as they choose so they do nothing flagrant. I would, having carefully day by day, canvassed with the Founder such points as I know he wished to teach, so teach them by incorporating them into my system of laws, so that the Professors when chosen *shall be chosen under them,* & liable to dismissal if not conforming to them.[57]

Raymond must have astonished Vassar with his plan for the control of teachers and the curriculum they would teach. Whether Vassar subscribed to this idea would be of considerable interest, but no account is given of his reaction. Raymond apparently had no intention of having his views ignored, and he fired off another shorter note within the week. Again somewhat later, he lambasted Vassar:

Now who is the author of the System which Mr Jewett prizes so highly, and which he hopes to gain credit for introducing into V.F.C.? I do not mean who made the system, *but who first suggested it for your institution,* and *accepted it as the thing best adapted to its wants?* If you did not do it, while Mr. J. was in Europe and before he knew anything about the details of the matter, then you and I are two very mistaken individuals.

As to the work of convincing Mr J. of the excellency of the System; of making out its details, and adapting them to his purpose, *I did all that,* not for his reputation, *but for yours,* and because I knew what would meet your views and wishes. You had certain ideas, often expressed in your conversations to me, which you wished carried out in the College you had founded. You needed help, for the habits of your life had been such that you were not familiar with the practical details of such work as organizing a college for young Ladies. Mr. Jewett never could have done what you wished, and therefore I did it for you through him. To whom now belongs the honor, Certainly to you, and to me if to anyone.[58]

This was too much for Vassar, who could see that he was being drawn into a controversy that could do his college little good. So he determined to shut off the stream of ideas that Raymond poured out. On 5 June he addressed his friend:

Sir I have held your last letter under consideration for several days, my feeble health forbiding me to enter into particulars respecting the contents, I must only say that having visited Dr Willard Parker at N. Y. last week, he was imperious in his advice "I must have rest", he also said the brain was taxed too much—I must think and talk less, I must give it up, therefore I shall follow his advice. The erecting of the College and endowing it is business enough for me. I have chosen a President in whom I have unshaken confidence, a board of Trustees equally as trustfully; with them the College will stand or fall. On the President I throw the great responsibility cheerfully. I am much obliged to you for the interest that you have expressed for the Institution and the proferred advice, but my health and the Doctors *Commands* will prevent me from participating any more in the plan of organization on these grounds I must be excused as my health is greatly suffering by reason of over taxation of the brain.

I cannot however let this opportunity pass without acknowledging your Kindness and the valuable suggestions & services thus far rendered in College matters and for which I beg you to accept my warmest thanks with the enclosed note of yours payable to my order, say $262 with interest.[59]

The final blow to Raymond came when he received a copy of Jewett's report, which had been made to the trustees at their meeting of 30 June 1863. Though the discussion was postponed by this body, they had authorized its publication as the *Report of the Committee on Faculty and Studies,* the plan for the organization of the college. Vassar sent a copy to Raymond, who did not acknowledge its receipt for some time. When he did, he blasted both the *Report* and its author.

Hamilton, Aug. 13, 1863.

Matthew Vassar Esq

Dear Sir

I have to acknowledge the receipt of a letter from you some time since with enclosure. My acceptance of the enclosure can only be temporary, & from force of circumstances, which now promise to be of short duration. Mr. Jewett had succeeded in insulting me quite grossly before your letter arrived, so I was not surprised at its tone.

Upon Mr. Jewetts former pledge to allow nothing materially in the plan of organization, which upon his importunity I made out for him, I wrote you *a private letter,* concerning the authorship of the plan. But I find the plan as now printed, so mangled, and defaced, and so much added which is crude and impracticable, & wholly ridiculous: that in justice to myself I must father the misshapen abortion upon Mr. Jewett. How much he knew a year ago of the principles and details of the system which he now professes to understand so well (and how he) had obtained the knowledge is revealed in the "plan"; you and I both know. But as he has reported and reproduced these principles and details, his plan is full of blunders; and as a working Schedule wholly impracticable. In a word "What is good is not new, and what is new is not good", and it is just such a mongrel affair as from his correspondence with me I was led to expect, and from which I tried in vain to save him. Now the thing is out, and challenges criticism—it shall have mine as freely as it invites it. And as soon as I get time, I shall address through the public press and over my own signature, one or more letters to your Trustees upon *the history and defects* of the plan of organization as submitted to them.[60g]

Vassar's reply to this show of displeasure was evidently designed to prevent such a display in the future. The letter, short and to the point, bore the date 2 September 1863:

Dear Sir

Your letter of 13th ulto. I found on my desk on my return from Newport after an absence of some four weeks to the SeaBord for the benefit of my health, which must be my apology for not replying sooner. I have perused the same with as much attention as my feeble state of health will admit, and regret extremely that your feelings should be in the least degree cool towards me as you say in the first paragraph "that you was not surprised at the tone" of my letter after Jewetts treatment &c towards you. Allow me to say very honestly and promptly that I have not had nor would I take any part in the private questions or contraversy between you and Prof Jewett. I was and have as far as I know been entirely neutral, that the latter has done the fair thing with you I am not prepared to say "Yes or No" as I have not seen all your correspondence that you have strove to render the College enterprise a *Success* by adopting your plan of organization. I have always acknowledged and intended the return of your note &c as a compensation for that trouble, and for no other purpose and I thankd you then and again at this time for it.[61]

Raymond's letter seems not only an ill-humored display of displeasure, but it was also badly timed and spiteful. He took unto himself the full credit for instructing Jewett and apparently thought that the president had no ideas of his own which could be used in adapting the university system for use at Vassar. To understand this, it is well to read portions of a letter Raymond addressed to Swan in January 1864 which gave Swan the historical background of Raymond's earlier relations with Jewett:

The history of the plan of organization for V. F. C. comprises the history of Mr J's. relations to myself. Our intimacy, never very cordial, commenced and ended with that history. This as you request it I will give you for your "personal edification".

Here hangs. . . . as I suppose, the secret of Mr J's peculiar conduct towards myself. The glory of the new system was to be Mr V's and not Mr J's. Mr. J. on the contrary wished to father it himself. If this is not a bone of variance, I don't know what it is. . . .

When Mr J. came home from Europe, I went to work at him, knowing that he had it all to learn, and that any plan of organization for V. F. C. must be given to the world through him. He consented to hear what I had to say. I commenced a series of articles which became at least *lengthy enough* to make a book of respectable size. He soon seemed interested, and urged me to go on, & write more. I consented with the sole condition that he would return my papers when I wished them, retaining only copies if he wished, as I had no time to copy them. My object. . . was to post him up thoroughly in the system for his own good. . .that he might have wherewithall to silence those who would no doubt gainsay the truthfulness of the premises upon which the system was based.

These papers & letters, if you can get hold of them, will best show what was done by me. . .at last he began to see the merits of the System I was advocating, and its salient points. . .then he began to be as greedy for facts, principles, plans &c as anyone could desire.

. . .I have his letters to show for it. He was at the first wholly ignorant of that which he now calls "his system". . .and it occurs to me that I was so disgusted with his ignorance, that in a letter to Miss Amanda I once let the thing out, quite inadvertently. . . .

He seems to have determined to squeeze me dry, and then throw me away. I was not therefore surprised when about the last of May, after I had sent the last sheet necessary to complete the course of study &c that he evidently cooled off wonderfully towards me. I had been very earnest in a letter, a copy of which I sent to Mr V. I believe, in urging him to forestall all objections on the part of others by placing Mr V. in the front rank, and present the plan of organization as Mr V's deliberate choice. . . .He wrote back a letter speaking of *his* "own system"*, and as one which he had adopted *in preference to the one I had proposed,* & spoke of *his own doings in a way* which made me think he was gone "clean daft" in the whole matter. . .I determined to drop the correspondence. I then wrote a very kind letter telling him I had done in the future with the whole subject. . . .This letter *he returned unopened, and I have heard nothing* since directly from him![62]

So much for the background of the Jewett/Raymond collaboration as seen through the eyes of the latter. Swan certainly showed this letter to Vassar, who already recognized a situation in which he had played a part. Evidently he accepted the Jewett report, since he backed his president in the meeting of 30 June 1863 at which it was presented.

At a later date, Swan received from Raymond another letter which was a long diatribe against Jewett. Some surprising facts emerge from it. Most of all, the letter showed that Jewett had not been discreet in his conversations with Raymond. In fact, the letter reads like a digest of portions of the *Origin* (1879). In a single paragraph that is very similar in feeling to two-thirds of the history, Raymond recounted what Jewett had told him of those early years of the evolution of the college idea. These remarks were not complimentary and showed how little judgment the president used at times. Raymond, for all his shortcomings, was conscious of the unkindness and lack of restraint displayed, for he wrote:

Now these facts may be partly true & they may not, but the representation of them to the world, even in a conversation, is to place Mr J. in the heroic attitude, and Mr V. in the mock heroic. Could a man who had a true sense of that delicate honor which should have shielded Mr V. before others, have taken Mr V's two thousand a year (Europe included) thus & show him through the reverse a telescope![63]

He went on to relate Jewett's discussions of the early financial problems and Vassar's "shocking handling of Them"—affairs very impolitic to relate to anyone, let alone Raymond. He continued his remarks:

Next came his disregard of Mr V's wishes with *regard to the Sectarian Character of the College.* He always prided himself that by his superior adroitness he has secured *a majority of Baptists* in the Board. And that it must & should be, really and virtually a Baptist affair. . . . He has vowed openly that no matter what Mr V. wishes *there shall be a chaplain in fact, if not in name.* This was in reply to my oft repeated statement, of the principle that Mr V's wishes should be law upon such matters, as the Sectarianism of his own College. . . he was determined to defeat Mr V's wishes. . . *he himself willed it to be so.* [64]

From January to June of 1864, Raymond persisted in tossing off letters to Swan, who apparently encouraged him to do so. There were some lingering hopes for the vice-presidency and Raymond told Swan what he would do for the college in such a position. With the appointment of John H. Raymond to the presidency as Jewett's successor, the correspondence seemingly came to an end.

There remains a curious letter in the Jewett/Sherman correspondence which referred directly to Charles Raymond and should be recorded as a part of this history. On 10 March 1864 Jewett wrote:

By the way, wife says you shook your head incredulously, when she was eulogizing "Charley" Raymond. Now, tell me, frankly, what you know,

1. In regard to his troubles in S. Carolina;
2. In regard to his *property* in the Ches. Fem. College, & his success therein, Tell me such facts as *you are willing,* I *should use,* if it becomes necessary to expose his true character, in order to protect important interests in the church or the community, hereabouts. You are aware, I have had good reason to change the estimate I formerly placed on him.[65]

Meanwhile, Jewett looked forward to 1864 as a year in which the plan of organization of the college would be accepted and a faculty might be chosen to carry it out. The idea of a college in full operation by September of that year was uppermost in his mind, and he was prepared to do battle with any forces that might oppose it. He took for granted that his plan of organization would be accepted without much change, especially since it was the result of considerable thought on his part and met with Vassar's approval.

Jewett had pushed forward from December 1862 to June 1863 to produce the plan and, judging from the report of his findings in England and Europe during those eight months in 1862, he found little there that he could use for his purposes in setting up a challenging and sound curriculum. The nature of and number on the teaching staff, of course, would depend upon the number and nature of the studies to be offered. If one takes the Raymond correspondence seriously—and there is no reason for not doing so—he furnished a complete plan, outlined in many letters both to Vassar and Jewett. In the Raymond letters, there are references to visits of Jewett with him during those months, too, although characteristically the president did not once acknowledge the existence of any collaboration in his *Origin* (1879), nor refer to any assistance that he had from the outside. He did claim that he sought the opinion of the members of the committee on faculty and studies, but that they were too involved in their own affairs to be expected to give much time to this important business. (Not to have used them more actively was a mistake because such men as Nathan Bishop[h] could have contributed much of value in setting up the plan and would have reduced the influence of Raymond decidedly. Bishop had worked with Francis Wayland in the revision of the curriculum of Brown University in 1849-50. Wayland was famous for the liberal and strong educational plan he had evolved. He had also written a concise little book[66] about his ideas for the arrangement of studies which much resembled the university system.)

Jewett quite cleverly adapted ideas which Raymond claimed to have given him into a useful document, fresh in its approach to the education of those young women Jewett hoped might enter Vassar College not only in September 1864, but in years to come. Raymond might say all that he would of the president's inability to grasp the essentials of the university system as he presented them to him, but the fact remains that Jewett used them by taking what he found to be useful and adapting ideas to his needs.

At the June meeting of the board of trustees in 1863, Jewett read excerpts of the report as coming with the blessing of the committee. Then, wisely, he proposed a resolution "that [the report] and resolutions of the Committee on Faculty and Studies now submitted be laid on the table and ordered to be printed,—to be taken up, at a meeting of the Board which shall be held on the last Tuesday of February next."[67] Such a published document would furnish each member of the board with a copy which they could study in preparation for intelligent discussion and action. The idea was also to submit copies to educators for their reactions and comments.

The adoption of this report was related to the opening date of the college, and that in turn would determine the selection and appointment of a teaching staff, apparently because Vassar opposed appointments to the faculty much before the opening date. For one thing, there would be no place for them to live but in the college building, and housing them might present problems if their living quarters were not in condition to receive them. Most of all, he felt it would be an extravagance to make appointments too far in advance of the time that their services would be needed.

There must have been lively debates on the question of what exact date could be set for the first classes. The founder himself wanted all things in order, so that students might enter a well-equipped college building, adequately prepared for heating and ventilation, and surrounded by trim grounds. There were some real doubts about meeting these conditions before September 1864 and there had been rumors that the executive committee was considering a later date for the reception of the first students. Jewett became much agitated by the possibility of postponement of the great day. His uppermost desire was to see the students arriving at college prepared to begin their studies in 1864. Any delay was unthinkable; it became a passion with him, absorbing his attention and driving him to extremes. He determined that he must have his way, and he set out on a campaign which could only lead to unpleasant and sad results for all and disaster for himself.

He was convinced that there was a plot backed by Matthew Jr. and, perhaps, Swift. At first, he brooded over this and out of his brooding came a letter to Vassar. He wrote it in late September or early October 1863. It was different from his other letters in that he used as some of his arguments, information and situations that properly were none of his business and were outside the jurisdiction of the office of president. His intention was clear but his motivation was difficult to justify. He simply saw no reason why his wishes should not be met. In this long letter, some six pages of hastily written argument, he began:

I have never given you any reason to doubt the sincerity & earnestness of my respect & affection for you. Of this true and devoted esteem, I have given you many proofs—not by smooth & flattering words, but by hard work, day & night, in assisting you to mature your grand and generous plans for the elevation of the gentler sex: laboring with voice & pen, to do justice to the benevolence of your character, the purity of your motives, the nobleness of your aims. Once, when certain interested parties would have dragged you down from the sublime elevation on which you stood, I rushed into the breach, and, today, instead of being known only in Dutchess County, as the builder of a city Free School, your name is hailed on both sides of the Atlantic, as the most liberal Benefactor of Woman which any country or any age has produced.

And, now, in my judgment, another crisis has come, which compels me to lift up a warning voice. My love for you, my jealousy over your honor, my desire to see all your remaining years pass in ever increasing respect & happiness, all forbid that I should keep silence. Will you listen kindly to my statements?[68]

From this point, he plunged into his argument about the disaster of a postponement of this great day. He gave every reason at his command to support his contention that the college buildings with all their furnishings and equipment could be made ready for a grand opening within the year and asked the question "Will the Executive Committee fail to perform their part of the work"—to see that all was in readiness for the reception of students, faculty, and employees? One telling argument for opening the college at as early a date as possible was a concern for public disappointment at a postponement.

Midway in the letter, he used a simile, a favorite literary device of his, to make clear his point of view. Here he wrote rather brusquely:

Suppose you had a gold mine at Pikes Peak, with thousands of tons of quartz rock waiting to be ground, that you might extract millions of dollars worth of gold from them. You have been nearly three years, at great expense, in erecting mills for grinding the quartz, & now they are nearly completed. You have beautiful mills, admirably adapted to your purpose—the envy & admiration of all the miners in the Gold Fields. You can easily complete your mills, & have them in full operation, another autumn, yielding to you, $5,000 to $10,000 a day in pure gold. Now, what would the miners say, what would all men of common sense say, if you should address them thus? "Gentlemen, these are magnificent mills; with the proper engines put in, they will crush the quartz & roll out the gold gloriously; I can easily finish them, by next fall, but I believe I will not put in the engines then, I will take another year to admire these buildings, & make myself happy in contemplating their beauty, and their adaptation to the end for which they are erected. To be sure, I have spent some $300,000 on these works, preparatory to the great object I have at heart, and all this will lie here, during the next year, unproductive capital, a dead loss; but there is time enough yet— there will always be quartz rock enough in these mountains to be crushed out, so I will let my splendid buildings, & all the capital I have invested, lie idle another year!!!" You can make the application.[69]

Vassar did not reply until late October. His letter repeated Jewett's arguments in his rebuttal of them:

I am first constrained to say, *your* want of experience in those matters which it chiefly embrac[d].—seemed to carry the *idea* that it was only to *will* and it is *done*, to *command* and it *stands fast—*you *forget* that there is much time taken up *unavoidably* in *preliminaries,* before the work can commence. He is a wise man who first sits down to count the cost before he begins to build his house and well considers his plans &c. As an illustration think of the amount of debates, opinions &c &c growing out of the apparent simple location of the Gate Lodges, which by the by, your consel with the Executive Committee reccommendations took up several consecutive weeks, waiting the plans of Daniels & Renwick, and then consider the time consumed in setting upon the Buildings to be erected for Heating & Lighting the College &c.

You know or at least ought to know, that I have always strenuously urged and advocated the policy (for the past year) of expending the College funds in all necessary & indispensable departments as fast as possible as they then was commanding advanced values—besides I was extremely anxious to press forwards not only to get our funds into Bricks Mortar &c, but to finish all the material structures to save other expenses and turn the current the other way, viz. earning an income, in its educational departments.—With due difference to your superior judgement in these latter matters, I am willing to yield, but in those of general business character, you nor any other man shall dictate to me my duty. Your life and experience has been one of an educational type—mine of business in general, you are practicaly in *your calling, I in mine,* and I allow no man to coerce or dictate to me in my course of policy. Your desires and ambition appear[s] to be baised entirely on the relations which the College will sustain to the *present—mine* to the *pre-sent* and *future.* You are for doing things up. . .in a day, I am for completing firmly, and leave the gloryfication of it to the future generations —You seem to predicate *your idea* upon the fact of its present *moral* influences, but I would respectfully ask wether there will not be "precious souls to be saved" after you and I are gone to our final resting places. You urge the opening of the College in fall '64, that the founder may see the *fruits of his labours* to "his honor & happiness", shurely if any human eyes would desire to see this consumation mine much more so. Generaly my fellow creatures give their wealth to charitable objects after their discease, but I have been permitted thro' God to cast my Bread upon the Waters while I live, and you are now Lecturing me why I dont give it faster!—If for the good of the enterprise, I am willing to forego the pleasure of seeing the College in opperation—shurely you ought not to complain.—Your *simile* applied to me in a California *Gold Mill* is *nonesense*. You take it for granted I have built the mill to grind *your Grist only*—I pray its benefits will extend far and wide. Another argument you propound for my consideration "The happiness I will have to walk out, over the broad grounds and *inspect* and *suggest improvements* &c &c." You *seem not* to consider that I am an old man nearly 72 years of age and subject to much more than the ordinary infirmities of age, but suffering with bodly as well as mental weakness—especially when over-taxed—It was only Thursday I came home took my bed at 7 P.M. could neither sleep nor rest, partly on account of a physical ailment, which troubls me much when I [am] taxed too much.—But to return again to some of your *Questions.*—*You* seem to *forget* that *I am not* the owener of the *College funds.* I have no more right *how* or *when* to use *them* than any other man on the Ex Comm— *True* out of respect to the Founder they have often yielded their own judgement, but I am not therefore willing to abuse it. I am unwilling to exact a tame submission to my authority. I have no more *official* power than any other of my associates, and then why should I place myself in an attitude to offend them &c—You say the College has lost money by *delays* as everything is now dearer? Ah—my dear Sir you have discovered *the fact after* and *not* before it *happened?* Why did you not tell the Committee that every article of building was a going to *grow* dearer after War was *declared?*. . .The facts show the contrary. Did not stocks and all securities decline? Did we the Committee not sell our first years funds to meet College payments *below par,* have we not made up our loss? and much more besides by not going faster? You forget the financial interest of the College. We have more than made up our loss by keeping along Moderately, but you say too *slow*. . . .You say there will be a greater *inflation* of *prices,* next summer, *now,* I think so too, and stocks at least some of them will perhaps be doubled in Value and if this should be so why spend our funds so rapidly, and especially when you have to pay 39 to 40 p^r c^t more for what you buy?[70]

There is nothing in this vigorous letter to suggest that Vassar was a doddering old man. What clearer warning could Vassar have given the president to attend to those matters which were within his province? Yet

Jewett so distrusted some of the committee's members and their influence on Vassar that he made it a question of who should prevail. The question of the opening date, therefore, became all-important to him.

A second warning came in December 1863 which, though it concerned a matter of slight consequence, should have put the president on his guard. Matthew Jr., who distrusted Jewett as completely as the president did him, wrote of an incident in his diary under the date of 15 December:

This day meeting of the Ex Committee—some sharp shooting by Chairman M.V. against President J—the Bill presented as expenses on Faculty—going N.Y. enquiring for some Teachers without consultation and without any use at present—J. has apologized & seen Error—making such charge of Expense $20—while is Receiving his $2000 for year salary &c.[71]

Such criticisms led Jewett to fear that Vassar was completely dominated by the other members of the executive committee. Had he read Vassar's letter dispassionately, he would have discovered exactly what Vassar considered to be his role as a member of the committee. He apparently could not do this, and as time went on, he became more and more apprehensive. He was convinced that all the arguments for an early opening of the college were on his side.

Anderson, of the University of Rochester, though he had had but a slight acquaintance with Jewett in 1861 at the time of the inaugural meeting of the trustees, had backed him for the presidency of the college at a salary larger than his own. Jewett was grateful for his stand on the salary question, and he assumed that Anderson was on his side against those whom he distrusted. The Andersons were in Europe during most of 1863 and returned in December of that year. Jewett began immediately to discuss his college problem with him with great frankness. This must have been embarrassing, for the letters were not very temperate. They named Matthew Jr. as the chief culprit, accusing him of wishing to postpone the opening of the college until 1865 or even indefinitely.

An examination of the minutes of the meetings of the executive committee during 1863 would lead one to think that the president had some reason for his feelings, for the dealings of the committee as a whole were carried out with protracted deliberation. They too often dealt with minutiae, for anything that involved the expenditure of even small sums of money had to be thoroughly investigated by the members of the committee. It took six months to come to a decision about the building of the Gate House and its exact location. An even longer time was needed to settle the problems of heating, lighting, and ventilating the college building itself. Everyone, including Jewett, became involved in it. The plans for the Observatory were completed by early 1864, mostly because Professor Farrar, in whose hands the details had been placed, pushed things through. One of the reasons for all the deliberation and cautious planning, of course, was the economic state of the country in the late war period. The uncertainties of the market and inflated prices had their effect on the value of the remaining assets of the college. Vassar looked into the future anxiously lest his funds be exhausted and little be left as an endowment. Matthew Jr. and Swift were apparently concerned with these problems, too, but they were anxious to curtail Jewett's influence over Vassar even if it meant his resignation. His anxiety over the state of affairs led to one indiscretion after another until a major crisis developed which was painful to Vassar and many of his associates, and disastrous to Jewett.

There were three problems that Jewett then faced. The first was the opening date of the college, which he was determined must be in the autumn of 1864. The second was the adoption of the report of the plan for organization, and the third was the necessity of the special meeting on 28 February 1864. The first of these was by far the most important in his mind—in fact, it had become an obsession with him. Acceptance of his organizational plan was almost assured. The meeting in February was a necessity if everything were to be shipshape by September.

The meeting was in question, however, and according to information the president had received, some members of the executive committee were considering cancelling it. A review of the minutes of the committee at this time reveals no discussion of the question. Yet Vassar had written to the Rev. E. Lyman Magoon, a member of the board of trustees, suggesting this possibility:

> We think of holding the February meeting, alltho' there is no special business save the examination of the revised plan or document of Organization & which could be without material disadvantage deferred to our *June Meeting.*[72]

One can almost hear Jewett snort at this. Writing to Anderson on 8 January, he lambasted his foes on the executive committee:

> They insisted Harloe [the contractor] couldn't finish the building by August; now, they abandon that ground & say, it will cost such an enormous sum to *furnish* the College, that they must wait for the fall of prices. Yet they dare not submit this gravest of questions to the Trustees, and, hence M. Jr. insists *there shall be no meeting,* in Feb.! He says: "The Ex Comm can send letters to the Trustees, saying that in the opinion of the Com., it is not necessary to hold a meeting at this inclement season". By badgering & bullying Mr. M.V. Jr. gets his assent, one day, but, on the next, Mr. V's good sense returns & he favors the meeting. The meeting *must be held* and *will be held,* at all hazards

. . . . If no meeting is had in Feb., *ipso facto,* the College *cannot* be opened, next Sept. M. Jr. knows this, & hence his determination . . . . If the Trustees meet, he knows *they* will control the College, if not, he *rules* it, for one year, if not for ten![73]

Jewett gave what he thought might be the general reaction of the trustees by quoting what Lossing had to say about the matter:

[Mr. Lossing said:] "If I should receive a copy of such a resolution [to cancel the meeting], I should return it to the Secretary with an expression of my opinion that such action of the Com. is an impertinence—it is a matter over wh. that Comm. has no control, & it is insulting to the Trustees for the Com. to assume to dictate, here". Swan I am sure, will take the same view; so, also, DuBois, I opine. No such resolve will be passed then: yet M Jr. will not give it up so. He will compel Mr V. *to play sick!* and will dispatch telegrams to every Trustee.[74]

If Matthew Jr. had set out on a campaign of this sort, he had met his match. One wonders how many messages written in this same vein were sent to other trustees. A search of the minutes of the executive committee meetings, however, during those days reveals nothing.

Anderson must have felt at some disadvantage because, at the time, he and Vassar were corresponding about the great question, the opening date. Writing to him a month before the stated meeting in February, Vassar placed one of his problems before him:

Now that our College Edifice is drawing near to completion, and Out Buildings & Ornamental grounds finished up or at least will be by the ensuing fall, the subject of furnishing & opening the College begins to engross our attention. We possibly *could* by strong pressure of our mental & physical muscles get prepared to fix the day on the 1st September next, but this must be accomplished by stirring & active efforts and at the Sacrifice of 30 to 40 perCent advance for war prices on all its interior equipment, beds, bedding, furniture, Kitchen & culinary appendages. The question therefore to determine is shall we go on regardless of difference in values between peace & war times or wait quietly a year or two for the suppression of the rebellion & return of Specie Currency. *True* our assets (some of them) are inflated by this paper currency, & will go down on the return of peace but not equal to the amount of other Kind values. Our College assets will now average an interest of 7prC. Pr Annum. Would it be wise . . . to take the last eggs out of their nest & put them into brick, Stone & Mortar. Prof Jewett is rather a "Young America[n]" he is for going ahead, our Executive Committee are for going slow, sure & strong, not for one day only but for generations after us, that is, lay our foundation so deep that it will endure for ages, not kill the Goose for sake of her golden egg. I suppose you have been informed by Prof Jewett of our contemplated meeting next month with its business objects, the chief of which will be the adoption of his plan for "Organization" and perhaps there may be some attempts at *official* appointments.[75]

Ten days later, he wrote again. This was a reply to a letter from Anderson, who had apparently discussed some of the problems associated with preparing everything for the reception of students in eight months. Vassar pointed out that the building needed "at least one Summer to thoroughly season the whole" and to dry the interior of the "massive structure of masonry, all inside partition walls solid brick work,"[76] to say nothing of the extent of plastered walls. He feared dampness in the walls and its effect on the health of the young ladies and the damage to the college should sickness result. At this time, early in 1864, the heating plant and gas works were not yet under construction, and the Observatory was still only partially built. All of these facts had to be considered, as well as the time required to furnish the building after all construction was completed. Vassar really questioned the possibility and the desirability of rushing the work so that the college might be prepared by that September date to receive students and faculty.

Jewett, nevertheless, continued his campaign for the September opening and just before the meeting of 23 February he did a most unwise and fatal thing. He wrote duplicate letters to each of five trustees, whom he trusted. He left little unsaid. He was feverishly desperate to get the trustees to act positively for the early opening of the college and for this body to assert its authority and power. It proved to be an unnecessary act, for 23 February came and according to the minutes of that day, the trustees acted in a thoughtful way, expressing concern only for the well-being of the college.

The secretary of the board recorded in the minutes that "Dr. Jewett from the Committee on Faculty & Studies desired in the first instance that the Board should determine when the College should open."[77] This was not considered as important, however, as the committee report upon the organization of the college. So the president reviewed the report and proposed three resolutions that had to do with the nature of the curriculum and its administration. He ended this presentation with several resolutions.

After the reading of the first resolution, Dr. Babcock from the Committee suggested that though the Committee had agreed to these resolutions, if the College was not to be immediately opened, he would prefer the recommendation of these resolutions for future reflection or

Perspective designed by Egidius C. Winter, Archt.

VASSAR FE

SITUATED NEAR POUGHKEEPSIE I
ERECTED AND O

Although Main Building was completed in 1864, it needed a summer "to thoroughly season and dry the interior of the massive structure of the masonry." Architect's drawing, including list of trustees. From a lithograph made in 1862.

E COLLEGE.

S COUNTY, STATE OF NEW YORK.
BLIC EDUCATION.

Ferd. Mayer & C? Lith. 96 Fulton St New York.

amendment. Mr. Kelly [the chairman] concurred in this suggestion and
there being no objection he called attention to the Resolution in regard
to the opening of the College in September 1864.[78]

There was great discussion of organization and of the opening date, and at
last, Lossing advocated that the college be completed so as to receive
students and faculty in the fall "to come." Matthew Jr. expressed strong
doubts as to such a possibility, and the debate was on. It culminated in a
resolution which was passed without a dissenting vote, instructing the executive committee "to exert themselves in completing the building and in
preparing for opening on September 14 next." Without taking an active
part in any of the debate, the president had won the day on the floor of the
board meeting. But his unwise letter sent out before the meeting to those
five trustees completely undid all that had been done that day.

No one can ever know the full story of all those events. Evidence points
to the struggle for domination of Vassar. He would have been completely
blind had he not known the political atmosphere that surrounded him. He
responded in his own way, ignoring as much as he could of what went on
about him. He had one goal, and he was determined to see it through. He
curbed the president, whom he still liked and admired, and tried to over-
look what must have been the obvious machinations of some members of
the board.

President Jewett gave his account of the history of the letter as follows:

A week or two before the February meeting I received a letter from the
Rev D_____ my friend who had partaken of the hospitality of my
house, and one of our most influential Trustees, who asked me to inform him what matters would be brought before the Board at the approaching meeting, &c.

Complying with the request I wrote him a private and confidential
letter, informing him of the subjects likely to be presented at this
meeting. I stated that the grand question to be decided, would be the
opening of the College the ensuing Fall, and gave him the arguments
for and against the proposition.

I referred to the desperate efforts which would be made by the opposition, and spoke of Mr Vassar as inclined to accede to their wishes.
I expressed the conviction, however, that Mr Vassar would readily
yield to the Trustees if the majority were decidedly in favor of opening
the College in the Fall.

. . . In further elucidation of this matter, it may be well to state,
after I had answered D_____'s letter of inquiry, it occurred to me
that other non-resident Trustees might like to receive information of
the same subject.

Accordingly I communicated to several of these, the substance of my letter to D^r _____.

And now occurred one of those unaccountable incidents which Providence sometimes employs to shape our lives and control our destinies.

After the adjournment of the Board D^r _____ one of the leading trustees, said to Mr Swan "He would like to write a letter", whereupon Mr. S. invites the D^r to go to his office, and furnishes him with the requisite materials. Having completed his work D^r _____ retires, shortly after Mr S entering the room where D^r had been writing, observes two or three sheets of paper lying on the table, he recognizes the familiar hand writing of the President.

He proceeds to read the letter which I had recently addressed to D^r _____ in answer to his inquiries respecting the meeting which had just closed. In opening my heart freely and confidentially to my correspondent, I referred to the difficulties that had environed me, and the obstacles which the malice of my enemies threw in my way, at every step. Added to these I remarked, Mr. Vassar grows more fickle and childish, every day. This was enough! Mr. Swan, thinking the letter was left in his Office for a purpose, and fearing he would be compromised by silence, showed it to Mr Vassar; my enemies now felt that they had in this letter the means to crushing the President at once.[79]

Surely, Jewett in retrospect must have thought that he was being quite candid in the retelling of the events of the early months of 1864. Even after fifteen years' association, he was unable to put himself in Vassar's place and to realize how devastating had been the effects of what he had written. It could matter little what motivated the letter or what interpretation Jewett's enemies made of its contents; it was a lamentable affair. Vassar was deeply hurt by it.

A week after the meeting, Vassar asked the Rev. Wm. Hague, the trustee who had inadvertently left the papers on Swan's desk, if he might keep the letter for a short time. Then, within a few days, Vassar wrote to Jewett. He seemed unable to do more than copy the president's comments about himself and college affairs. A short concluding paragraph, that was his own, brought to a close the association and friendship of the last nine years:

Poughkeepsie March 2^d 1864

Prof. M.P. Jewett L.L.D.

Sir. A letter in your handwriting and in your signature lies before me from which I make the following extracts:

viz.

"M.V. Junr is to put off the opening of the College, first till the fall of

'65; then under some pretext to '66, and so on, indefinitely. Meanwhile M. Vassar has become more *fickle & childish* than ever—He wants the College another year for a *play thing* to amuse himself with. M.V. Jr. tells him, 'when the College is once opened the President & Faculty will have all the power and all the glory—you will then be nobody'— Like a child, M.V. must have every new excitement to keep alive his interest. If then the College can lie still 12 Months and M. Vassar have nothing to do about it all the autum, Winter, & Spring, he will cease to care for it, will become disgusted with the whole thing, will change his will, giving his money to 'the Boys' during their lives & applying it in connection with *their* fortunes (already so appropriated by *their* wills) to the erection of a vast Hospital in Po'keepsie, for a *family* monument.

"For some months past M.V. Jr. has openly declared 'the College *shall* not be opened next fall'. To prevent the opening, he had gained the consent of his uncle to have no meeting of the Trustees in Febʸ. He *dared* not submit the question to the Board.

"M.V. Jr. admits this (opening of the College) can be done 'if we choose to give all our time and attention to it but we wont'. Precious little time has *he* given to the subject except to try hard *not* to do it.

"But M.V. Jr. and Swift had secretly agreed to a *denier* resort. I discovered this two weeks ago. The plot is to bring before the Trustees a Report on the cost of completing buildings, furnishing the rooms & showing so enormous an aggregate that it will be best to wait another year hoping for a fall in prices. Why do they desire concealment? why are they afraid to have the Presᵗ see their figures. Because they wish to make up a false issue—to impose on the Trustees leaving no chance for detection and experience. My old friend Dᴿ Babcock, whom I sincerely pity, will aid the *conspirators* with all his force and cunning. He assumes the pastorship of the first Church here (salary $750) for the sole purpose of getting the ear of M Vassar and revenging himself on the President. But Dᴿ B. cannot influence more than two votes at most, and when the *yeas* and *nays* are called for I suspect he will find himself alone. This is a poor World. What a mean nasty thing is the love of filthy lucre! From its defilement may the good Lord deliver us. P.S. For three years I have lived in the midst of plotting and counterplotting, mining and counter mining. I am often heart sick and ready to abandon the whole enterprise but to say nothing of the higher considerations, my '*old Adam*' wont allow me to give this selfish and contemptible faction a triumph so signal, a joy so exquisite.

"How come the Ex. Com. to take the matter of constituting the Faculty out of the hands of the Committee to which the Trustees had confided this important trust? and why did the Ex. Com *secretly* send out the slip from the Ladyˢ Book to the President & Principles of Institutions over the country asking an expression of their views of the practicability of finding Ladies prepared for the heads of the Departments in this College—any names you may suggest, &c—As a collateral matter subsiduary to their design they will oppose the elections of any Professors *at this Meeting.* They will also hasten to have their Report on the cost of furnishing refered to a Com. *to report at the June Meeting.* A measure *fatal* to the hopes of the Petitioner. Again they will dictate to M. Vassar opening address getting him strongly to commit himself & thus compel the Board to follow the founders lead. Finaly when they wish to frighten him out of his wits, *they will then threaten to resign!"* The remainder of this remarkable document, Sir, is of the same tenor. I[t] seems to preclude the possibility of explanation—You will doubtless see at once the impossibility of any further confidence or harmony between us. I forbear to state the circumstances under which I placed you where you are, and these obvious traits of your character as since developed, which renders it past hopes, that you can longer be useful in your present position. The only alternative for me is to ask your resignation in proper hands without delay. Whatever further communications there may be between us they must be in writing. I remain Yrs &c.[80]

In his indignation, Vassar forgot that it was not within his power to ask for the president's resignation—a fact that he later fully recognized. The realization on Jewett's part that Vassar had seen his letter and felt that he had been betrayed seemed to have shaken him. In his perplexity, he turned to another trustee, Nathan Bishop, in whom he seemed to have found a person to whom he could speak freely and without restraint. On 8 March he sent Bishop a résumé of the history of the case:

My dear Doctor,
"Cease from man"—"Put not your trust in princes"—These words have been in my mind & on my heart, many times, within the last 36 hours. As you are aware, before the late meeting of the Board, I wrote, confidentially, to Messrs Anderson, Bishop, Raymond, Robinson, Hague & Magoon—putting them in possession of such facts as I deemed of vital importance to a proper understanding of affairs as they would come before the Board. My letters, written under great excitement; when I was smarting under official & personal insults; & in view of (what I believe to be) purposes & plans fraught with danger to the very life of the enterprise to which I have given my whole heart & soul. These letters were full & strong; handling men & motives with no gloved hands, & pouring out all my feelings of love & anxiety for the College, with an entire forgetfulness of self-interest & self-preservation. I was writing to true & honorable men; to *christian* men: how *could* the thought of *treachery* enter my mind? It never did occur to me. Yet, one of *these*—my own familiar friend, *has betrayed me!!*

Returning home, Saturday night, after a week's absence, I found a Note from Mr. Vassar, dated March 2, in which he says there was then lying before him, in my handwriting & over my signature, a letter from which he quoted extracts as follows, &c. These extracts embrace, substantially, all I had ever written or told you, respecting the designs of *R. Doe et al.*

Mr. V. says, after this discovery there can be no further confidence between us, & asks me to place my resignation in proper hands, without delay. All further communications must be in writing, &c.

I have answered, kindly & tenderly referring all I have ever spoken, written or done, in reference to the College, to my zeal for its welfare & for the true honor & happiness of the Founder. As to resigning, I say that a matter involving not only the interests of the College but also my own *reputation,* must be decided only after the maturest deliberation.

Deeply as Mr. V. is wounded and the matter has made him almost sick, the breach may be easily healed if his true friends can get access to his nobler impulses & his better convictions.

My present purpose is, assiduously to devote myself to my official duties; and if the matter of my resignation be pressed, to bring this letter before the full Board and after giving a complete history of my connection with the College, & of every official not of mine to-gether with a perfect ventilation of the doings of R.D. & Co., *ab inito,* I will submit the question to the Trustees.

Will you, my *fidus Achates,* my mentor (would that you had spoken sooner!) give me your views as to my best course?. . .

(P.S) I see among the St. Nicholas "Arrivals", Hon. William Kelly. I have reason to know he feels kindly towards me, & appreciates my labors for the College whatever he may think of my *prudence,* in letter writing! Can you show this to Lathrop & Raymond, & then burn it? Or, shall I limit my communication to you alone?[81]

How little he understood the great wrong which he had done his trusting friend Matthew Vassar! He did not consider the consequences of writing so devastating a letter to five people predicting events that never were to take place. He claimed that he "was smarting under official & personal insults." Did he destroy Babcock's reputation by his letter of 1862 to Vassar for similar reasons? What purpose did he expect his letter inquiring about Charles A. Raymond to serve?

Bishop answered within a week in a way that made unmistakable the mood which might well have been that of many trustees:

This evening after receiving your letter of the 8th inst. I was engaged, but the next evening called at the St. Nicholas, and learned that Mr Kelly had left. Remembering that Smith Sheldon Esq. was spending the winter there, I sent my card up to him, who seemed to be better acquainted with what has occurred at Poughkeepsie, than I was.

Reliable information received from different Sources, authorizes me to assure you, that *no one* of the Trustees, named in your letter to me has "betrayed" you, but that one of them, while in Poughkeepsie, *lost his papers.* Mr. Swan will, I presume, give you the whole story showing how they came into Mr. Vassar's hands.

As soon as I read your long communication, which you spoke of in your last, as "handling men & motives with no gloved hands", I felt sure that such severe expressions would do great harm, if, by any accident, they should ever fall under the eye of those parties whose motives and conduct were so strongly censured. With the impression that such documents could not do any good, but might do a great deal of harm—I *"burned"* what you wrote me on the Subject, on which you were then so *much excited,* and after receiving another letter in the same tone, I ventured to caution you against such unguarded expressions of your opinions of other men's motives & actions. I am sorry that you think my caution came too late.

In your last letter, you ask me to give you my views as to the best course "for you now to pursue". At first, I thought I would decline to say anything on this very delicate matter, but after some reflection, I felt that no true hearted man would desert his friend in such an emergency. Hence, I have decided to make the best suggestions I can, as to your course in this extremely embarrassing case.

After a careful survey of the whole field, I do not see but *two* courses that you *possibly can pursue.* You must either continue in your present position, paying no attention to Mr. Vassar's letter requesting you to resign, or, you must comply with his request, and offer your resignation, subject of course, to the action of the Board of Trustees. As I do not see how one of these courses can affect the final choice of the Board any more favorably than the other, your choice between these two courses must be governed by your *own personal feelings.* Not knowing how *you feel* on this point, I can speak only for myself.

If I were in your place, I would present my resignation, for the purpose of placing myself before the Trustees, and before the public, in the most gentlemanly attitude. Then if the Board should see fit to sustain me, they would, of course, request me to withdraw my resignation, & thus, I should stand on a better footing than if I had not offered my resignation.

And on the otherhand, if the Trustees should not sustain me then they have only to accept my resignation, and I should stand before the world in a much more dignified position than if their action *forced me* to resign.

You must decide for yourself what to do, as no one can act for you in this bad looking case. I say "bad looking case" because there is no use in attempting to conceal the facts that this "lost paper" is seriously damaging your standing before the Board of Trustees.

When you read this you must not be displeased with me, but remember that "Faithful are the wounds of a friend; but the kisses of an enemy are deceitful."[82]

Jewett responded within a few days as if he thought that the situation might be resolved. In fact, he thought it had been!

No, my dear Doctor, I am not "displeased" with you, for your fidelity, in your last. I honor you, more than ever, & the love I bear you has been growing stronger & stronger, the last few months, just in proportion as I have known you more intimately.

After writing you, I resolved to see Mr. Kelly. I placed in his hands Mr V's letter, with my reply. I gave him a sketch of our enterprise, since the winter of 1860, when it barely escaped shipwreck. I unfolded the manifold embarrassments—the open opposition, the secret plottings, the *sinuosities,* with which I had contended especially during a year past. He saw my difficulties & appreciated my motives, while he condemned my imprudence. I "ought not to have written such a letter to any man"—especially to a man of whose possible weaknesses, I am totally ignorant.

Mr. K. saw Mr. Vassar—found his feelings towards me kind & tender: he was *grieved*—deeply grieved, by the cruel letter. Mr. K. explained, how I could have no possible motive but the best good of the College, whose interests I believed to be seriously threatened; I did not intend any reflection on the Founder, &c. Mr. K. insisted on the necessity of harmony among the friends of the College, and on the injury which would result from a rupture. Mr. V. cheerfully assented to Mr. K's suggestion that Mr. V. should permit me to call on him & offer my apology, in person.

To-day, we have had a private interview, & *all is right* again. Mr. V. apologized for alluding to my resignation, having done so under "excitement". He did full justice to my motives, & accepted my apology, promising to forgive & forget.

According to Mr. K's view, I have been in error as to my official rights & privileges. Hereafter, I shall confine myself, strictly, to the duties of the Presidency, & of the Chairmanship of the Com. on Faculty, &c—always holding myself in readiness to respond to any call from the Ex. Com. for such suggestions, and other services, as my experience may furnish.

The painful affair has taught me a lesson. I shall not soon forget—
"Never too old to learn", you know.

"If", says Mr. _____, "the leaving of that Letter on the table *was*
'an accident', it was one of the most extraordinary, I have ever known"!
But on this accident, or on the course of the man who put the letter into
Mr. V's hands, the writer of so indiscreet a letter has no right to comment.[83]

But he was too sanguine about the outcome of the interview, for Vassar
wrote to William Kelly completely upsetting this impression. He clearly explained his position after first assuring Kelly of his gratitude for his devotion to the enterprise and thanking him for his assistance in the present
crisis. Believing that Jewett had misinterpreted the outcome of their
meeting, he hastened to correct the impression that the chairman of the
board had given him that all was well between him and the president.
Vassar went on to describe Jewett's role in the whole process of planning
and building the college and his early confidence in him which had been
slowly undermined by the president's recent behavior. "It is with extreme
regret," he wrote, "that I am compelled to admit that I have not obtained
from him practically that assistance or that counsel which has assured my
own mind as to the clearness of his judjment or his power to organize or
control its immense interest."[84] He had hoped continually that he might
show these traits, and went on to write:

Prof Jewett has been always entirely mistaken as to the extent or
violence of any prejudice upon the past or of any member of the Ex.
Com. against him so far as I am able to judge. It is impossible that
there should have been this hostility to him or to the enterprise which
he has fancied without its coming to my knowledge. You may depend
upon it they are unreal—at all events up to a verry late period and even
now they do not take any shape beyond what must be the natural consequences of Prof J's own conduct and expression.[85]

He explained that all he desired was the success of the enterprise and the
presence of someone to preside over it all with "his mental and moral
power as a controller of other minds and a leader in an undeveloped pattern." He ended this long letter saying:

I have thus fully expressed every feeling and desire I harbor. . . . I cannot and do not ask your personal favor or friendship to me to control
your conduct. But I do anxiously ask you to give this subject your full
reflection and that you judge and act as if the Presidential chair were
vacant and Mr. Jewett if you please & others the best men whom you
know were in the canvass for that place—who of all the men you know

would or should receive your endorsement—Mr Jewett or any other person.[86i]

Vassar saw that he must deal with Jewett so that there would be no question as to their future relations. With this in view, he wrote to him on 19 March:

> Friday Morning
> March 19, 1864
> Sir the note you handed me yesterday morning and of yesterdays date accompanied with explanation and apologies you then made seems to demand from me some reply thro' the same medium and found, me in the way of a preliminary that after sleeping over it one night and reflecting upon one day with small prayers to my Heavenly Father to guide me aright. I this morning place some thoughts before you for your consideration.
>
> Alluding as I did in that conversation to the circumstances that led to our early intimate and warm attachment continuing thro' a course of several years, and ending in the noble enterprise of Building a College for the elevation of woman and altho' frequently interrupted by our opposite arguments for the purpose of eliciting truths and strengthen & not weaken the conception.
>
> I little thought that you would or could as a Christian man calmly sit down in your study and deliberately pen and forward to a member of our Board of Trustees, such a cool and unblushing slander & falsehood as said letter contained which only fell into my hands by a Providential circumstance.
>
> Yet after hearing your explanation of yesterday and seeing your contrition for the consequences and your seemingly heart felt appolog in extenuation to me & the Com. I was ready to say to you as I did that I should *overlook it* & your continum in the Pre[t] of the College in and after the meeting in June must be decided by the Trustees—Therefore I have nothing further to say to you on this point, but nevertheless, I do not wish nor will I depart from the true Character of a man but extend to you when we meet, the ordinary civility &c that becomes a true gentleman.[87]

This letter was not sent, but a colder one, written three days later, was. Its meaning is unmistakable:

> Poughkeepsie March 22[d] 1864
> Prof. M.P. Jewett Dear Sir. Yours of the 17th inst is before me and I have delayed a reply thus far hardly conceiving that one was necessary or perhaps expected—Upon reflection I have satisfied myself that one is due to you for the right understanding of our present position and to

prevent any possible misconceptions. You speak of being "encouraged" by the Hon Mr Kelly to renew the assurance of your regard &c I do not of course know to what circumstances that encouragement is due and it is but fair to you to say that our positions are in no respect altered from what they were when I wrote you on the 2^d inst. at least for the better as I have since heard (if true) much to widen our difficulties.

It is impossible that we shall ever again occupy the same relation to each other hereafter, and a sense of self respect require me in honesty & candor to leave the expression of them just as I have already written them to you as I cannot nor would not disguise my feelings.

I subscribe myself Repectfy.[88]

Clearly, Vassar was deeply wounded. He could not ask for a resignation, but he made it quite evident that the relationship between them could never again be the same. Jewett's recollections as told in the *Origin* (1879) were somewhat at variance with these letters. He continually wrote about a plot and was possessed with the idea—so much so, that he seemed to have forgotten that he had the interview with Vassar arranged by Kelly—the interview reported in the last letter to Bishop at which he thought all had been forgiven and forgotten. In fact, he suggested that a plot had prevented this meeting. In the *Origin* (1879) he gave little information about what might have happened between mid-March and mid-April when he gave up. He had reached the conclusion that he could not go on without "the full confidence and cordial cooperation of the Founder." So on 16 April he sent a letter of resignation:

Hon^b William Kelly Chairman, &c
Dear Sir
The entire harmony of views and feelings which has subsisted between the Founder of Vassar Female College and myself, from the first inception of the enterprise, having been recently interrupted; and that harmony being essential to my usefulness, as well as to my happiness, I deem it proper for me to withdraw from a position I accepted only for the sole purpose of co-operating with the Founder in maturing his generous plans.

I beg, therefore, through you, to tender to the Trustees my resignation of the office of President of the College.

You will also please present my resignation as a Trustee of the College.

Cordially thanking the members of the Board for all the marks of confidence I have received at their hands, and for all Kindness and courtesy extended to me, officially and personally, I desire to assure them that I shall continue to feel the deepest interest in the institution: and I shall be most happy, at all times, to contribute to its prosperity, by any service which it may be in my power to render.

With sentiments of the highest consideration I am, dear Sir, . . .[89]

After Jewett had submitted his resignation, he wrote one last letter to Bishop on the subject. As usual, this is a long letter full of advice and suggestions about college business:

Since forwarding my Resignation, on the 16th, I have not had one moment of despondency or dejection. I feel so fully persuaded that this step is necessary to save the College from death or paralysis, that I *cheerfully* sacrifice myself for the good of the cause.

Your sagacity anticipated this result, while, to my mind, the *data* before me failed to warrant any decisive step in this direction—a step, too, which would have been in opposition to the decided convictions of my friends in the Board here, with the light then before them. On Tuesday (19th) following my resignation, Mr. Buckingham called, to report to me his interview with Sheldon and yourself. . . .

One word more about myself: *if* the Board should accompany the acceptance of my resignation with any kind expression, I don't want Babcock, or any of his clique to have a hand in preparing it. It would be characteristic for him to desire to kill me, by placing a chaplet of *poisonous* flowers on my brow! If there be any thing let it be simply true, just, modest.

And, now, will it be improper for me to suggest a few points for your consideration, respecting the College?

1. The President. Before I went to Europe, I named Dr J.H. Raymond to Mr. Vassar, as the best man I know of, to succeed me in case I should never return. From a further acquaintance, I am more strongly persuaded he is the best available candidate for the post.

2. It seems to me of great importance that your Com. on Fac. & Studies report next week, such *essential* points as may be embodied in a Circular & embraced in Advertisements—inserting the latter in all the leading secular & religious papers of the West as well as the East.

3. I think the Professors should now be elected, & so settle this contemptible "woman question" forever.

4. The Board should give to the Pres., in connection with the Com. on Faculty, power to engage Lady Instructors. These ladies are now engaged, as a general thing in institutions, & they *must* make engagements for another year by the end of June, or risk being *thrown* out of employment altogether. The Pres. will always be welcome to any knowledge of candidates, I have. . . .

6. In my opinion, founded on statements of N.Y. workmen 4½ months is ample time for correcting the *almost fatal* error of Renwick in regard to Heating, & for completing all things. . . . Excuse me, if I am too officious—can't stop, *instanter!*

And now it only remains for *me to thank you from my heart of hearts,* for all your manly frankness, your true Christian kindness, manifested toward me.[90]

The special meeting of the board, requested by the five members of the executive committee, and Bishop and S.M. Buckingham, was held on 29 April. Nineteen[j] of the twenty-nine members of the board were in attendance. After some preliminaries, the letter of resignation was read. On the motion of trustee Swift seconded by trustee Bishop, it was resolved that the resignation be accepted and after some discussion, the vote was unanimous.

Jewett was disappointed. He wrote in his *Origin* (1879):

At a special meeting of the Board convened on April 29th 1864, it [the resignation] was accepted. After the vote of acceptance Mr. B. J. Lossing was about to present a resolution appropriately referring to my connection with the origin and progress of the Enterprise, but Matthew Vassar Jr objected, and a substitute was prepared, couched in the most general terms and meaning nothing.[91]

This is sad because there was no note of any objection to the resolutions proposed by Lossing in the minutes of the day. Nothing could suggest more clearly the depth of Jewett's disappointment over the outcome than this statement of the three resolutions which were passed without a dissenting vote:

Whereas Milo Jewett, L.L.D. has resigned his office as President of Vassar College and that resignation having been accepted, therefore
Resolved that the Board of Trustees entertain a high appreciation of the industry, zeal, and energy which President Jewett has uniformly evinced in the discharge of his duties, while connected with this College.
Resolved that on leaving his place of active cooperation with us in the great work of female education, he carries with him our cordial good wishes for his happiness and prosperity.
Resolved that the Secretary is hereby directed to present to Doctor Jewett, a Copy of these resolutions with the Corporate Seal of the College attached.[92]

Jewett had been in touch with his old friend Sherman throughout these worrisome days. He kept him informed of the highlights of what he called his "devil of a fight" about the opening day of the college. On 26 April confessing to Sherman that he had lost, he belabored the members of the executive committee for what he called being "deliberately determined they would not open the College with Jewett as Pres., Mr. Vassar assenting."[93] By mid-August, he had rested and had time to consider this unfortunate affair, but he wrote Sherman again—a terrible letter in which he attacked some of his friends on the board:

> The Baptist Trustees had axes to grind every one. Anderson expects $20,000 from Mr. V. for Rochester Univ. and Bishop wanted his friend Raymond as Pres. Dr Hague operated for the interest of his brother, J.B. Hague &c. &c. Dr. Magoon, his Art Gallery to sell.[94]

How ironic that Jewett in 1860 and 1861 was the one who wanted a majority of Baptists on the board! Furthermore, each of the men, excepting possibly Magoon, was one of those to whom he had gone for advice and help. They had not been unresponsive to him.

And how about Matthew Jr. and the rest of the conspirators? Matthew Jr. made some entries in his diary, two or three of which are worth consideration in that they show something of his feelings:

> Feby 29 Meeting Ex Committee College—resolution for progressing with College and purchase furniture and other matters particularly of the Hypocrisy and unfair acts of Presdt Jewett—his intrigue, cunning, Jesuitical preceedings against M.V. & others—his *would* be one man power—which is showing itself time will prove his evil attempts
> Mch 1 engaged at College office this A M with Committee on matters pertaining to business of M.V. connection with Jewett—the latters evil attempt to injure the Committee as also the Founder
> April 5 Called on Mr. Sheldon, N.Y. and talked over College affairs, the acts of Jewett and his deception & Hypocrisy and unfitness for office all of which is fully known by the Board and now seen as has always been seen heretofore.[95]

Jewett was exhausted and, in his way, he was suffering for his indiscretion which was so unnecessary and so ill timed. It is sad to think that he had no part in the active college life at Vassar, the result of the great vision that he and Vassar had had and worked so strenuously to make a reality. Yet in spite of this, in spite of his mistakes, no one could take from him the knowledge that without his influence and his zeal, there could not have been a Vassar College.†

Vassar was saddened by this series of events and to a degree he seemed bewildered by Jewett's attack. He must have recognized that without him, he could not have found this magnificent cause on which to spend his fortune. In spite of the necessary postponement of the opening of the college until September 1865, Vassar still had two years of happiness remaining to walk through the halls of Main Building greeting his young ladies, to

†Appendix 2

wander through the grounds of the college, and to visit his friends, Maria Mitchell and her father in the Observatory. He wrote to his nephews in a manner that left little doubt of his intention to see his plans completed and asked for their cooperation. This eloquent letter speaks for itself:

Mar. 5, 1864

To my honored Nephews Matthew & John Guy Vassar

Dear Relatives. Feeling sensible that my days are fast being numbered at least for business purposes of life, I therefore improve the waining Moments briefly to address you, and I need not by the way of preface remind you that I trust in God that he will so influence your hearts to insure the full and complete development of my long cherished hopes in the reiliseation of the College enterprise—Let not my Glory be turned into shame by the "plotting and counterplotting" of selfish and unprincipled men. The College is a *fixed fact for weal or for woe* and the name of the Founder with all his intimate associations stands or fall together.

As we made our wealth in common let us *unite* in one common purpose of humanity in its employment,—like a wise master-Builder I have laid the foundation, it now remains with those that comes after me to crown it with the *Crest of Glory*.

The edifice now stands with the family name of "Vassar" engraved on tablets of marble in the foreground of the building. There is no doubt that through diversified circumstances I have arrived at an event in the history of woman that will descend down to the remotest period of her future destiny and all I hold dear in this life and that which is to come conveys to my mind and heart that nothing short of Divine Interposition has guided me to these results.

May I not then implore your counsel, your favorable influence, *present* and ultimately, in all the means within your power to extend them, and I would therefore kindly suggest in this connexion that you jointly unite either in the erection of another monument on the Grounds of the College for a Gallery of Fine Arts, (similar to that of our friend Revd. Doct Magoons) or use that now designed in the Building—In no way could you use your reluctant means so worthily, so honorbly, so benificially,

My thoughts almost runs into *extacy* when I contemplate such a powerfull influence!

Unlike any other benevolence, its grand beauty is its *indefinite* expansion—its ruffled waters will never cease to flow till its creasted foam reaches the shores of Eternity! Will you not my dear Nephews take these suggestions kindly to heart I dont wish *present action* but only when you cease to have power to use your means they may flow in this channel so that your names may be identified with mine to descend down to all time.

With these reflections which may be my last to you on the particular subject, I

Remain truly & affectionately

Your Uncle,
Matthew Vassar.[96]

Chapter III

Vassar and Mrs. Sarah Josepha Hale:
A Problem of Semantics

A story appears periodically in the press, claiming that Mrs. Sarah Josepha Hale,[a] "editress" of the *Godey's Lady's Book,* helped to organize Vassar College. This truly Victorian lady would deny the story were she still with us, but she might agree modestly that she had had some influence in the affairs of the developing college. As a staunch believer in improving woman's lot, she worked for bettering her opportunities within the limits of Victorian propriety. The discovery of plans to found a college for young women that promised them an education equal to, if not better than, that offered to young men by the colleges and universities of the day, delighted her.

Matthew Vassar, as far as one knows, did not consult Mrs. Hale in those early days of decision when he and his confidant Milo P. Jewett sought out the opinion of educators throughout the land. Vassar made up his mind to embark on his grand enterprise, and Vassar Female College was incorporated by the State of New York on 18 January 1861. This momentous decision involving his large fortune faced one great question: would it be successful and effective? But his mind was made up. After that January day, he never thought of failure. So at the age of sixty-nine, he began his glorious and stimulating experiment. Until his death seven years later, he gave every moment to it, and to all who watched, it was apparent that these were the best years of his life. Like many of his contemporaries, Vassar had little formal education. He was to use his native shrewdness and ability to develop a keen intellect through reading, discussion, and study of everyday problems associated with his large business enterprises; all contributed to his self-education. Maria Mitchell wrote of him at his death: "As he built up so grand a structure; it so grew upon his hands, and he so grew himself, that genius could only have been the base [of it]."[1]

The enterprise was not without its national and local critics, some serious, some amused, and some intolerant. Such criticism saddened Vassar, but he was immensely cheered by the universal applause of the press. In spite of this, there remained the problem of bringing the news of the institution to the women of America. Their sympathy and understanding were essential if he was to have the backing of those who might influence young women to attend Vassar College. Imagine, then, his pleasure when Sarah Hale wrote not only to congratulate him, but also to offer what assistance she could to the college during those early years. She even put a short notice in the *Lady's Book* in her famous column, the "Editors' Table."

Here was the answer; Mrs. Hale would be a safe promoter of the grand enterprise. As the cautious editor of a Victorian periodical, she might be depended upon to present the news of the college in a favorable light. Her many years of association with the *Lady's Book* gave her an assured place of honor and power. Her editorials, articles, and reprints from many sources had a large audience. They were generally factual and often argumentative in a way that gave no offense to her readers. She stood for no nonsense and when all other arguments failed, there was always the Bible to fall back upon.

112

Sarah Josepha Hale's attitude toward the roles of men and women in life was a continuing source of material for her editorials. It is perhaps best summed up in an article, "Woman: in Her Marriage Relation" published in her column. Sharply differentiating between the powers of man and woman, she spoke of man, the creator:

> True, he cannot absolutely make or create a single particle of matter; but he can, by new combinations, create innumerable differences in the particles...and make apparently new elements and new things.... Woman cannot create or make like man. She has not his constructive genius, and there seems an organic difference in the operations of their minds....Woman never applies her intuitive reasoning to mechanical pursuits....She works on mind, and for immortality.[2]

Mrs. Hale considered man and woman to differ in many other ways—modes of thinking, application of thought to the solution of problems!

> Hence it is sure that those who are seeking to elevate woman through industrial pursuits and competition with man in the arts will never succeed. The wife cannot work with materials of earth, build up cities, mould marble forms, or discover new mechanical inventions to aid physical improvement....She works in the elements of human nature; her orders of architecture are formed in the soul....She must build up these elements in the characters of her children.[3]

Humility should be a trait of both men and women, she thought, each in quite different spheres, man remembering what woman has done for him as teacher and moral preceptor; woman dependent on man, humble before him for his protection. Woman was first of all the educated wife and mother and teacher of the young. She might choose medicine or editing as a profession, or there was the wide mission field, but Mrs. Hale would decidedly limit the opportunities by her ideas of what was a fitting endeavor for her sex. She must have raised her hands in horror if she read the urging that the editor of *Vanity Fair* gave Matthew Vassar to seek the best in education for women "not forgetting the fact that life is—or may be—a brave, strong, earnest career, full of great objects glorious aims and not a mere husband-hunt and endless housekeeping or 'society'-ing."[4]

Vassar needed no such urging. He was closer in his thinking to the editor of *Vanity Fair* than to Mrs. Hale. After all, this lady had her public to placate and though she often wrote sympathetically of the plight of woman and was genuinely interested in any plans to increase her educational opportunities, she was inhibited both by her own thinking and by the limitations imposed by Mr. Godey. Not so Vassar; he had nothing holding him back. He had devoted "his best powers to the study of the subject for a number of years," not only to how it was to be done, but why it needed doing. He could use Mrs. Hale not only for what she could do for the new institution in her column but also to get a woman's point of view, a view he sadly needed in his man's world.

So Mrs. Hale's letter came as a pleasant surprise: "I am much interested," she wrote, "in what I have learned respecting your plan for a new Institution on a very liberal scale, for the Young Ladies of America. . . I feel solicitous to know more of the plan, in order to make it known to the readers of the 'Lady's Book'. . . .Therefor I take the liberty of applying directly to you, Sir—as the only person who can give me authentic knowledge on this subject."

She assured Vassar of the importance she attached to woman's education, human happiness, and Christian character. As the correspondence developed over time, she often enclosed in her letters reprints of her writings to drive home some point that she wished to make. This letter was no exception; it ended with a long paragraph that is worth quoting:

I shall be rejoiced to aid in your good plan, by making the readers of the Lady's Book your earnest friends, as they cannot but honor a gentleman who is thus earnest to promote the true cultivation of femin[ine] talents. We want true women, trained to the full use of their *powers* of mind, heart, soul, and taught to devote all to their duties as women. Then the world will be better as well as wiser, for their cultivated talents, and they will enjoy the full reward as they give to God, their country and their families the sweet fealty of womanhood in its beauty of virtue and piety.

She signed herself "Literary Editress of the 'Lady's Book' " and added a postscript, "Any prospectus or plan of yours will be welcome. I should like to honor your College."[5]

The assurance that Mrs. Hale through the *Lady's Book* stood ready to help in securing new friends and supporters of the project must have pleased Vassar immensely. Here was the beginning of a correspondence[b] which lasted through the remaining years of Vassar's life. In 1864 and 1865, seventeen notes or editorials dealing directly with Vassar College appeared in Mrs. Hale's column. There were at least seven others bearing some relation to it which she called to the attention of her correspondents at the college. All of these were excellent publicity, introducing Vassar College to her special public in an attractive and appealing way.

Vassar replied to the first letter within a week. Blaming one of his periodic spells of ill health for the delay, he apologized for not having responded earlier. He showed great pleasure at being so esteemed and in having his plan so highly praised:

First page of Mrs. Sarah Josepha Hale's first letter to Matthew Vassar, 30 April 1860

I am honored in finding my own views so much in harmony with the Sentiments found in [your] Editorials. . .and will avail myself of an early opportunity to secure the Biographical Dictionary &c to which you have alluded, to aid me in the more enlarged Sphere in that department of Knowledge.

In regard to details respecting plans, organization &c of "Vassar College" I deem it premature to present to the public anything further than what has already been commented on in those articles furnished you by. . .Professor Jewett. I shall be very glad to see in the Lady's Book. . .such suggestions as your mature reflection and practical knowledge of the subject may. . .prompt you to make.[6]

Jewett, as president of the new college, had sent her an announcement of Vassar's intentions.

The first really important Vassar-related editorial appeared in the columns of the "Editors' Table" in October 1861. It began, "While clouds and darkness overhang the land, we naturally welcome with double pleasure whatever promises permanent good for the future."[7] This is one of Mrs. Hale's very few references to the Civil War during its four long years. There followed a glowing report of Vassar and his great enterprise. The editorial, picking out pertinent quotations from Vassar's address to the trustees at their first meeting on 21 February 1861, was all that Vassar himself could have wished, and he reacted with grateful pride. His letter to her dated 13 November began:

I am just in receipt of your esteemed favor of yesterdays date and it gives me great pleasure to notice the deep and continued interest you take in our Enterprise the V. F. College and more especially as its incipient beginning has fallen amidst our great national troubles which absorbs all other minor interests, under these considerations your kind Co-operation to aid my Scheme comes with peculiar satisfaction at this time.

The rest of the letter dealt with news of the enterprise, of progress in the early stages of building the college and of Jewett's tour of eastern colleges, universities, and libraries. Vassar ended it with:

Please to say to Mr. Godey to send me his "Book" as a regular subscriber, commencing with the October Number, and for which I herewith enclose $3 in Advance—the Article enclosed to me in your letter I have caused to be placed in my scrap book with Sundry other articles pertaining to the V.F.C.[8]

The way was now opened for this unique correspondence. Mrs. Hale's interest in the well-being of the enterprise, and knowledge of public reaction to many ideas, gave Vassar an opportunity to sound her out on a few issues to which he and his advisers had given some thought. His assurance that he valued Mrs. Hale's opinion made it easy for her to embark on three crusades, the purposes of which were close to her heart.

Vassar learned very soon how demanding was the task to which he had set himself. He knew that his college must be successful from the outset. He recognized the worth of his trustees—"such a combination of talent is rarely to be found in any Board,"[9] he wrote. But often, he wanted to present to his board issues discussed only with the president or, perhaps, the executive committee. They were not of tremendous importance, perhaps, but they could affect public opinion; so he naturally sought the reaction of someone such as Mrs. Hale, who was ever very conscious of the public.

The first problem was about uniform dress for students; the second proposed a calendar for the academic year; the third suggested an endowment plan that would encourage women to support Vassar College.

The question of uniform dress arose in early discussions of what sort of institution the college should be. He wrote to a trustee in 1861: "I would go even further and insist upon a *Uniform* Costume for all the young ladies to be furnished by the College and here again we make a saving to patrons."[10] A month before this, he replied to enquiries about the college and among other questions he answered one about scholarship students: "Yet none but the President of the Institution will ever know who are beneficiaries or who are paying pupils, nor can they ever be distinguished by their Costume, as these will be furnished at the expense of the College, exacting pay only to such who are *paying pupils* in the School."[11]

Nothing further was heard of this issue until 1865, when he explained to the editor:

For some months last past my thoughts have at intervals been occupied with the idea of adopting a uniformity of Costume for the pupils attending V. F. College—The object of which is first, to prevent jealousy which usually arises in the minds of young persons in the articles of Dress—Secondly to Secure more comfort and convenience to them while in School or at their playfull recreations. Your fertile mind will readily suggest what these should be—their make and material— something that will be desirable, least needful of repeated washings repair &c, and to consist of something like the "Bloomer Dress" which would give freedom to their persons whether in School or out of School for exercise. Will you please take this matter into considerations and at your early convenience inform me—Of course these garments are only for School house and need not be expensive so that they will be available to all the pupils—with those suggestions.[12]

Mrs. Hale's reply came within a fortnight:

And now a few words on the subject of dress in Vassar College. I have heretofore considered this subject and written several articles in explanation of my views. If I can I will look up some of these papers for you: or I think of writing another article for my Eds. Table, which may be more satisfactory.

In the meantime—I do not consider sumptuary laws of much use in the service of morality or of economy. Children are not taught to walk well by keeping them in leading strings. The individual will must act with conscience, judgment must regulate taste or there would be no real improvement of the pupils. Besides the distinctions of rich and poor are all around us; there will be *richer* and *poorer* in Vassar College. Would it be well to enforce an equality of personal appearance there which cannot be found in Life?—Is not the training in your Institution intended to prepare young ladies for their duties in the world—as it is?

It seems to me that *character* not *costume* will be the test of merit in Vassar College, and that thus the pupils will be best prepared for their duties of life. It might be well to announce that simplicity and appropriateness of dress will be expected of the pupils—and that any superfluous jewelry is disapproved. But I should not counsel uniformity of apparel.—And any hint approaching the Bloomer standard would, I greatly fear, be a serious injury to the College.

Pray pardon my frankness; I write to you, my friend, as to a brother. The best good of the institution is my only aim.[13]

This answer emphatically closed the issue. Vassar did not present his views on the subject of uniform dress to the trustees at their next annual meeting. (There must have been some continued discussion, however, because some months later, Mrs. Hale sent John H. Raymond, when he had succeeded Jewett as president, a copy of an editorial[14] on the subject.)

Raymond and Vassar had frequently discussed "[the] arranging of the College terms and vacations so as to maintain a just proportion between the periods of rest and labor and at the same time to secure for collegiate uses the largest possible amount of that season which, in our climate, is the most propitious of the year."[15]

In March 1865 Vassar asked Mrs. Hale for an opinion on a proposed calendar:

It would be exceedingly gratifying to me to have your opinion on another question equaly novel, viz: The division of School or College terms. It is proposed by some of our Trustees to divide the periods of tuition thus:

To say—   months
    First Term from 1st April to 1st August   4
    Second "   " 1st Sept to 20th Decbr   4
    Summer Vacation   1 mo
    Winter   "   Janury, Febry, March   3   "   4

The advantages of this division of time will allow the young ladies whose parents or guardians reside in the Country or rural districts to avail themselves of the long winter evenings assisting the pursuits in their household duties at home, studying their text books &ca and making up new and repairing their own wardrobe, while the pupils of parents residing in Cities or large Towns and perhaps in better pecuniary circumstances will have the opportunity of doing the same and attend intellectual and polite entertainments usually held in large towns and places in the winter months. The College, as you are aware, is already provided in its arrangements for Winter conveniences by an extensive heating apparatus so that it is not out of economical considerations that this change of School terms is suggested, but rather on account of health and comfort to its inmates, for it is the late fall & Winter Season in our clime that causes most of the malady^s common to the northern latitudes and should we have a large share of them, the public would ascribe it to an unhealthy location of the College, besides which extensive arrangements are made on the grounds for gymnastical or athletical exercises in Summer and for the Study of Floral, Botany, Trees &c^a by *living existences,* these would be comparatively lost to pupils in the winter Season. It is not however our purpose to insist in the *entire dismissal* of *all* the pupils; Such as has no parents or homes can remain, but the Season of general Instruction ends at these several terms and those that remain will only be required to pay simple board &c^a. I will not however extend these remarks, as your fertile mind will readily supply or detect pro's or con's of these suggestions.[16]

In her reply, mostly negative, Mrs. Hale answered:

It seems to me that there are some serious objections to the plan of having a three months vacation in the winter. That season is the best time for study. In the hot summer months pupils cannot be confined to book studies. Then the plan takes out *four months* from the year for vacations, leaving only eight months, 32 weeks (or thereabouts) for school.—I do not know any Seminary for young Ladies that has such short sessions. Would the plan be popular?—I have not had time to think much on the subject.[17]

Vassar apparently agreed with Mrs. Hale—that she had had insufficient time to think about it, for his address to the board at a special meeting in April 1865 dealt almost solely with this topic. He outlined its essential features and gave several arguments in its favor. The minutes of the meeting record rather succinctly, "By invitation. . . Mr. Vassar caused his address to be read [by] the Secretary which was heard, recorded and placed on file."[18] Nothing further was done. The subject was not raised again in his lifetime, and the calendar adopted at the opening of college more closely corresponded with Mrs. Hale's notions than Vassar's.

The last item that Vassar presented to the social arbiter for her opinion concerned money:

Now as we have begun a new era for Woman, and my reputation as pioneer staked for its consummation I am desirous to avail myself of every suggestion, and thought arising in my own or other minds to

secure the hopefull end. We have daily precedents of public benifi-
cence and millions of dollars flowing into those channels, would it
therefore be unreasonable or impolitic for the College to open an
avenue whereby the flow of Womans generosity in behalf of her own
sex might center? What I would suggest is that a series of articles
should appear in your valuable "Lady's Book" as preliminary, suggesting the idea of the Ladies or women of America leaving by their wills,
Legacies for special endowments to the College, for Professorships or
otherwise, stipulating the department of Studies to be applied.[19]

It so happened that in the March issue of the *Lady's Book*, there appeared an editorial, "Men receive great gifts: women need them."[20] As a
subscriber to the *Lady's Book,* Vassar must have read this editorial. He
realized that a series of carefully prepared articles on the college could
pave the way for an appeal for funds. There is no letter, however, from Mrs.
Hale in answer to his. Perhaps she was unwilling to use the pages of the
Lady's Book to promote the special interests of a selected college.

Her editorial provides a lucid statement of her beliefs regarding woman's
mission in the world. Defining the occupational limits she felt must be
recognized by any educated woman, she would have woman "engage in no
profession that would wound the delicacy of her mind or derogate from her
womanly dignity of fame."[21]

Certainly, Mrs. Hale treated Vassar's three questions straightforwardly
enough. Yet, she had her own ideas about features of the plan which, if
modified or changed, would improve it. She is best known for her successful attempt to change the name of Vassar Female College. She is less well
known for her efforts to have a majority of women appointed to the faculty
as professors and to introduce a course in domestic science into the curriculum. The vigor of her attack on these three issues was that of a crusader.

Her most pressing crusade—also the first—was against the use of
"female" in the title of the college. Two editorials on the use of "female" as
a synonym for woman appeared in the "Editors' Table" two years before
the announcement of Vassar's intention to found the college. To the dis-
cerning reader of her column before 1855, these two articles may have
come as something of a surprise, because Mrs. Hale had used the word
often enough in the sense to which she objected. Before that year, one
might read a heading, "A Female Elected Register of Deeds," and her use
of female as an adjective was uninhibited. She wrote of female vanity,
female intellect, and female emigration. The present-day reader may look
for an explanation for this sudden reaction against the use of the word, for
in these first articles, Mrs. Hale gave no references to books or papers that
she might use as authorities, although she quoted some later in the 1860s
when her attack was well launched.

It began with a note appearing in her column: "Females—Is the Term

Proper to Designate Women?"[22] Essentially it pointed out Mrs. Hale's distaste for what had become common usage. She called it "inelegant" and "absurd." Queerly enough, she did not "object to the term when used, necessarily as an adjective; but many, indeed most writers employ the word as a noun, which, when applied to a woman is improper, and sounds unpleasant, as referring to an animal."[23] Within a year, a leading article of her column began with a quotation from the Bible: "She shall be called woman because she was taken out of man."[24] The attempt here was to show how absurd, degrading, improper, and vulgar was the use of "female" as the "name of woman." A footnote to the editorial reads: "The custom has become prevalent of styling 'colleges for women' 'female colleges,' 'female institutions' &c. This is quite vulgar, if not improper. A school cannot be *female,* though it may be for that sex."[25]

By the next year when interest had been aroused in her readers, she had more ammunition ready and, as a lady of the mid-nineteenth century, used the Bible to make her point—first by specific references, then by taking verses and substituting 'female' for woman. "Man that is born of female" is an example. Mrs. Hale did the same with lines from Shakespeare—"For none of female born shall harm Macbeth." Such usage, she declared, could only degrade woman and deprive her of man's sympathy and respect. She called her editorial "Grammatical Errors."[26]

"Woman! her Name and its Significance,"[27] rehashing arguments and adding some new material, was followed by an editorial citing Vassar Female College. It showed the inappropriateness of "female" in the name, concluding with: "Does it seem suitable that the term *female,* which is not a synonym for *woman,* and never signifies *lady,* should have a place in the title of this noble institution? The generous Founder intended it for 'young women.' The Bible and Anglo-Saxon language mark, as the best and highest style—VASSAR COLLEGE for Young Women."[28] "Line upon Line"[29] was a long diatribe which quoted from the *Queen's English* by Henry Alford,* the dean of Canterbury Cathedral, and ended with a list of masculine titles and their feminine equivalents, such as writer-writeress, professor-professoress, American-Americaness. The last article appeared in 1865 when Mrs. Hale's crusade was at its height. Called "The Royal Names of Humanity,"[30] it was, she thought, very fine and she sent copies to all the Vassar trustees. Its argument was largely biblical. In it she wrote:

> Man was to subdue the earth and reign over it. Woman, by her moral virtues, was to subdue man, and, by the aid of the Holy Spirit, imbue him with faith in her promised seed. . . .Thus was Man and Woman restored to their royalty of name, and the whole Bible is proof that the human race are never to be confounded with the animal. To use the word *male* as the synonym for *man,* or *female* for *woman,* degrades humanity and strikes at the root of Christian faith.[30]

*Stratham & Co., London, 1864

Poughkeepsie, N. Y. December 4th 1865

My dear Mrs. Hale,

Yours of the 2d current was duly received enclosing articles for the "Editors Table" in the forthcoming January Number of the "Lady Book", I have read the same with pleasure and satisfaction, I am happy to see such able treating on the feminine mind and rights so out-spoken by so able and dignified a mind as "John Ruskin" of England, when such distinguished writers & scholars wield their pens in behalf of womans Mission in the world, we may hope that her intellectual meridian has come, and henceforth a brighter era awaits her future destiny. and I may add that already is this sentiment pervading the minds of our Young Ladies pupils & inspiring them with more fervent industry of study in our College.

I notice your suggestions in regard to increasing the charges of tuition &c — Our Trustees had already anticipated the policy of deferring it untill another year term, altho it is quite evident from our past experements that the present terms are too low and must ultimately be advanced.

The liberal provissions made for the physical, and intellectual comfort and culture of College life demands it — Encouragement to future benificiarys examply demand it — and in fact duty to ourselves demand it, and we must therefore advance our terms to 450 to $500 another Year.

Now as we have begun a New Era for Woman, and my reputation as pioneer staked for its consummation I am desirous to avail myself of every suggestion, and

Letter of Matthew Vassar, 4 December 1865, proposing that Mrs. Hale in Godey's Lady's Book *suggest that women leave legacies to endow professorships*

thought arising in my own or other minds to secure the hopefull end. We have daily precedents of public benevolence, and millions of dollars flowing into those channels, would it therefore be unreasonable or impolitic for the College to open an avenue whereby the flow of Womans generosity in behalf of her own Sex might Center? What I would Suggest is that a Series of articles should appear in your valuable "Ladys Book" as preliminary, Suggesting the idea of the Ladies & Women of America leaving by their Wills, Legacies for especial endowments to the College, for Professorships or otherwise, Stipulating the department of Studies to be applied.

As it is now quite evident, from the experience already attained that the Gallerys of Art & Science &c must be enlarged, number of Teachers increased, to accommodate the prospective applications — We have now Some 150 to 200 learning the Art of Drawing & painting alone, and more daily applying — You will perceive from our last "Prospectus" that all these Branches of Study are Extra, and therefore aid the income College revenue very materially.

But I must now Close my remarks for this Morning as my old head divining admonishes me, only adding I do hope you will redeem your promise to honor us with a visit next Summer.

I remain dear Miss Hale
Your Friend &c
M. Vassar

Mrs. Hale asked her readers to consult Cruden's *Concordance* and there to count the number of times male and female are used in the Bible and under what circumstances. This would direct one's thoughts to good and bad usage. Then, she asked: "Is it proper to say the 'male mind'? Might not the elephant claim, justly, to be included?"[31] This was one of her favorite examples of the absurdity of such an error.

With these arguments and these papers, she bombarded many of the trustees of the college. Her one letter to Vassar on the subject was no different. It was plain that Mrs. Hale had come to abhor the term in its common usage. Eventually, she won Vassar to her conviction as she did many of the trustees, though she must have exasperated them by repetitious argument.

Vassar had first acknowledged that a movement was on foot to change the name of the college in a letter to the secretary of the New England Female Medical College in Boston in 1863 when he remarked:

> I am reminded of the Criticism now going on among several of our Litterati regarding the Etomology of the Vassar Female College, several of them advising a change to "Vassar Girls College" or College for young Ladies as the term "female" more directly apply to the brute creation, &c[a]. I cannot however at this moment enter into the merits of the controversy, suffice to say as we have adopted the customary name to designate the character of our Institution. I hardly think it of sufficient importance to change its title at this late day, notwithstanding the criticism of Mrs. Hale Editrice of the Godey Book & others.[32]

At a meeting of the board of trustees on 30 June 1863, a committee had been appointed to study this whole matter. Writing Jewett a week before the February meeting of the board of trustees in 1864, Mrs. Hale advanced an argument continued from an earlier letter. Its slightly acid tone expressed her displeasure with Jewett's reception of the idea, for he indicated that like Vassar, he thought the change neither necessary nor timely. So she wrote:

> I have been rereading your letter of the 2d Jany. . . . As you agree with me that *female,* used as a noun or *name* for *woman* or lady would not be a fitting term;—that you "would not use it";—there is only one point to consider in this question.
>
> You say—"We have, I conceive, the highest authority for the use of the *obnoxious term as an adjective—as we employ it*"; &c. You mean . . . in the style of *Vassar Female College.*
>
> Pardon me, but I think you are mistaken. Is not *English* authority the highest to which we can appeal in settling questions regarding their own language? Are there any places of education for Girls or Young Ladies in England that have this term *female* incorporated in

their style or title? Did you, my friend, find any *"Female College"* or "Female School" in England? The educated classes of Great Britain know too well the importance of a title to allow the *lowest designation* for woman to be ingrafted with the name of places where their daughters are educated. The term *female* with the English people, is applied only or chiefly to women of the lowest grade.[33]

Whatever Jewett thought of the attack, he was not moved, and if he showed the letter to Vassar and discussed its contents with him, the latter was unprepared to take a stand for or against the change. He didn't even refer to it in his long address to the board at the opening of their meeting of 23 February 1864. Yet in a letter a few days after the meeting, he wrote to the crusader:

> Your wishes in the matter of change in the College name was fully discussed. B. J. Lossing and several others strenuously advocating its adoption and others opposing—the most efficient of these latter was Dr. Bishop of N. Y., Dr. Anderson of Rochester & Dr. Raymond of Brooklyn. The final question of its adoption however was deferred until the regular meeting in June.[34]

He gave no indication of his own feelings and avoided any mention of Jewett's reaction. Vassar was not the least overawed by the lady and sent her an abstract of his address to the trustees at that February meeting. It might, he thought, be the basis for an article on the college and, indeed, it subsequently appeared as "Vassar College: Woman's Own,"[35] a page-long article. Mrs. Hale did not show any hard feelings even though Vassar thoughtlessly referred to a competent "female" in his letter; she would take that point up with him later. The address summarized arguments for a phase of college organization which she wished to exploit.

When Jewett resigned the presidency and John Raymond was appointed his successor in June 1864, she immediately communicated to him her ideas on woman's education in a letter welcoming him to the presidency and touching lightly on the change in the name. She tactfully enclosed some of her editorials on the subject which she expected him to read. She hoped, she wrote, that the title would become Vassar College for Young Women—she doubly underlined these five words and called the institution "this Queen of Colleges."[36]

The annual meeting of the board of trustees of 27 June 1864 came and went. Vassar had other points to make in his usual address to this body at that time; so he did not specifically call attention to the discussion of a change of the title. He avoided it in his letters to Mrs. Hale. During the rest of 1864, her letters were sober discussions of many ideas, but she did not bring up the question of the title again until February 1865. In a letter to Raymond that anticipated the April meeting of the board, she wrote, "I enclose five papers. Some of these you have seen I think—at least *one* you read yesterday, 'Grammatical Errors' but Mr. Vassar has not seen it."[37] Raymond had called upon her in Philadelphia, and it was at this time that she had given him a copy of her editorial. Her letter continued:

> Perhaps he [Vassar] would be interested in that paper. I shall write to him suggesting that Mr. Lossing take charge of bringing the matter before the Board. If Mr. V. will only allow his approval of *the change of name* to be known, and President Raymond will unite with the Founder; I do not think there would be any serious objection urged against it. If this "consummation" so deeply deserved—even devotly supplicated, should be reached before the College is opened, it will add a bright ray on the fast deepening twilight of my life.[37]

She was not sure of Vassar. Up to this point he had not been altogether helpful in the crusade, but he gave her a beautiful opening and she pounced upon it.

Poor Matthew Vassar! In his quiet way, he had sent Mrs. Hale a real essay this time, hoping that she might see fit to use it in her "Editors' Table." But it never appeared, for he made a fatal error and gave Mrs. Hale her chance. She began her letter:

> Thank you for your Essay—it has valuable hints and noble sentiments, —but I cannot notice it under its present title—*"The Female Mind."* What *female* do you mean? Not a *female donkey*. Must not your reply be—*"I mean a female woman"*? Then, why not say—*"Woman's Mind"* at first?. . . In your Essay I find this degrading term applied to woman *seven* times beside the Title. Pray look it over.[38]

She called the present title unpleasant to eye and ear.

> Reflect on the thousands of times in our one year which this imperfect, and worse than useless word *"Female"* would have to be used. Certainly this would be loss of time, taste and propriety to put the matter in its gentlest form.[38]

After this it was not Lossing who introduced the subject at the meeting of 13 April 1865, but Vassar himself. He still refused to take full responsibility for it, however, but referred it to President Raymond and the gentlemen of the board who were "intimate with the long discussion for the past two years in some correspondence on that matter."[39]

In committing himself to a course of action Vassar wrote:

It is needless for me to repeat that I have it in my heart to change the title of the College by omitting or dropping the word "Female", which is not only useless but absolutely vulgar in the connection which it stands. I shall insist on this change at the coming meeting 27th June.[40]

Mrs. Hale, at last, had a positive response; yet it is important to remember that Vassar, though willing to face the issue himself, wanted the final action of the trustees to be based on full discussion and a conviction of the majority of the board. In fact, he did not refer to the issue at the opening of the meeting of June 1865 and again there was failure. He sent the sad news to the editor a week after the meeting, reporting matter-of-factly:

> The subject of change of Title to the College came up for discussion . . . and was warmly debated and closely voted. Yeas 6 & Noes 7—7 out of 20 members present declined to vote not having their minds made up. We shall carry our points at the next meeting of the Board. The nonvoters out of regard to the feelings of the Founder would have voted in the affirmative if he *specially desired them,* but not otherwise, until further persuaded of the propriety of the change. Of course, I would consent to no such compromises and thus the affair passed off at the meeting.[41]

How frustrated Mrs. Hale must have felt! Nevertheless, she did not give up. Late in the summer of 1865, she reminded President Raymond and Lossing that she had Vassar's word that the change would be made. At the same time, Vassar wrote urging patience, predicting victory at the next meeting. He had assured her earlier in the year *"I know we are right* in asking for the *change* and besides which I have in my last Will and Testament devised another portion of my Estate to the 'Vassar College' making it imperative on the Trustees to change the title if they wish to secure this last gift."[42] Mrs. Hale was reassured, but she recognized Vassar's desire for a decisive vote. She laid plans for one last-ditch effort in late August 1865, addressing Lossing at that time:

> Mr. Vassar writes me that the style and title of the College will be changed at the next meeting of the Trustees.—*When do they meet?*— Pray write me on this point and also I enclose a list of Trustees; please mark, as I have indicated the *names* of those who voted for the change thus *O* Those who voted against *X*—and return the pages. I am intending to write to each man of them and enclose my "Royal Names" &c. I now send you a copy, altho' I think I did send you one when I last wrote.[43]

In another letter to a trustee, dated two weeks before the annual meeting, she wrote:

As a discussion has arisen [on] your Board, respecting the omission of the word "Female", in Vassar College, I have taken the liberty of enclosing some printed papers from the "Lady's Book", where the whole subject has been considered at length.

Let us hope that you may find time to examine these; it seems to me that they coincide with the object you have at heart:—the elevation of woman's education in *language,* as well as in other studies.[44]

Vassar's quiet, sensible remarks to the trustees a week later were devoted to the importance he attached to changing the name. Very concise and most convincing, he used some of Mrs. Hale's arguments and added some of his own. He avoided reference to the Bible, to Cruden's *Concordance,* and to most of the religious arguments, though he called the use of 'female' unscriptural. But he had caught the editor's sense of dignifying woman through the words with which one spoke or wrote of her. In its calm way, his was a masterful, but touching address. He concluded it with:

> It does seem to me that no one can look at the title of our College calmly and without prejudice, and not feel that it contains a word too much; a word which we are constantly tempted to drop, and which our young pupils invariably do in every instance when they can, not only because it is too long, but that there is an innate feeling, whether acknowledged or not, that it mars the meaning of the title, because it does not fully describe the class of persons for whom the College was or is intended.
>
> My friends, I wish you to look at this matter, and I beg of you to agree, at this meeting to change the title of the College...so that it may be presented to the next Legislature...and thus make "Vassar College" in name, as we hope to make it in fact, the blessed means of raising woman to her true position physically, intellectually and morally.[45]

Mrs. Hale had accomplished her purpose of overcoming Vassar's earlier indifference and making him the champion of her cause. When he realized the implications of the change, he took it up. In the end, it made him review all his deep feelings of what it meant to him to be involved in this great enterprise. He carried the day as he wished to do—without dissension and hard feelings among those men whom he had chosen to guide the college through the first difficult years. In a letter the next day he said to Mrs. Hale:

> I hasten to inform you that the great agony is over, your long cherished wishes reilised....Woman stands redeemed, at least so far as Vassar College is concerned from the degrading vulgarisation in the associated name of "female", that...has long and extensively grown up in our society....I was call[d] on for my customary address which I read,

one essential portion of which was to urge the change of title of the College.[46]

The legislature approved the change in the winter of 1866, and "Female" was removed from the white chiseled plaque on the facade of the Renwick building. The event was announced without fanfare in *Godey's Lady's Book.*[47]

Mrs. Hale's second crusade, of short duration, was almost over before it began. Her belief in what Vassar was attempting to do, led her to disagree with what she believed to be the intention of Jewett and some of the trustees in assigning most—if not all—of the professorships to men. She though it illogical, a bad example for women's colleges which might be founded in the future, and a disservice to the organization of Vassar College itself. From existing letters, it seems that Mrs. Hale began her campaign for women professors a few months before the great plan of the organization of the college was discussed in detail by the trustees.

She was certain of Vassar's purpose to do everything within his power to elevate the position of women, but his wait-and-see attitude was not always very reassuring. She knew too well from forthright statements he had made that he would never force his opinion on the majority of the board. He had called such action arbitrary—in fact, downright insulting. She knew, therefore, that she must try to influence Jewett and as many of the trustees as she could. Letters to them, or even better, a straightforward article in the "Editors' Table," might carry the day.

An offhand statement regarding the composition of the teaching staff had been made by Jewett in a report read at the first annual meeting of the board of trustees on 25 June 1861. Buried in this grandiose report is this single sentence: "To secure fifteen or twenty suitable Instructors, one half of either sex, is a task of no trifling magnitude."[48] The report antedated Jewett's travels in America and Europe where he visited institutions and talked with educators. Some months after his return from Europe in 1862, he read a report of his experiences to the board. In itself, it does not seem to offer very much that would be significant in planning college organization.

At the regular meeting of the trustees in June 1863, he produced the outline of studies to be offered. His plan—a university system, as he called it—suggested the division of studies into nine schools or departments, each under the supervision of a professor with a number of assistant teachers. Vassar mentioned this suggested organization in his address to the trustees at this meeting:

> For two years past, the President has given his earnest attention to the matter [of college organization]; and, for the last six months, his whole time and thoughts have been employed in elaborating and maturing the details. The plan which will be submitted to you has received the sanction of several of the most distinguished educators of our country. The President has conferred freely with the Founder on every feature of the system; and while I can not claim any knowledge and decline all

responsibility in relation to matters purely literary and professional, yet, so far as I am capable of judging, the great principles contained in the report met my cordial approval.[49]

Trustee minutes of this meeting indicate that only an abstract of the plan was read and that a preamble to a resolution recognized that trustees needed time and leisure to digest its contents before acting upon the full report. It recognized as well the values to be gained from expert opinion outside the college. This resolution called for discussion and final action on the report at a special meeting of the board to "be held the last Tuesday of February [1864]."[50]

Mrs. Hale made her strategic moves about the number of women professors to be appointed to the staff between these two dates—30 June 1863 and 23 February 1864. She was to use letters to Jewett and Vassar to reach all of the members of the board. In her column, she planned to publish an article on this subject written by an anonymous reader. Vassar and she exchanged letters before January 1864 dealing with the problem of the proportion of women to men of professors on the college faculty and in that month he wrote her:

> I am in receipt of your kind and valued note p[r] President Jewett of the 19th Current and have read it over and given your suggestions the most profound consideration.[51]

The founder's letter suggested that Mrs. Hale had communicated her feeling about women professors to Jewett, only to be rebuffed by him. Vassar continued:

> The subject of Women Professors & teachers is now fairly before our Trustees, who at the Meeting 23[d] proximo will report their views, and decide if it can be safely adopted in our College at the opening. The only question that can possibly arise, is whether we *can obtain* prominent distinguished Ladies instructors to fill the several chairs.[51]

Mrs. Hale sent two letters to the president three or four days before the February meeting. The first, clearly presenting the issue, asked "Shall Vassar College be organized on the plan of employing men only as professors? Or shall some of these highest honors be offered to women?"[52] She enclosed extracts from a note by her son, Horatio Hale,[c] to present his arguments in case Jewett had not read the anonymous article in the *Lady's Book* of February. She told him that she had sent his letter and also that of Vassar to her son for comments.

Horatio Hale was direct. "It certainly strikes me that President Jewett is mistaken in his opinion that women cannot be found who are qualified to take the professorships at present."[53] He then proceeded to produce

Members of the original faculty: upper left, *William T. Knapp, professor of ancient and modern languages, 1865-67;* upper right, *Charles Hinkel, professor of Latin and ancient history, 1869-90;* lower left, *Charles Farrar, professor of mathematics, natural philosophy, and chemistry, 1865-74;* lower right, *Truman Backus, professor of rhetoric and English, 1867-83.*

arguments similar to those set forth in the article appearing in the *Lady's Book*. Mrs. Hale used her son's communication as a springboard for several references. She considered her son one "whose opportunity of understanding the subject he discusses have been of no uncommon order." The younger Hale questioned the value of a celebrity as a professor. He argued that young women with experience would be fitted for the positions, and that when openings were announced in some of the journals, many applicants would respond.

Mrs. Hale ended this letter in a blaze of glory:

> We do not want scholastic ladies, ambitious and unsatisfied with woman's lot, from Vassar College; but we do need them wisely instructed and thoroughly accomplished in all womanly knowledge of Science, Art and Literature. . . . May Vassar College earn for its noble Founder and learned officers the good praise of training the daughters of our land to excel in these excellencies of character is the earnest wish of my heart; and I have faith that God will bless your constant endeavor.[54]

Her second letter contained a paragraph which had to do with salaries:

> It has never seemed to me that a lady should claim the same amount of salary as a gentleman professor. The man is forced by his manhood to sustain Government and participate in its duties; he is the soldier, the juryman, etc.—and then, the maintenance of others, besides himself, is laid on him. In short, he must do the hard work of the world, and if he does his duty the wealth should be his. I know that women are left in conditions that, sometimes, make the man's duty devolve on them; so far as their own families are concerned.[55]

She conceded that in the case of a widow with children, the college should pay the full salary of a professor. But, for her, there were limits beyond which one should not expect to go. Salaries for women equal to those of men in the same position were seldom expected by women in those days.

The article by Horatio Hale already referred to which appeared in the February issue of the *Lady's Book* was designed to reach a larger audience than the Vassar trustees. The idea of choosing her son to write it anonymously as though it came from a gentleman reader of her column was excellent strategy for it would seem to have no partisan point of view. It appeared a bit late in the crusade, and it is doubtful that it influenced any of the trustees who read it, but it couldn't do the new college any harm, for public opinion was divided on the issue. To those readers of Mrs. Hale's articles, it must have had a familiar ring.

Her son's article, "Vassar College: the Plan of Organization Examined;

Only One Defect; and this may be easily Remedied,"[56] began with a brief, factual exposition of the university system, and then proceeded to discuss the "one defect" so easily remedied. Although there was no definite statement in the Vassar report that men were to be preferred above women, there was some implication that this might be so; yet all the young Hale's arguments centered about this point. He scoffed at the supposition that the scarcity of women having intellectual and professional requirements for the highest positions in the college was a real one. He also stated:

> We have no desire that women should occupy political offices, or should be professors in colleges for young men. But it is peculiarly proper that woman should be the teacher and guardian of her own sex. The different qualities of mind and character in the two sexes render this imperative. Nature forces this law in giving the mother the training and tuition of her daughter; and when she surrenders the trust, it should be only to a woman fitted to continue the same important and dedicated office.[56]

He believed that Vassar College might be excluding its own graduates from positions in their alma mater if it assigned professorships only to men, and that it would lose those "who bring to their office not only genius and learning, but an ardent love for the home of their studious youth, such as no stranger can feel."[57] The pedantic article echoed his mother's thoughts and often seemed to use her very words.

Vassar's approach to this subject in his address to his fellow trustees at that special meeting in February had a freshness and eloquence that brought together those thoughts on a subject with which he had been preoccupied for many years. Give a woman a chance for the best in education and for a leading part in the process of this education and then let her future develop in any fresh ways open to her. In part, Vassar said:

> Gentlemen, . . . I do wish to lay before you frankly, . . . my views upon the general subject of appointments for your future reflection. . . .
> It is my hope. . .to inaugurate a new era in the history and life of women. . . . I wish to give one sex all the advantages too long monopolized by the other. Ours is, and is to be, an institution for women—not men. In all its labors, positions, rewards, and hopes, the idea is the development and exposition. . .the martialing. . .and the preferment of women, of their powers. . .demonstrative of such capacity as may surpass those of men. This. . .may be fully accomplished within the rational limits of true womanliness. . . .
> We are. . .defeated before we commence, if development be in the least dangerous to the dearest attributes of her class, [or] if it be hazardous for her to avail herself of the highest educated powers when

that point is gained. We are defeated, if we start upon the assumption that she has no powers save those that she may derive or imitate from the other sex. . . . [or] if we recognize the idea that she may not, with every propriety, contribute to the world the matured faculties which education evokes. We are specially defeated, if we fail to express our practical belief in her pre-emminent powers as an instructor, of her own sex especially.

Gentlemen, no superior power. . .will give us, an exclusive patent for originating the ability or genius of women out of nothing. We must proceed upon the conviction that these are in the world before us. We shall fail to make all coming women what many already are. We can and shall fill up many valleys, elevate many plains, and build higher many natural summits. But we can scarcely hope that every future height shall wear our family crest alone. Go as high as we. . .can hope to do, and genius, which will not call our College mother, will stand all the time abreast of us. It is my wish to recognize. . .the *fact,* of that genius and those high abilities at the very outset. Let us prove the certainty of woman's higher possible future by the best examples from the present. . .and honor her existing talent ourselves first, before we demand that recognition from the world. . . . Let us not add another to the examples of man's want of generosity, or of half hearted recognition of the powers of one half of the world. We should be ashamed to do it, at least under the mask of an institution which professes to be her peculiar champion, and which is to be dedicated to her benefit alone.

We cannot hope to maintain our belief before the world, when we voluntarily oppose it to our practice. We are. . .to illustrate our idea at the very start; . . .this idea, since the commencement of our enterprise, has unfolded itself immensely. I have therefore no fear of its failure. Only aid me judiciously in the selection of the best instruments to be found among the highly educated and accomplished women of this country, and let them take the hazard. . .I, at least, have gone too far already to allow me to shrink one instant from sharing, or being intimidated, by that risk. Let woman at least share the most prominent and responsible positions in our gift, and let them be proffered her accordingly, as her unquestioned right, as far as she can fill them equally as well as man. . . . I verily believe a generous partition between the sexes of all the professorships, is due no less to the idea underlying this enterprise than to woman herself, and the immediate and permanent success of our efforts. Inaugurate woman's elevation and power, genius and taste, at the same moment you open the door to her sex; for it is vain to educate woman's powers of thought, and then limit their operation. . . . Let the foremost women of our land be. . .the most advanced guardians of coming women, and I cheerfully leave my name to be associated with the result. I do not urge this point from any consideration of an economical nature. We must pay fairly. . .whatsoever instruments we use.[58]

His speech came directly from his heart.

The trustee minutes for the day reported that the address was received with some praise. Nevertheless, there was no indication that his speech was taken as a directive for future action on faculty appointments. A single, cold, matter-of-fact resolution recorded in the trustee minutes left the matter ambiguous:

NO SECTARIANISM. Mr. Bishop moved that the communication be filed, & at the same time suggested that the Committee on Faculty and Studies had already concluded that no sectarianism should be allowed to influence their selection and that in all cases where women could be found equal to the positions they should be preferred.[59]

Vassar sent Mrs. Hale a copy of his communication to the trustees and requested that it be given a place in the *Lady's Book*. She published those portions dealing with women as professors, adding:

Such are the enlightened views of Mr. Vassar. If these are faithfully carried out, his College must become the glory of Christian civilization. From it will go forth an influence essentially subserving the cause of peace and good-will among the churches of our land and of all Christendom. This power of womanly influence has never yet had proper training, right direction, or ample encouragement. Let all women thank God and Mr. Vassar—"and take courage."[60]

Before Vassar College opened in September 1865, eight professors were appointed—six of them men and two women. It is interesting to note that Mrs. Hale received a letter from a reader of her column complaining that all of the high offices of the college were given to men—with the exception of Mrs. Hannah Lyman, the principal; Maria Mitchell, professor of astronomy; and Alida Avery, professor of physiology and hygiene. The reader asked: "Why should six gentlemen hold professorships in a college designed for the daughters of America, and only two ladies have like rank?"[61] Mrs. Hale replied that she assumed no other ladies were found who qualified and explained that of thirty-five assistant teachers, thirty were women.

All that could be done at the time had been done and Vassar had spoken truthfully and well. Within a month, he wrote to Mrs. Hale:

I feel happy to have one by my side whose *idea* is that woman's mental powers in this world are *unappreciated* or, if appreciated, Custom has

Mrs. Hannah W. Lyman, principal, 1865-71, one of three high-ranking women on original staff of 38 at Vassar

Maria Mitchell, famous astronomer from Nantucket, who lived with her father in the Observatory. Her compensation did not equal that of the male professors.

Vassar students in first class in astronomy, 1866, with Mary Whitney '68, seated at table. Helen L. Storke '68, S. Louise Blatchley '68, Mary Reybold '68, Sarah Glazier '68, Clara E. Glover '68.

The Rev. John H. Raymond, a charter trustee, became Vassar's second (but first functioning) president in April 1864 after the resignation of Milo P. Jewett.

prevented her from employing them. It is this *idea* that has given rise to much discussion between President Jewett and myself, he was willing to grant to me all my claim in this particular if, I left him the majority of male Professors in the College, while I desired and have since demanded that every chair possible should be filled by women. . . . My desire is now and always has been to make our College, not only a College to educate women but a College of instruction by *women*.[62]

Vassar was reluctant to become too involved in the academic organization of the college. He had spent one summer discussing its problems with Charles A. Raymond, but he said quite firmly, "My business is to build endow and outfit the College and I shall have nothing to do with its internal organization."[63] It is true that he had outlined a possible course of study at the first meeting of the trustees in February 1861, so that they might know what purpose his college was to serve. The outline had summarized his discussions with Jewett and the opinion of educators with whom there had been correspondence. Among the studies listed was domestic economy, "practically taught. . .in order to prepare the graduates readily to become skillful housekeepers."[64] In 1863, Jewett's report on his travels abroad dealt in part with the teaching of domestic economy in European institutions, but only a year later, he did not include it in the formal studies outlined in the organization of the curriculum. When the minutes of the special meeting of the board in February 1864 listed nine professorships, a chair of domestic economy was conspicuously absent.

Mrs. Hale was quick to notice the omission in material sent her about the organization of studies and made quite a point in an editorial on domestic science. She felt that it was a suitable and necessary study in the curriculum of any young ladies seminary. Her arguments stressed the need of young women to prepare to fulfill the role of wife and mother, the need of any such institution as Vassar College to continue the education begun in the home. She called Vassar College remiss in failing to recognize the study and in not giving it the place it deserved:

It was natural to suppose that a subject of such importance, which had thus been brought into prominent notice, would have been kept in view in the system proposed for Vassar College, which aspires to be deemed, and we sincerely trust will hereafter prove to be in fact, the head and model of Young Ladies' Seminaries in our country, if not in the world. We might have expected that a Professorship of Domestic Economy, and a method of practical instruction in household knowledge and duties, would have been deemed a desirable and essential part of the system. In looking over the Report on Organization, however, we find no trace of anything of this description.[65]

She concluded her paper with an amusing picture of the neglected husband of a Vassar alumna appearing in the morning in a wilted collar and greeted with an indifferent breakfast and general chaos.

Mrs. Hale's third crusade lacked the vigor of the other two. Her letters on the subject to Vassar were often gentle reminders of impending editorials in the "Editors' Table." Correspondence with Raymond was given over almost exclusively to her views on women's education, her own strange ideas of man's relation to and treatment of woman, and the long arguments against the use of "female," and those supporting women as professors. Little wonder that Raymond wrote to his wife after a visit with the editor in Philadelphia: "Saw Mrs. Sarah J. Hale, who agreeably disappointed me; nothing of the 'strong minded' in her manner whatever; simple, quiet, ladylike, but bright and sensible, full of conversation and running slightly to enthusiasm on her favorite topics of Woman and the Bible."[66] In only one letter did she propose a course in "Domestic Education," but one suspects she was more intent on proposing a candidate that might fill the bill as a competent instructor in the subject, a woman "who devised and organized the system of Diet Kitchen service for the Christian Commission."[67]

In the *Prospectus of the Vassar Female College*, a forerunner of the college catalogue, one section dealt with "Extra-Collegiate Departments." Domestic science was among those departments listed. The *Prospectus* explained that formal courses in home economics would detract from liberal studies, but that plans had been made "to maintain a just appreciation of the dignity of a woman's home-sphere: to foster a womanly interest in its affairs; to teach correct *theory,* at least, of the household and its management, and to give some practical training in such domestic duties as admit of illustration in college life."[68] The description was copied in the editorial that Mrs. Hale called "Unfinished Education." The article congratulated Vassar College for the steps it was taking and deplored the fact that other institutions continued to neglect a subject so full of usefulness to young ladies. Too often, she said, such schools turned out frivolous young things, unready to assume the leadership in the family, a role that Mrs. Hale would assign to every woman. She was satisfied with the attitude that the college had taken as pictured in the *Prospectus* and quoted generously from it.[69]

Mrs. Hale may have been satisfied, but not Vassar. He withheld comments until he opened the annual meeting of the trustees in June 1867. His address was a review of the accomplishments of the past year and made recommendations for changes and improvements in the future. He urged the erection of a building

. . . for special training in the knowledge of the culinary art, where pupils, with the consent of their parents or guardians, may be instructed how to make a pudding, boil an egg, cook a potato, prepare a dinner, and, in fine, arrange in a proper manner the affairs of a household. Simple as these suggestions may appear, they are the fruits of long thought and reflection. There is nothing more needed than order and fitness of things in domestic economy; for without such provisions all is discord and confusion, like Hogarth's burlesque perspectives.[70]

The trustees did not act upon these suggestions then, so on 23 June 1868 Vassar tried again.

I renew, gentlemen, my wishes heretofore intimated and expressed about the erection of a building...for the purpose of instructing pupils...in a thorough knowledge of domestic economy.[71]

At this point his voice faltered, he sank back in his chair and died instantly. In the sadness and confusion of the moment and in the subsequent formalities surrounding his death, the project was overlooked and at an adjourned meeting, a week later, no action was taken. The cause was given up for it had lost its leader.

Vassar over those years of association with Mrs. Hale never met her. At first, the lady firmly refused to visit the college as long as "female" remained in the title. A year before he died, Vassar wrote to her: "I am fearfull we shall never greet each other in this life and if we should be so happy as to meet in the world of Spirits, how are we to recognize each other there, not withstanding the spiritualist theory of sympathies, &c."[72] Vassar recognized these sympathies—helping women in a way that they had not been helped heretofore. They could agree on the widening of women's horizons and improving their lot though each held divergent views on how these things should be accomplished and how far they should be carried. His point of view was dynamic, ever growing and expanding; hers was static, remaining essentially the same through the years. Vassar was clear and concise in expressing his ideas; Mrs. Hale more often than not invested hers with a grandeur that confused. Vassar's horizons expanded as he dealt with the multitudinous affairs of founding a college which was his daily occupation; Mrs. Hale's remained virtually unchanged, for she had not the stimulus of watching an idea become a reality.

Yet Mrs. Hale could write with affection and delight about an idea that held her imagination. She sought perfection. Her letters stimulated Vassar to make new and continued appraisals of his grand enterprise. Though he used her to bring Vassar College before an important audience of women, she used him in improving the articulation of goals of women's education. He had become her unconscious and willing student, who in the end went far beyond her.

Nothing better illustrates the difference between Mrs. Hale's thinking and that of Vassar on some aspects of the opportunities and rights of women, than the response of each to woman's suffrage. Mrs. Hale in a long editorial on the subject set down several arguments against it. She attacked the problem by contrasting woman's sphere of influence in the world with man's:

> Would the true Wife desire to supercede her husband? Would the good, intelligent mother, who has trained her son to the glorious ambition of serving his country and gaining a noble fame—would she, were it in her power, pluck the laurel from his brow and place it on her own? Would she be willing that any woman should enter the lists against her son? If not, is it right for this mother to encourage the competition of her own sex against the sons of other mothers?
>
> Greatness is most perfect when it acts with the least reference to self; power is more efficient when moving the will through the heart. Let us American ladies cultivate the virtues, the knowledge, the accomplishments which will influence, imbue and aid men to do the work of the world to the glory of God; then the woman will truly shine forth as "the glory of man."[73]

A short time after this, in a letter on the subject, Vassar wrote:

> I received last evening. . .your note of yesterday[s] date, and were glad to hear that you and all the other Young ladies of the College were pleased with Miss [Anna] Dickinson[d] lecture last evening and before I had passed the Gate-Lodge after leaving the Observatory I was sorry we had not remained to hear the Lecture. . . .
>
> The subject of "Womans Suffrage" or "Idiots and Women", was correctly quoted from the Law[s] granting the right of them to the ballot Box, and when I read the law some years ago I was equaly supprised to find our Fair Sex placed in so shamefull category as "criminals, paupers, Idiots &c", which if the Law was right by this classification I think it is full time that my 300 Daughters at "Vassar" knew it, and applied the remidy.
>
> The truth is it is all *nonsense* and irreconcilible with Divine truth in regard to the Mental Capacity of Woman, nothing but long prejudices with the dominering spirit of Man has Kept woman from occupying a high elevation in literature & art, but mens tyrany & jelousy, and wilful usurpation of her normal rights &c.[74]

Chapter IV

Matthew Vassar Acquires
Elias Magoon's 'Gems'

Strength clothed in beauty

In 1865 at Matthew Vassar's request, Benson J. Lossing wrote an informal study of the founder and his college. His description of Main Building given in this book was fairly exhaustive and from it one can get a feeling for the complexity of the task of designing one single huge structure to house almost all of the activities of college life. In James Renwick's detailed plans of each of the four floors, reproduced in Lossing's work, it is possible to locate the various parts of the college building. For instance, the chemistry laboratory was located in the basement—now the first floor—to meet the requirements of fire insurance companies. The main entrance was reached by staircases on the outside of the building that led to what is now the Rose Parlor on the second floor. Directly over this main entrance, on the third floor, is a room with three windows across the front. In 1865, these looked out upon the main drive, lined with tiny fir trees, down to that delightful Victorian gate-lodge, which was torn down early in this century to make way for Taylor Hall and Taylor Gate. This third floor room, 33-by-35-feet, was designated as the library room. Even on the first day of college, 23 September 1865, it was totally inadequate to serve the purposes for which it had been designed.

On the floor above this, the fourth story, and immediately over the library, was a large, airy room adequately lighted by skylights and nine windows which overlooked the town of Poughkeepsie to the hills and mountains on the west bank of the Hudson River. This room, designated as the art gallery, Lossing described as follows:

> Opposite the gallery of the Chapel is the entrance to the Art Gallery. This admits us to a room thirty feet in width and ninety-six feet in length, lighted from a dome in the center that rises about forty feet above the floor, a sky-light in each wing, and windows along the western front of the College. In the greater portion of the apartment, the walls, from the floor well up toward the cornice, are hung with pictures, all adapted by their size and character to the purposes of instruction.[1]

He said nothing about the magnificent view to be had from its windows. Unfortunately, the old art gallery has since been divided into several smaller rooms. Nothing remains to give us any idea of its splendor. The library room, however, is as it was in 1865, but it is now used as a student game room with a pool table and several easy chairs in an alcove.

Jewett had more than a little to do with the first plans drawn by Thomas A. Tefft. Indeed, he wrote in his earlier *Origin* that in the summer of 1856, he traveled to Providence, Rhode Island, to lay before Tefft the ideas for the college building. In the *Origin* (1879), he was more explicit in reporting the part that he played:

Maria Mitchell and her father, who lived with her in the Observatory. Matthew Vassar called on them frequently after he had resigned from the executive committee.

Henry Van Ingen, professor of painting and drawing. When Vassar opened on 26 September 1865, Henry Van Ingen taught in the School of Design, an extra-collegiate department of the college.

Mr. Vassar asked me to visit Mr Tefft [to] present my ideas on the subject, [of the college building] and engage his services, the result was, the drawings which are now in Vassar College.[2]

Tefft's death in Rome that year made it imperative to select another architect, and the professional services of Renwick were sought. Though the latter's new plans in no way resembled the earlier ones, there is no doubt that the general idea of the number of rooms, their sizes, and locations came from Tefft's drawings. It is difficult to see why Renwick did not discover how totally inadequate the library room was and why he did nothing to correct it. But then Renwick, for all his expertise, made no provision for closet space in student rooms[a] and his specifications for heating, lighting, and ventilating the rooms of the college were sketchy at best.

Those intensely busy years between the first meeting in February 1861 for the organization of the board of trustees and the opening of college in September 1865 used every bit of Vassar's imagination and his skill at getting what he wanted and needed. Problems of heating, ventilating, and lighting the vast structure that was under construction during those years were a source of much discussion in the executive committee. Correspondence and conference went on for months. The letter book in which Vassar kept rough copies of most of his correspondence reveals how much of his thinking and energy went into securing systems that would insure a healthy atmosphere in which his young ladies might live and study. Yet he never forgot the importance of an adequate library for use by both faculty and students. In his early letter analyzing the probable cost of the new college, he thought of most things. Of the total of $685,000, $30,000 was allotted for the library, art gallery, and "philosophical apparatus"[3]—a sizeable amount in the 1860s. Moreover, as the building took shape, Vassar was liberal in spending money from his own pocket for special projects. This money, of course, was aside from the initial endowment of the college, which was in the control of the trustees. The purchase of an art collection and the art library that it included is only one example of such a special project.

The problems associated with the selection and purchase of books were fairly simply solved. That a sound education depended upon an adequate library was recognized by all members of the board as well as by Vassar and Jewett. Vassar felt in the early days of his planning that the college must open with a library of at least 10,000 titles. Jewett was of the opinion that no self-respecting institution could begin with less.[4] Fortunately, this number was not reached until 1875, and in the ten years between 1865 and 1875, the inadequacies[b] of the library room were corrected. The changes involved a very simple rearrangement and assignment of rooms. In spite of the fact that two library catalogues[c] had been prepared in 1862, they were apparently not used in the selection of books, for the library consisted of a

Entrance to Main Building, showing staircases to second floor

A 20th-century restoration of the Founder's Parlor in Main Building. From a photograph taken by Margaret de Muth Brown, photograph archives, Special Collections.

rather indifferent and miscellaneous collection. Some books, however, were and are still of great interest. Many are on the shelves today and include collections purchased by Jewett[d] through agents in London during his sojourn abroad in 1862.

Perhaps the recognition that the faculty must have a voice in selecting books which would meet their needs and those of their students led to the decision to wait until a staff had been appointed before trying to meet the goal. This permitted teachers in the various disciplines to have a say in the purchases made. At any rate, the result was that the college opened with a library of only 3,000 titles. The first college catalogue stated:

> The library is yet in its infancy. It numbers about three thousand volumes, comprising many valuable works of reference. It will be the policy of the Trustees to foster its growth by annual appropriations, expended so as to meet the actual wants of the several departments of instruction. In this way, they hope to diminish the great risk of inappropriate purchases, and gradually to form for the College a good working library.[5]

The number did not include an art library of more than 450 titles, which was a part of the collection purchased by Vassar from the Rev. Elias Lyman Magoon in 1864. Magoon was one of the men selected by Vassar in 1861 to act on the Vassar board of trustees, probably because he was a life-long friend of Rochester's Anderson. As a charter member of the Vassar board, Magoon attended the first meeting of that body on 26 February 1861 and was appointed chairman of the committee on the art gallery, associated with such men as Benson J. Lossing and Samuel F. B. Morse in the early years. He remained chairman not only while he was a member of the board, but for the rest of his life.

Magoon wrote a letter to Vassar in mid-January 1861, possibly as a result of Vassar's approaching him as to his willingness to serve on the board of the young college: "[I am filled] with rapture while my mind glances at what seems to be your purpose in the edifice you are going to build, the cultivating forces you accumulate within, and the mild splendors you design wisely and most beneficiently thence to diffuse through all classes."[6] Magoon ended with:

> Surely the evening of a busy life could in no way be rendered more cheering and delightful, than in perfecting what you have so well begun. May younger hearts, heads and hands become the prompt and genial coefficients of your plan. Let chaste intellect and sober elegance imprint themselves at the outset of the prospective College and its Gallery of Art, Library and Halls of Instruction, will at once become the central attraction of your beautiful town, and the wide admiration of mankind.[6]

A perspective drawing of the original buildings

The library, fourth floor of Main Building

Main Building

The letter was typical of many that were to follow.

One of the most original of the first trustees, Magoon was born in Lebanon, New Hampshire, in 1810; so he was fifty-one years old when he became a member of the board. His early life was not one of ease and indulgence, for his father, a successful architect, apprenticed his son to a bricklayer and mason when the boy was sixteen. He prepared himself for college in the evenings after a strenuous day's work and entered Waterville College (now Colby College) in Waterville, Maine, in the early 1830s. During vacations, he followed his trade, applying his earnings not only to finance his years at Waterville, but also to make possible his theological studies at the Newton Theological Seminary, Newton, Massachusetts, from which he received a certificate in 1839. At this time, he was ordained a Baptist minister and during his active life, served a succession of pastorates at Richmond, Virginia; Cincinnati, Ohio; Albany, New York; and finally, at the Broad Street Church in Philadelphia. Magoon retired in 1884 but continued his Vassar connection until his death in 1886.

He spent fourteen months of 1844 and 1845 in Europe to absorb European culture. A letter of 14 July 1845 to Anderson described his travels through the British Isles and on the Continent, concluding with "For purposes of mental improvement, give me Paris above all other places in the world."[7] He returned to the United States on the *Great Western,* satisfied that he had accomplished what he had set out to do—lay the foundation for future collecting of art objects and a library in art history "around the mother thought of *Christianity Illustrated by its Monuments.*"

In April 1854 he made a second trip abroad to renew old acquaintances. On this occasion, he enjoyed "fresh as well as invaluable facilities furnished by that noble Cicero of our Union, Edward Everett."[8] Through Everett, he met men of letters and "the foremost of British architects and artists." The way for collecting books and works of art was opened to him, and he took advantage of his opportunities. Among others whom he met at that time was John Britton, author of the fourteen-volume study, *Cathedral Antiquities of England.* Britton was an old man in 1854—he died two years later—yet Magoon found his aid invaluable in selecting hundreds of original works. Others helped him in seeking out and selecting pieces of art and illustrated books and manuscripts, which would carry out the great plan that had been uppermost in his mind for over a decade.

After a summer of collecting, he nearly lost it all as he explained sometime later:

The entire expenditure of that summer was stored in Liverpool, to come with the owner, in the Collins steamer of Sept. 20th. But a merciful Providence prompted a delay of ten days, to gain some choice antiquities in Normandy. We read our obituary, in a Brooklyn paper, written from Paris, by one who a month afterwards learned that we did *not* come "by the Arctic."[9] †

†Apparently Magoon originally booked passage on a vessel which was shipwrecked sailing from Liverpool by the Arctic route.

Benson John Lossing, author of Vassar College and Its Founder, New York, 1867, and an original trustee of the College, 1861-91

Elias Lyman Magoon, trustee, 1861-86. Matthew Vassar purchased his art collection to found the Vassar art gallery.

Directly over the dining hall in Main Building was the chapel. In front of the organ, the copy of Raphael's La Vierge de Foligno *by Emma Church reposed when the college opened.*

Magoon also commissioned first ten, and then many more, American artists in New York to paint pictures for his growing collection. He displayed his collection first in New York City, after which he moved it to his parsonage at 66 Philip Street, Albany, during his pastorate there.

Clearly, Elias Magoon was no ordinary clergyman. A photograph taken in the 1860s shows him to have been a man of character. He looks as though life were without any great cares, as though he were an amused and an amusing man. Unlike many of his contemporaries on the board, he was clean-shaven and his strong, intelligent face was surmounted by a mop of white hair. One Vassar College story survives that gives a clue as to the sort of impression he made on his contemporaries. Frances Wood, an early librarian of the college, said of him, "He looked and we all thought him slightly crazy, but we came to appreciate him and delight in his ardor."[e10] He was a self-made man and never forgot the debt he owed to his own hard labor as a mechanic. As one of his biographers said, "The first brick ever laid by him was taken from its position in the wall of a house long after it was first laid, and is now converted into an inkstand, ornamented with bronze, and occupies a prominent place in the possessor's library."[11]

The later years of his life were devoted to his beloved avocation as a collector of art and literature. He made many gifts to art museums, institutes, and libraries.[f] In the early 1880s, he wrote to Anderson:

More than a thousand intelligent admirers crowded my parlor to study the seven pictures by the great and noble Richards, during the ten days, they were on view. It is hoped that to-day they are safely at Vassar College, where they will be a valuable force in education, so long as their beauty may endure to feed and fashion intellect.[12]

In 1861, the trustee minutes told of his appointment as "Chairman of the Committee on the Art Gallery" and his association on this committee with Lossing and Morse, as well as with John Guy Vassar, and John Thompson, a New York banker and publisher.[13] He, Jewett, and Nathan Bishop were appointed a special subcommittee to make arrangements for the painting of a portrait of the founder by Charles Loring Elliott.[g] A note from Vassar to Swan dated June 1861 dealt with this matter: "You will please to inform your gentlemen Committee Messr M. P. Jewett Profr Doct Nathan Bishop, and Revd E L Magoon whom have the same in charge, that I will be prepared to sit at the Artist Studio at any time most convenient to himself."[14] Incidentally, the finished portrait gave Vassar great pleasure. For a time, it was hung in the Baptist church for all Poughkeepsie to see and admire, and now, of course, it hangs in the Vassar College Art Gallery.

Magoon and his subcommittee during 1862 and '63 were apparently mulling over and discussing the needs of the art department and how the gallery might be used to the best advantage in the teaching of art. At the

February and June meetings of the board in 1864, reports of the committee on the art gallery showed that they were now prepared to present their ideas to the members of the board for their discussion. Since both reports involved the selection and purchase of art objects and books for an art library and since Magoon was at the center of it all, it is necessary to review some happenings of the years 1862 and 1863 as revealed in pertinent letters and documents.

Perhaps Vassar's first worry was lest the college should possess a fine gallery, but have nothing to put in it at the outset to show of what high quality the instruction in art would be. The acquisition of telescopes, lenses, and the like for the observatory, apparatus for the laboratories of chemistry and physics, and the purchase of cabinets for the study of geology and zoology was relatively simple; but the selection of materials which would serve as teaching elements in the study of art posed a problem of which Vassar was all too aware. What is more, the art gallery must be a place that would be used and respected by the community. How did one go about collecting pictures, statues, and all such costly objects? Their number must be large enough so that the gallery did not look bare and unfinished.

Charles A. Raymond, always so ready with ideas about college organization, made some suggestions on the subject in a letter written early in 1863. In all seriousness, he set before Vassar a plan which he thought quite ingenious and original. The idea was to start with a small, select nucleus of pictures about which a collection might be built. It called for the appointment of a professor of painting:

This Prof[r] must *be a first class artist,* not a teacher of painting, and the special contract made with him, would be that he is to paint for your gallery, at a fixed salary, and you hire all his time.

Such a position would be a paradise to most Artists, and you would have no trouble in procuring any one almost. Historical Landscape Painters alone would suit the position, and they are not often sure of their bread.

The advantage to the pupils studying painting would be, that they would see this Artist paint daily and this is the only way to learn how to paint viz. *by seeing some one else paint.* . . .

Think what a collection of pictures under judicious management you might thus have in ten, twenty, fifty years: and at really no increased expense.[15]

Vassar apparently didn't see fit at the time to dignify this ingenious plan of Raymond with an answer; at least there is none in his letter book.

Anyway, he was already in the midst of negotiations with Emma Church,[h] an American artist in Rome. He hoped that these negotiations would lead to a partial solution of the problem of the collection. First of all, he had been assured that her copies of the masters were fine reproductions. Jewett had been introduced to this artist when he visited Rome in the autumn of 1862. He saw and admired her work and he assured Vassar that this woman was unquestionably one of the best copyists in Rome and had a fine reputation. In this first letter to her, Vassar wrote as though she were already under contract to copy several pictures for the college. He said further: "Prof. Jewett speaks in the highest terms of your genius. . .and purity of character, and of the many warm friends you have in Rome which gives weight & additional value to your pictures."[16]

The minutes of the meeting of the executive committee on 25 May 1863 show:

> Mr Vassar reported that himself & Dr Jewett had some months since contracted with Miss Emma Church an American Woman at Rome for four oil paintings the subjects to be selected by herself without fixing the Cost one half payable in advance. That recently information had been received that two of these pictures awaited our order at Messrs Monroe & Co in Paris & that Miss Church was awaiting the payment for the same & an advance on the two unfinished. That in view of the urging of the Case he had advised the Treasurer to send forward to Miss Church at Paris $750.
>
> The Treasurer thereupon reported that he had given Dr Jewett a Check for $1200 with which to purchase exchange & send the avails as above and desired the approval of the Committee.[17]

Members of the executive committee could hardly do other than approve something that was an accomplished fact. The surprising thing in all of this is that Vassar allowed Jewett to make such arrangements. There seemed to have been no formal contract establishing a probable cost of each copy. Apparently, too, no provision had been made for the costs of framing each, crating it for shipment, and paying the shipping charges between Rome or Paris and Poughkeepsie. Why should this artist have been treated differently from anyone else supplying materials for the development of the enterprise? Did Vassar rely solely on Jewett's assurances of her high character and her professional worth, so that he considered a contract unnecessary? This was quite out of character.

Two months later, Vassar reported to the executive committee that two of these copies had arrived at Poughkeepsie and that they were hanging in his house. He invited all members of the board to come to see them and pass judgment on them. In November Vassar laid before the committee "the letter of Miss Church in regard to the 'Foligno' she is now copying & for which she asks $1200"![18] This price for a single reproduction, even of this famous *Madonna of Foligno* by Raphael, shocked them all; they did not know how to proceed with it. Discussion followed discussion at successive weekly meetings of the executive committee for the next four weeks. At each meeting the matter was tabled until it became imperative to take some action. On 14 December 1863, "Mr Vassar submitted a draft of a letter from himself to Miss Church in which he absolves the College from any obligation to take the picture she is now executing & agrees to take it himself personally & absolves the Committee & the College from any responsibility therefore."[19] By the time all of the extra charges were added to the cost of the painting, the total was $1553.39, an impressive and sizeable sum for Vassar to pay out of his own pocket. Eventually, the board of trustees considered the matter and voted to take over the entire cost. There must have been some discussion of the part Jewett played in the early negotiations with the artist, but no record was made of it in the minutes of the committee.

Vassar's correspondence with Church during this period adds little to the general story. It gives no indication of the struggles going on over the "Foligno"; in fact one would be led to believe that the price was quite acceptable,[i] but some small difficulties of another sort are revealed in a letter dated 15 December 1863, written by Vassar to Church:

When Prof. Jewett was in England & Rome in the Summer of 62 he wrote to me *not* as Chairman of the Ex. Com of V.F.C., but *personally* avoiding all acts that more properly belong^d to the Committee on "Fine Arts" which is composed of Prof. S.F.B. Morse, Benson J. Lossing (Historian) E.L. Magoon D.D, Honb^l Jno Thompson and Jno Guy Vassar, and in as much as the Chairman of that Committee [Dr Magoon] had not been advised or consulted, a little feeling of jealousy was created, so much so as one or two of them have since declined to cooperate and they have not seen your first pencillings....Seeing this matter *hangs fire* and unwilling to widen the breach I informed the Board of Trustees yesterday that to remove all trouble, I would take the picture now in process of execution (Foligno) off your hands and present it to the College *gratis* sooner than to have any further trouble or feeling upon it.[20]

While these particular difficulties were being unraveled, Vassar found himself deeply involved in other troubles of the same sort. The attention of the members of the executive committee had been directed to a catalogue of engravings and prints that were for sale in Cambridge, Massachusetts. No action leading to acquisitions was taken at that time, but a second notice, six months later, caused a flurry of activity, as well it might have. Vassar wrote immediately to Anne S. Toffey, an agent connected with the sale:

Samuel F.B. Morse, distinguished scientist, artist, and trustee of the college, 1861-72

I received this morning letter &c from my friend & townsman Prof. S.F.B. Morse respecting a Collection of valuable antique engravings which are for sale by Mrs Clark widow of the late E.P. Clark of your City and which collection he recommends to the attention of the Trustees of the V.F. College. I shall lay the subject next week before our Ex Committee and write you the results of their deliberations immediately thereafter.[21]

Professor Morse as a member of the committee on the art gallery might well have called the attention of Vassar to the sale of these objects, but he did this without the knowledge of the other members of the committee. Within a week, Vassar was in communication with the Boston agent indicating that the matter had been referred to the executive committee. Its members had indeed instructed him to write asking Magoon to investigate the Clark collection. He wrote Magoon promptly:

Enclosed you will find letters received from Miss Anne S. Toffey Cambridge by Prof. S.F.B. Morse respecting a Catalogue of valuable Unique Engravings now for Sale by the widow of the late E.P. Clark...The Executive Committee regarding the matter as properly belonging to the Committee on Art and as you are the honble Chairman with propriety, they have authorized me to say and especially in view of your high taste and culture in these matters, that you visit Cambridge, examine the Collection and learn what specimens of these fine engravings would be important for the College to possess, if any, and what price they can be obtained at private sale.j22

He ended with a postscript about the cost of Church's "Foligno."

Magoon's retort came as a thunderbolt to Vassar, whose immediate reply called it "quite spicy and pointed." From the context of Vassar's letter, there is no doubt that Magoon had a low opinion of copies of masterpieces and objected to the acquisition of Church's work, about the existence of which he had just learned from Vassar's letter. Vassar did the best he could to smooth things over. He wrote, "As soon as I could I stopt it, only 2 has come to hand, the other two ordered from Miss Church will not be finished before next fall."[23]

In another letter to his friend, just before Christmas of 1863, Vassar wrote sorrowfully that he had heard from the board's secretary, Swan, that Magoon had sent in his resignation from the board. In short, this letter expressing genuine concern lest the board lose so valuable a member, he asked for a reconsideration of this action, concluding with "I cannot consent to part with you."[24] A week later, Vassar, still concerned lest Magoon persist in his intention to resign, wrote a second time. He did not want to lose him:

The more I have reflected upon your proposed resignation, the more I am convinced it will operate to the serious disadvantage of our enterprise. We have among us many good *sort* of people that are often shrugging up their Shoulders accompanied with significant gestures as to the final success of the College enterprise and whom in the event of *failure* would *not* sob aloud with *regrets* or griefs.

Oh for *humanity poor humanity,* but is just here as elsewhere, we are not *worse* (tho' I say it with some reluctance) than those on whom the Tower of Silean fell. Do my dear friend think *twice* before you act *once.*[25]

Thereupon, Magoon answered with a twelve-page letter. It must have been more reasonable than Vassar had expected, but while the latter's response the next day was cheerful and showed that he was somewhat relieved, Magoon had to be appeased. The letter also contained an admission:

We want a Gallery of diversified actualities in artistic Elegance &c, to illustrate the loftiest principle and refine the heart.

Now my dear friend tell me how to do this thing best? I am no connoisseur myself, nor do I know of any one in our honb^l board besides yourself that can, but how can I expect you to leave your sacred and gracious calling "to serve tables" but some one must, our President cheerfully would, but like myself has not the Capacity or he would not have ordered from an *undistinguished* american artist four pencillings of so *large a size* at so great a cost to *adorn* the walls of V.F.C. had *their* cost been paid in *several original copies* (as you suggest) by different celebrated artists.[26]

Magoon had not been gentle in condemning the purchase of copies. He had much higher ideals for the gallery. Vassar, accordingly, not completely at his ease, agreed to go with Swan to see Magoon in Albany. Two days later he went.

Express to Albany with C. Swan on Trustee commission to see Magoon. Returned same Evening. Saw Mrs. Magoon....We (Mr Swan & self) went over the whole ground, and before leaving him had all matters straightened & much satisfaction—But it was quite a task.[27]

Vassar blamed no one but himself for this impasse. He could have censored Jewett for his part in ignoring the gallery committee, but he didn't. He treated the affair as though it were an unfortunate lapse on his part. But some good came out of it as revealed by Vassar's chatty letter to Magoon dated 15 January 1864, two days after their difficult conference in Albany.

Since our short and pleasant interview at your domicil on Wednesday I have been exercising my thoughts on the Suggestions you then made as to the manner of making up our Gallery of Art, convinced as I am, [that] if properly and artistically arranged, [it] will do more or at least as much as any other appropriation to the College in securing a favorable public estimation of the Institution and therefore as you just-ly remarked its special purpose should be to elevate and imbue the minds of the pupils with the most refined and perfect specimens il-lustrating that science. I do not now speak of its advantages in its moral bearings; which by so doing would extend these remarks beyond my present purpose—Suffice to say I want our College to *possess your Collections,* but as that is a matter that more especially belong[s] to the Committee in that department I shall wave further considerations upon it till this next week meeting.[28]

It would appear that Magoon had made use of the mellow mood of Vassar at the close of their conference, to impress upon him the importance of the Vassar art gallery and the use to which it would be put. Vassar, who had ap-parently not seen it all before, could not help but be astounded at the extent of the Magoon collection, only a part of which was on display in the house in Albany. Here was the answer to the perplexing question of how to have the gallery prepared for the teaching of art before the opening of the college in 1865. Vassar was convinced that the college must have Magoon's collection, but Magoon was to play about with the idea of selling it for a while before committing himself.

On 23 February 1864 Magoon made a stunning report to the trustees at their meeting in the name of the committee on the art gallery. George T. Pierce, a member of the board, presented a resolution, seconded by Vassar "that 500 copies [of the report] be printed for the use of the Trustees."[29] The published report was bound between blue papers with *Report of the Committee on the Art Gallery of Vassar Female College* printed in gold letters on its cover. In a brief twenty pages are set down the thinking and conclusions of the five authorities who were members of the committee—two of whom were art collectors; at least two more, artists; and the fifth, a cultivated man of the world. The form and expression of the report were due in no small part to Magoon and reflected him at his best.

The report has a fascination simply in the use of words which convey, with some elegance, the most elevated of Magoon's thoughts. Only a small part is given to problems of the art gallery and their relation to the study of art within a curriculum in which a rather strong emphasis was to be given to science. Magoon threw out for his listeners' consideration a certain few suggestions "on Art, on Original Art, and upon American Originality in Art."

It is almost impossible to paraphrase the whole without destroying it. His definition of art, for instance, as "petrified poetry, or concrete rhetoric" is amusing to say the least. Three-quarters of the whole is definition. He explained, "Mere ornamentation is to art what words are to thought," and "Art is diviner than science, the latter discovers, this creates." He went on from this to say:

It is the highest sagacity and purest exertion of human nature. The study of it possesses this great and peculiar charm,—that it is absolutely detached from the disgraceful contests of sordid ambition.[30]

About "Original Art," he had much to say but lost himself in the beauty of nature and at first did not seem to be making his point. Yet he managed to remark on the sterility of copies:

Take the gem of your prospective college, under the full sway of legitimate education. Draped in enraptured unconsciousness, her bosom swells, cheeks flush, eyes sparkle, and thrilling inspiration gleams on her brow, as all that is receptive and immortal within responds to the living words of a competent teacher expounding facts in the presence of things. Now take her dead, in yon coffin, obtuse to the flowers that glow in her marble hand, and blind to the pictorial charms that used to waft her soul near heaven. Such is copyism compared with originality,—lightening painted with charcoal—the avoirdupois of gun powder weighed against its explosive force.

You may double your expenditure in monumental structures, or in lifeless apparatus, and yet not attain an iota of educating force. *That* is not a medicinal bath—something soaked in—but latent ability educated forth. When all other tools of inert erudition are at hand, give them to a substratum of LL.D.'s, with a superstratum of D.D.'s, and all you will thereby accomplish is the dignified extinguishment of what little capacity for excellence yet remains in American youth, as you might smother a swarm of young bees under a cart-load of autumnal leaves.[31]

Then, he laid out for their inspection what the art gallery would need if it were to be a success as an educational force. He even managed to include in the necessary items "Etruscan remains, Roman relics and ancient coins," all of which were represented in his collection.

But to get the full flavor of Magoon's argument and his dissertation, the whole report must be read. The ending is typical of the man:

In conclusion, your Committee would remind the Board that no worthy monument was ever built, or enduring thought conceived, that was not inspired by and dedicated to woman—Minerva or Mary. But let us remember that the former sprang from the brain of Jove, not from his belly; moreover that she was clad in armor, and not in crinoline. Marble polished and not mere polishings, we need in the structure of the social edifice; and your College will attain the end desired, only by such educating force as strength clothed in beauty can employ.

At the Creation, God gave his image to man; in Redemption, woman gave her image to God. Let us, with sagacious zeal, repeat the process of Godhead, and, through virginal purity exalt mankind.[32k]

The report of the committee was all very well, and most likely it moved many of those twenty-nine members of the board. Nevertheless, the most practical and vexing of all questions requiring an answer was not even brought forward. How could an art collection worthy of the name be obtained within the next few months without drawing heavily on the college funds? This problem had to be faced sooner or later. Magoon alone had a solution, which he vaguely hinted at in the report when he listed the materials that a self-respecting gallery must have available. They were all there in his house in Albany.

A letter from Magoon to Vassar recalled the events that led to the purchase of his collection:

When I rode to the College with Swan, Matthew, Babcock and your honorable self, I had not the slightest intention of offering you my Art Collection. Leaning against the window (in the Gallery) where your portrait is to hang, my heart in true sympathy with your own purpose, first breathed to your confident (Mr. Swan) its reluctant consent to part with treasures which no wealth can create, for the nominal sum of twenty thousand dollars. You accepted on the spot.[33]

Some months later, Vassar quoted from his "memorandum book" his own matter-of-fact interpretation of this meeting:

Rode to College with Magoon, Swan, & Matthew & Babcock on matters of Library Room & Art Gallery—Promised to give Magoon $20,000 for *all* his complete collection of *Art,* he is first to send me "Catalogue" of them, then if approved I am to pay him $10,000 Cash & $10,000 yearly payments of $1000 to suit my convenience.[34]

The first steps officially offering the collection were taken on 30 May 1864 by Magoon, in a long letter giving the history of the development of the collection and its purpose, to "illustrate human progress under and along the Divine purpose,—*Christianity, Illustrated by its Monuments";* and hinting to Vassar that the collection should not be broken. He knew that somehow and somewhere "the good God would provide a safe depository for the priceless treasures."[35]

For several paragraphs, Magoon quite lost himself in the heights of a prose ecstasy, but he pulled himself together and began to plan the transfer of his collection to Vassar. By early June, the matter was so nearly settled that some formal agreement was necessary. He drew up a rough contract, proposing:

First, to sell [Vassar] the collection of oil paintings at 66 Philip street, one hundred and twenty-five, or more.

Secondly, the collection of water-color pictures now hanging under the same roof, one hundred mounted under glass, and framed. Moreover a large variety of other like works, mounted under glass, and stored in cabinets for want of wall-room.

Thirdly, a great variety of original drawings in sepia, india-ink and other media comprising the aggregate of original art.

Fourthly, illuminations, missals, armor, arms, coins, and original antiquities.

Fifthly, antiquarian works, printed, and illustrated by numerous engravings on all the great departments of monumental history.

Sixthly, a copious library on art, embracing every form of Aesthetics, or the Science of Beauty.

Seventhly, a vast number of engravings, beginning with the revival of art, and showing the progress to the pres[ent] and the treasures accumulated since.

All of the above I propose to surrender to you as it stands for the sum of $20,000—twenty thousand dollars, ten thousand dollars to be paid me on the 29th of June, 1864, and the payment of the other, as to time and form, to be arranged by yourself.

Magoon wrote further that he would supervise the packing and unpacking of the collection and "direct the final arrangements of the same."[36]

Vassar's answer arrived within a few days. He wanted it clearly understood that he was to have the *entire* collection—"printed and otherwise." Anything which served the purpose of art education was to be included in the sale.

We need no express contract. I rely upon you as a christian man. . . . In regard to payment—I wish it delivered first. The Building will not be in such a state as to warrant the placing of these articles any longer before the 1st of August than to enable you to hang them by that date. The payment of $10,000 should therefore be made on that date. The balance as we shall not disagree about as you leave the times for future payments much to my convenience.[37]

If there was any vagueness in the general statement of what was entailed in the sale, Vassar made quite clear what he expected for his $20,000—all of Magoon's art objects and all of the literary works that had any relation to art.[1]

Vassar was pleased that the problem of the gallery could be solved so easily. He wrote Emma Church about it, "I wish to make our Art Rooms a decided attraction at once with the hope of course that it may continue to grow in beauty, value & in educational and refining power."[38] Vassar presented the Magoon Collection to the board of trustees at the regular meeting on 28 June 1864. In the report of the committee on the art gallery which showed how the general ideas and ideals embodied in the report of February 1864 had been met, Magoon rose to the occasion. He took the opportunity of acquainting the members of the board of trustees with the history of his collecting and purchases in 1844 and 1845, and again during the spring and summer of 1854.[m] A great many of the most valued pieces were purchased at these times. He was extremely proud of the methods he followed in his researches and of the results obtained, all of them so soon to be displayed in the Vassar College Art Gallery. He spoke of hazards and finally the proddings of the Providence which had placed his collection in Vassar's hands:

The seventh of last January [i.e., 7 January 1864] fire suddenly arose in the very midst of the central gallery (in my home). Providence again saved the collection, but admonished in regard to greater security. Another mind had from on high been prompted to kindred ends through other avenues, and it was unmistakeably revealed when and where we should coalesce. By this new gift, Mr. Vassar has done much to perfect his great endowment, and crown it all with consummate glory.[n]

From beginning to end, the chairman was in his element in making this report and in hearing a resolution proposed, accepted, and carried without dissenting vote, thanking Vassar for the "munificent donation of an Art Gallery. . .in addition to his original foundation fund. This College & the world owe him an enlarged debt of gratitude."[39] The members of the board then voted unanimously to reimburse Vassar $1535.28 for his expenses in connection with the copy of the Raphael "Foligno."

An easy friendship developed between Vassar and Magoon—much more informal on Magoon's part than on the part of Vassar. Magoon addressed Vassar as "Dear Sir," "Dear Uncle Matthew" and, of course, "Dear Founder." He even took to signing his letters with his initials—thus "Elm." His sentimentality sometimes overwhelmed him and caused Vassar to respond in kind. In mid-August when all was progressing so well, Vassar closed one of his letters with the following:

It is not often I allow myself an indulgence of grief—but I confess my spirits failed me yesterday on reading the closing portion of your note—viz—"When our hearts are both dust may the print of our toil still feed the myriads of immortal minds &c"—the sentence brought me down with tears, considering how many eyes will hereafter be gazing upon these *Gems* while the Collector, and donor bones lies mouldering in the grave.[40]

It is true that Magoon's letters sometimes became a bit acid when he felt that he was being put upon, but usually the "dear Sirs" and "very respectfully yours" which appeared at such times, gave way to the more intimate forms.

Magoon had hot summer work cut out for him to prepare the collection for shipment and get it hung, but he had the assistance of the very able Mr. Foord[o] whose name appears in those summer letters. In early August, they listed the number of cases needed to transfer all of these works of art—four cases of engravings, two cases of water colors, two cases of books. It took forty-seven cases to pack all of the oils and water colors. Eighty-nine pictures "had to be glazed, that is covered with glass and framed."[41] Finally, Vassar wrote to Magoon on 19 August:

All safe—the steamer arrived 1/4 4 .o'cke—6 spring Waggons in attendance at Wharff—at 5 P.M.—all safe in College.[42]

Slowly, Foord, at the direction of Magoon, hung the pictures on the walls of the gallery. Vassar might write—as he did—that some of the framing was defective, that pictures had fallen from the walls, or again, that the varnish on some of the oil paintings was cracked and had a whitish cast. Such difficulties were amicably settled, but in late September, Magoon sent an undated letter to Vassar saying:

> [T]he completeness of your library on the theory of art can as yet have but little impression on your mind, because you have had no occasion to appreciate its invaluable worth. Time will help.
> My heart is joyful before God for what is already within the walls of your Art Gallery, and I shall rejoice at the advent of the most sagacious lovers of Beauty to feed upon and scan its worth.
> Our great and unexpected approach to perfection, in this department creates in me an intense desire to see the superlative attained so that your hand may strike twelve at the outset from your Central throne.
> First of all, in that Inner Sanctuary let there be nothing "common or unclean". Pure original art, in all varieties, and sound writings on artistic theories are now in hand to an extent that may well challenge a parallel on this continent if not in the whole world.
> What I would respectfully propose is, the *Transition from Art to Literature,* and a collection of *Illustrated Literature* to the fullest possible extent. As I once said in the Board "no books should go there save those that either inculcate the theory of Art or are adorned by it."

After some further remarks, he listed thirty books under the general subject of art and good taste. These comprised some twenty works of from one to three volumes. Next he mentioned twenty books of French literature, comprising seventeen titles in one to two volumes each. He listed about three hundred titles which he headed Literature of Antiquity. The noteworthy thing about this collection was that some of the illustrations were by famous artists or were reproductions of beautiful sketches, drawings, or paintings. In all, there were "ten thousand engravings worth at least a dollar each, and yet I offer the entire thirty-five thousand, three hundred and eighty articles . . . for the nominal sum of five thousand, three hundred and fifty dollars."

He went off into one of his charming, fanciful descriptions of how he would enshrine the portrait of the founder in the gallery. If Vassar was not confused by this whole thing, there is little doubt that he was indignant. His anger is not to be wondered at and the concluding words of this letter from Magoon could have done little to assuage it: "Dear Sir, it was only yesterday that I began this plan, and now I leave it at your feet, to do just as you please, and may God bless you."[43]

Vassar's reply on 30 September was puzzled and indignant, but very firm:

The long communication without date forwarded by you to me...has been received & very carefully read. I learn from it that you have still in your hands a large collection of pictures, illustrations, engravings, &c[a] &c[a] a list of which you furnish at length in your letter & which you strongly recommend should be placed in the Art Gallery of our College. I entirely concur in this view, and it was because I thought so that I have already purchased them of you & given them to the College. I can scarcely believe I read that part of your letter right which seems to look as if you were expecting another purchase for these articles. If this is so, I shall insist that the College which now owns the collections you speak of, shall take measures to secure their property. At present I have only to say that your letter of 4th June to me, stating to me your understanding of your contract with me, & mine of June 8th to you, in terms most positive and conclusive, cover all the catalogue you now mention. Before another step is taken, I beg you will refresh your recollection as to what has passed, both written & verbal, between us in regard to this subject.

In the belief that you are laboring under a wide misapprehension or misrecollection of the facts, I call your earliest attention to them.[44]

It is of some interest to note here that Vassar called Magoon's attention not only to the written contract but to any verbal agreements that the two men might have had. Taken together, these were vague at best, particularly since no complete catalogue had been furnished with the sale. Magoon was plainly taken aback by Vassar's reaction to his letter and responded with dismay immediately:

Dear Sir:

I am at this moment in receipt of yours of Sept 30th

If I sent without date, it was because I wrote without guile. In all my dealings in this matter I am perfectly conscious of an upright intention.

I sold you my art collection, that is my original works of art, and works on the theory of art, properly so called.

But my literature, dear Sir, my library for personal work and use, is entirely another thing.

The chromo-tints, or facsimilies, which were never included in "art" as it was shown in my collection is another thing also. In my frank communication to you I stated how we can fill *that* department as well as the other. Before God, our country and your own conscience, dear Sir, do you wish to oppress *me?*

He added a postscript:

I beg you, Dear Sir, read my writing, and review our action for yourself. I rely on *your own* calm judgment, and leaving you to reflect on what immense results are connected with our mutual labors. Will you *please* be actuated by what springs up in your heart when you are nearest to God and least moved by external influence? ELM.[45]

These three letters considered together certainly baffle the reader. The undated one of Magoon, the first of the three, made a definite proposal. Vassar responded on 30 September indignant that Magoon offered him something, the purchase of which, he thought, had already been made under the terms of the original loose contract. In fact, he had gone through the final step of presenting it as a gift to the college. Magoon immediately answered—horrified that Vassar would rob him of his "library for personal work and use." Vassar treated the matter as a contractual affair between himself and one of his trusted friends[p] and he believed that Magoon was indeed "laboring under a misapprehension of facts."

Magoon was now on the defensive, perhaps realizing that the battle was already lost for him. On 4 October he began a letter of retreat from an untenable position with "My only fear is that you do not understand my aim" and continued with:

and my nature is such that I value your sympathy infinitely more than your money.

I sold you my Art Collection, and I knew very well that you had more than double the worth of your honorable payment. There it hangs. Taking simply what is now on view, let any competent judge estimate the oil paintings alone, and I will answer for the amount less than the whole cost. And I do not care for that. Mr. Koegler, Goupil's successor, the first art dealer in America, told me the day after the "Turners" were hung, that they alone four little drawings in your collection of hundreds, are themselves worth $20,000. It sounds an exaggeration, but it is certainly near the truth, in the market of London, if not actually here, nor do I care for that. Mercenary thoughts never were coupled with the accumulation or disposal.

Magoon stressed his love for his collection and made the point that he desired only the good of the college:

But the long list of "illustrated Literature" you cannot possibly confound with the "Art Collection" you originally bought. Let John Raymond or John Thompson, or any other literary man, go over the list with you, and they, or any other competent persons will at once tell you that Literature is the staple, and Art only an accident. All the latter might be removed, and all the first is yet complete. The illustrations are valuable, indeed, and are of so much value over and above.

Moreover these are mostly choice, original editions, now out of print, and very costly. A large portion of them were in hand long before I owned a single picture, and bear numerous traces of my mental progress up to the intense artistic feeling that now impels me. . . .They are as *uncommon* as they are elegant, and I pant for their continued union with the Art Collection, with which they have no other connection than that which God has permeated all realms of Beauty—identity. . . .

O, my dear Sir, will you understand my heart, my convictions as to soul culture, and my most ardent desirè to put into the hands of your educators, of whom I shall never be one in person, the true means of the mightiest influence?

Art treasures I am done with in my own house, tearing away, as I do, every choice thing even from my wife's affection; but literature I *must* have. If, for the sake of furnishing what no other man can, I place at your disposal, in this frank and disinterested manner, the precious accumulation of my life, are you unwilling to give me back the means of replenishing with some literary matter the shelves, I most generously empty for you?. . .

If I may complete your Hall of Beauty, with all the diversified resources I can command, what are you willing to pay me over and above?[46]

It took a great deal of writing to lead to the asking of a simple question—the answer to which would settle the whole affair.

But Vassar's next letter, dated two days later, was written before he got Magoon's and he repeated the seven clauses of the original contract. He claimed no more than that he wanted his due:

No more is asked of you than that which any fair mind would decide to be clearly covered by your written statements & what you have repeatedly expressed to me, to my nephew, to Mr Swan & to the Board of Trustees, and so much you will not hesitate to grant. It would be very unfortunate should this subject fall into other hands as it must inevitably do, unless we can dispose of it upon the broad principles which govern men in all affairs of life.

Now in closing allow me to say that so far as I am individualy concerned I would drop the subject here sooner than to have any misunderstanding or differences with one whom I have ever cherishd as one of my best friends, and in regard to the interior adornment of the College with Art & Litterature of which you were the Suggestive Organ and whose name with the Founder must descend to posterity, never let it be inferred that you have not done all you could or all you agreed to do, to be worthy of a record in its memorials.[47]

On 7 October Magoon wrote, "My original profer was honest, and your recapitulation of it is exact. In open day, I stand by it, my dear Sir, in every iota. Do you think me so capable of the contrary?" And then he added, respecting point six of the contract:

6th The "library on Art" is as copious as a devoted and zealous life could render. If I have an additional volume belonging strictly to that department, I am unconscious of it. The discussion of monumental, sculptoral and graphic Art, I gave you to the fullest extent.

But rhetorical works, discussions in all forms touching linguistic forms, yet remain, and constitute the "Illustrated Literature" I have offered you. With the exception of Harper's reprint of "Greek and Roman Antiquities" which I procured and had bound since the original bargain, I can think of nothing that does not relate to Classical Topography, as illustrating Classical Literature, with all the varieties of Language, History of Races, Prose and Poetry, Biography, Belle Letters, &c &c &c

"Christianity illustrated by its Monuments" is yours, I have nothing to add.

Finally, he got to his point:

Our only child, Frank, keen in his taste for literature, and especially my most valuable works, expects that of course to be his very own, and so does his fond mother. *I* desire to see it all removed to Vassar College, and only ask for a fair apology for broaching the scheme. Therefore, have I frankly proposed a bargain which will be most auspicious for you and your foundation. I have no purpose but such as I am prepared to review at that tribunal where we are soon to appear. When I ask you to give a nominal return for this great addition to the original purchase leaving it all to your own mode of payment, it is not for gain to my pocket, God knows, but for domestic happiness and the general good. When done, I wish to visit your college as a grand shrine, where my soul may adore in gratitude and love. And I wish my wife and son, if they survive me, as probably they will, may there contemplate my life's labors duly appreciated and devinely employed...

Again I ask leaving me to execute the fullest possible good for your

College, what are you willing to give, as the means of rebuying a library for my family and myself? I end just as I began with you, with a gushing heart of mutual consecration. Tell me, in a word, your intention, and, in God's name, let that end forever all correspondence between us that shall be of a character in the least to arouse your excitable nature or my own.[48]

Vassar wrote his reply promptly the next day:

I most solemnly believe what you say in your letter of the 7th Inst: viz "My original proffer was honest" &c[a]. I never for a moment doubted it, or thought you otherwise capable, but you well know we can be as *sincerely* wrong, as *sincerely* right,—the only difference is motive or intention. I believe with all my soul you *intended* to give me just what you wrote in your letter of the 4th June—and still believe it, but your keeping no memorandum & in the midst of your multiplied and arduous duties escaped your attention. Never—no never, have I distrusted your fidelity or honest purposes—how could I when I knew you were bound up with me in my great work in placing your Gems of Art, therein, where for ages to come posterity might gaze and commemorate your Reverend name with the Founder of the Institution—and permit me to remark that in all my correspondence with you I have taken "no counsel and used no precautions" other than were suggested by my mind as a business man, and no one knows them to my personal knowledge save my Clerk M[r] Schon who takes copy of my letters.

With regard to your Suggestions of a further renumeration &c[a] Such as to afford a specific for that case I would respond with an overflowing heart, had not things changed with me since the failure of the College builder M[r] Harloe which circumstance may require a further pecuniary advance to complete the work where all of this worlds interest with me is concentrated—Still if there is a nitch open when done—your suggestions for a family Library will not be forgotten &c.

You will excuse my brevity—my stooping posture after a few minutes writing is attended with vertigo, and obliged to desist. I remain dear Sir.[49]

Magoon seemed to be satisfied that a solution to his problem had been found. He wrote on 11 October that he would rather "rely on [Vassar's] own generous appreciation of [his] cooperation and in giving a dazzling fame to [the] College, than to the written bond of any man." And he concluded with:

I hold in my mind and heart a literary completeness within the walls of *your* Hall, intimately associated with the artistic perfection, and yet distinct from it, and its invaluable counterpart. And *that* I am determined to see in place, at whatever sacrifice of purse and painstaking. I am favored by God with the power of combining around you more varied treasures than any other man, and every attractive feature I can procure or now possess *shall go.*

Your kind note this morning received is perfectly satisfactory. . . .We will hope to stand together yet in the centre of a Collection of Art *and* Literature, such as, in all your yearnings to live in the gratitude of posterity you never dreamed of actually seeing under your own hand. It shall be a perpetual joy to you to show to others and walk amidst yourself, and that shall be no small part of my own reward.[50]

Afterword

He was growing when he died . . .

Matthew Vassar, c. 1865-66, still actively interested in the college in his later years

Early in 1865, Matthew Vassar began to realize that the executive committee, composed as it was of five astute businessmen, was nevertheless not competent to act on questions of educational policy and college organization which would be continually facing them, particularly in those months before the college opened its doors to the students who were to be in its first classes. Vassar knew that most of the educational planning—perhaps all of it—would be the responsibility of President Raymond, but that officially it must be presented to the executive committee for discussion before it came to the board of trustees for their action. The results of consultations with board members and with Raymond, whom he respected and liked greatly, formed the basis of a letter that Vassar addressed to trustee Bishop on 27 June 1865:

> The first stage in the development of the great enterprise to which I have devoted a large portion of my fortune and the latest labors of my life, is now drawing to a close. The erection of the College edifice and its equipments with the material apparatus for instruction will soon be completed, and with the coming autumn, its interior life, as a great educational establishment will begin.
>
> Thus far the great work of the Executive Committee has been in a great measure, that of a Building Committee and I have cheerfully shared its perplexities & toils from a conviction that my long experience in the management of material affairs would enable me to give them important aid. Although a Kind Providence has blessed me with more than ordinary health and vigor for my years, yet I begin to feel sensibly the wear & tear of these numerous and ever-multiplying details, and since the business of the Executive Committee must hereafter pertain more than heretofore in the internal regulation of the College, I have felt a strong desire to be relieved by some gentleman, who. . .[possesses] the general qualities of business capacity, high proficiency and practical Knowledge in the management of an institution of learning.
>
> With this view I have not only looked carefully over. . .our list of Trustees but extended my view through the entire range of my acquaintance; and among all within my reach or *beyond* my reach, I find no one who possesses those qualifications so immenently and so entirely as yourself. It is my desire, therefore, at the approaching meeting of the Board of Trustees, to resign my present place as chairman of the Executive Committee, and my earnest hope is that you will consent to accept and discharge this honorable trust.
>
> I have requested Pres. Raymond & our mutual friend Mr. Stephen Buckingham to be the bearers of this communication and to give any further explanation of my views (of which they are fully informed) that you may desire.[1]

Henry Van Ingen, professor of painting and drawing, in the art gallery

The lodge and gate house, also designed by James Renwick

Bishop agreed to accept the assignment and at the meeting of the board of trustees later that month, Vassar's resignation from the executive committee was accepted and the appointment of Bishop in his place was confirmed.[a]

Vassar did not, however, sever his connection with the college. Still a member of the board of trustees, he often drove out to the campus, walked through the corridors of Main Building, visited the art gallery, and looked in upon the science laboratories. He visited the Raymond family and often, too, he went to the Observatory where he saw Mitchell and his brilliant, unconventional daughter, Maria. Frances Wood recalled meeting him in the long gallery where geological specimens were displayed:

> I had gone one day by myself to wander about looking at specimens of minerals when the door opened and a benevolent white haired old gentleman entered. There was no mistaking the man of the portrait with his old time dress,—ruffled shirt front, diamond pin and wonderfully kind expression—and I went forward to pay my homage. He seemed familiar with the collections, pointing out whatever was especially valuable and curious as we walked around together. "I often come up here to see these", he said smilingly.[2]

A Vassar student of the first class in 1865 remembered him well:

> It was not an unusual event to meet [Mr. Vassar] walking alone in one of the corridors. The impression he invariably conveyed was one of dignity and benevolence. His white hair, his regular features, suffused with benignancy, his manner never in the remotest degree conveying the idea of self-importance, won the hearts of the students.[3]

But Vassar was tired and, more than ever before, felt the physical limitations of age. He was amazed that at his age, he had still been capable of so much concentrated effort in seeing the first stages of the college planning successfully completed. The truth was that he had become quite fatigued in those hectic months just before the board's spring meeting in 1865. He complained of dizziness and physical exhaustion. Early in January of 1866, he suffered another one of those slight strokes that had so often incapacitated him to a small degree. Recovering, by 30 April 1866 he was well enough to be able to take part in the inauguration of Founder's Day. It was a grand surprise and he was moved to tears by the reception he received. He loved the music, the poetry, and the pageantry of the exercises prepared in his honor.[b]

In late August of 1866 he wrote:

Maria Mitchell in the Observatory, with her telescope

I am spending the hot months among the Evergreens & flowing water-brooks at Springside, our average temperature some 8 degrees less than our city residence, my health is fair—that is, only subject to occasional oscillations resulting from my last attack of slight paryalysis, otherwise I would scarcely feel the ordinary infirmities of advanced years. . . . I take a ride to the College every pleasant day inspecting the progress of the general work, all of which will be completed by the 15th proximo.[4]

He had a "bad cold and fever" and was unable to accept an invitation to have Thanksgiving dinner with the teachers and students at the college in that same year. His spirits revived in late 1866 and early the next year he seemed in improved health, and his energy returned. But by 10 April 1868 he explained his failure to call on Cyrus Swan: "It is with difficulty I can *get in* or *get out* of Carriage & walking is out of the Question and if you had call[d] and seen me during the last 5 or 6 weeks confinment to my house either my Doctor or myself would have explained the cause."[5] He knew that his activities must be further curtailed and so he prepared to retire from the board of trustees in June of that year.[6]

The time for the seventh annual meeting of the board was set for eleven o'clock on the morning of 23 June. It was the day on which the festivities of the second commencement of the college were to begin. Vassar, Raymond, and Anderson drove from Vassar's house through the town to Arlington and then along the new road to the college; Vassar noted that the road was in fair condition after a rather hard winter. The trees were very green and the weather was that of a typical late June day in the Hudson Valley.

Promptly on the hour set, Kelly, the chairman of the board, called the meeting to order. The Reverend Rufus Babcock opened it with a prayer after which the roll was called. A few matters of business were discussed and acted upon before the chairman turned to Vassar to read his annual address. From this point, the minutes of the day tell the story concisely:

Upon invitation of the chairman Mr M Vassar Founder proceeded to read his annual address. M Vassar requested that he might retain his seat while reading and then proceeded to read from his manuscript which consisted of 14 pages of note paper and was reading from the eleventh page when he failed to pronounce a word which was upon his lips, dropped the papers from his hand, fell back in his chair insensible, and died, at precisely ten minutes to 12 o'clock AM by the clock in the College Tower.

There was no apparent pain, no convulsion. . . but an instant passage from life to death. . . .

Upon order being restored the Secretary by request finished

reading Mr. Vassar's manuscript address.

By request of the Chair prayer was offered in reference to the event just transpired by Rev. E.L. Magoon. . . .

The Board then adjourned to three o'clock P.M.

Believing. . .that Mr. Vassar, could he have been allowed to express a wish on this point would not have desired any suspension [or] not even any material change in the usual closing exercises of the collegiate year the committee would recommend that the exercises appointed for tonight & tomorrow be held as already announced.

It was further

Resolved that the Chairman of this Board be and is hereby requested to announce the death of Mr. Vassar at the close of the Commencement exercises in such remarks as he may deem fitting.[7]

The closing paragraph of the founder's address was a farewell and a leave-taking of all his friends. It was so like him, so filled with his spirit that all who heard it read by the secretary that day must have been deeply moved.

And now, gentlemen, in closing these remarks, I would humbly and solemnly implore the Divine Goodness to continue His smiles and favor on your institution, and bestow upon all hearts connected

The Observatory, with students playing croquet on the lawn

The Riding School and Calisthenium, completed in 1866, designed by J.A. Wood, architect. Instruction in riding was given by Baron Leopold von Seldeneck, who had served as a cavalry officer in the Civil War. The riding academy closed in 1872 because of the expense, and the remodeled building after its dedication in 1875 housed the museum of natural history, the art gallery, and the music department. Louisa May Alcott was a guest at the dedication. After the 1918 fire in Main Building, the Wood building was redesigned to include an assembly hall, theater, and four classrooms and renamed Assembly Hall. Renamed again in 1931, this time Avery Hall in memory of Alida C. Avery, professor of physiology and hygiene, it has since housed the English, classics, (and now) drama departments.

herewith his love and blessings, having peculiarly protected us by his providence through all our college trials for three consecutive years, without *a single death in our Board* or serious illness or death of one of our pupils within its walls. Wishing you, gentlemen, a continuance of health and happiness, I bid you a cordial and final farewell, thanking you kindly for your official attentions and services, not expecting, from my advanced years and increasing infirmaties, to meet you officially again, and imploring the Divine Goodness to guide and direct you aright in all your counsels and social business relations.

Yours truly, etc., etc.

M. Vassar.[8]

Of all the things that were to be written or said as memorials for Matthew Vassar, Maria Mitchell's entry in her diary the day after his death is one of the most eloquent in its quiet way:

Matthew Vassar is dead! I am sorry. I have met him at least once a day for three years and I never saw him cross or ill-natured. . . .

Mr. Vassar had a fancy for size. He must build the biggest building, he must have the largest number of students and so forth. The girls must be taught everything. His schemes were innumerable, but he grew as the building went up, and he seemed to me, although not a small man when I first saw him, almost a great man when he left us. He built up so grand a structure, it so grew upon his hands, and he so grew himself, that genius only could have been at the base. . . .

He was growing when he died. I think he would have been willing to see women among the Trustees.[9]

NOTES

Introduction

a. Benson J. Lossing (1813-1891) wood-engraver, author and editor, was a charter member of the board of trustees of Vassar College. At that time, he was a successful author and resided at his home, The Lodge, in Dover Plains, N.Y. He was born in Beekman, N.Y. of Dutch parents who both died when he was quite young. His early life was one of hardship and difficulty. After three years of formal schooling, Lossing was apprenticed to a watchmaker in Poughkeepsie. He educated himself by reading everything he could lay his hands on. His particular interest was in history. At twenty-two, he became the co-editor of the *Poughkeepsie Telegraph* and the *Poughkeepsie Casket* and learned wood-engraving from the illustrator of the latter publication, J.A. Adams. At twenty-five, he moved to New York City to establish himself there as an illustrator. Soon he was editing the *Family Magazine.* From this point, he became involved in writing and publishing. Within the next thirty-five years, he wrote and published more than forty books. *The Hudson River from the Wilderness to the Sea; Pictorial Field Book of the Revolution; Pictorial History of the Civil War;* and several biographies and histories were among these.

b. Vassar served as a village trustee on seven occasions between 1819 and 1835. He acted as president of the village board in 1835. See Edmund Platt, *The Eagle's History of Poughkeepsie from the earliest settlement in 1683 to 1905.* Poughkeepsie, N.Y. 1905, p. 304.

c. It was reported that "a large and respectable meeting of the citizens of Pough-keepsie in favor of the speedy construction of the Hudson River Railroad, [was] held at the Village Hall on Saturday evening, January 23rd, (1847), Matthew Vassar, Esq., was chosen president." Ibid., p. 311.

d. A notice in the Poughkeepsie press of May 1850 announced that Miss Frances Ann Kemble "has selected Monday and Tuesday evenings next (May 6 and 7) for her readings. . . [she] proposes *Romeo and Juliet* and *Hamlet".* The *Bulletin* of 9 May 1850 reported her great triumph in Poughkeepsie.

e. Rufus Babcock (1793-1875) was born in Colebrook, Conn. He was educated by his father, a Baptist minister and later (1817-1821) attended Brown University from which he graduated with a Bachelor of Arts degree. For three years, he acted as tutor at Columbia (George Washington University) in Washington, D.C. At the same time, he studied theology with the Rev. William Slaughter. He was the second president of Waterville [Colby] College in Maine where he served for three years and from which he resigned in 1836 because of failing health. Babcock held pastorates in various cities, among them Poughkeepsie, where he served two terms, one from 1839 to 1845 after his ordination, the other from 1865 to 1875. He founded the *Baptist Memorial Magazine;* wrote a *Memoir of Andrew Fuller; An Immigrant's Mother; A History of Waterville College* and others. He was reputed to be a man of great energy with great devotion to the cause of religion. Babcock was chosen to be a charter member of the board of trustees of Vassar College and served thereon until his death in 1875.

f. Samuel F.B. Morse (1791-1872) was not a local man of letters, but his scientific activity would have made him a friend of the founder. His estate, Locust Grove, which he used most of the year, was on the old South Road a mile or so south of Vassar's Springside. The house still remains surrounded by meadows and woods. When Morse was close to forty, he became fascinated with the idea of transmitting messages by telegraph and devoted himself to a study of the problems associated with it. He applied for a patent for some of his ideas and, though he was successful

181

in obtaining it, received no governmental financial aid. Recognition of the worth of his patent was not really made in this country until 1842, when the Congress granted him $30,000 to develop his ideas further. Success was then assured. To write only of his scientific accomplishments would mean a neglect of his ability as a painter. On his graduation from Yale College in 1810, he went to Europe to pursue the study of art which he had begun at Yale. He worked with Washington Allston in London and also met and was advised by Benjamin West and John Singleton Copley. Though his work received favorable critical comment, he found that he could not make a living from the sale of his paintings. Back in the United States, he devoted his talents to portraiture but again he was unsuccessful financially. It was then that he turned his talents to scientific ventures. Vassar asked his neighbor to serve on the first board of trustees of his college, a trust which Morse accepted and maintained until his death.

g. Andrew Jackson Downing might well have become the landscape architect for Vassar College had it not been for his untimely death in 1852. On 28 July of that year, he embarked with his family and some friends from Newburgh, N.Y. on the Hudson River steamer, *Henry Clay*. The captain of this vessel entered into a race with another river steamer and the *Henry Clay* burst into flame off Yonkers, N.Y. Many of the passengers were burned or drowned. Downing remained calm throughout it all, gave instuctions to frightened passengers, threw chairs into the water to assist those already struggling there. He was an excellent swimmer but in attempting to save his friends, he lost his life. He was thirty-seven at this time.

Chapter I

a. Martin B. Anderson (1815-1890) was closely associated with Vassar College affairs and in many ways aided Vassar in those early years of decision (1861-1865). Anderson had an interesting career. As the son of a farmer in Maine, he early found it necessary to seek employment in a shipyard. With the earnings from this employment, he supported himself as a student at Waterville [Colby] College in Maine, where he received a bachelor's degree in 1836. After a year at Newton Theological Seminary, he returned to Waterville as an instructor in classics and mathematics. He was appointed professor in 1843 and remained in this post for seven years, when he resigned to edit the *New York Record*, a weekly that he had acquired. Through this paper, he had great influence on Baptist thought. He accepted the presidency of the newly established University of Rochester in 1853, the same year that Vassar was elected a trustee of that institution. Anderson remained president until his retirement in 1886. As a versatile man of wide cultural acquaintance, he influenced Vassar. His selection as a charter trustee of Vassar College was a wise one for he had much to offer as advice in those years of building and organizing the college.

b. Maria Mitchell (1818-1889) was born and lived her early life on Nantucket, a community in which there was unusual freedom of action and independence of judgment. Her life reflected these qualities. She began early to develop those characteristics which were to make her an independent observer of the heavens. She came to Vassar's attention through Rufus Babcock, who had visited and admired her. She soon became the founder's choice for the professorship of astronomy in his new college and was appointed to that position in 1864. She came to Vassar at the age of forty-seven and was the only member of the faculty who had a national and international reputation. Yet she was always the teacher, willing to work hard with any young woman who was serious and dedicated. Her reputation among students was great; the faculty, however, found her indifference to foolish convention a bit trying. She had no patience with deadly formalities. She was genuine in all

182

that she said, taught, and believed and because of it, became a most beloved teacher. Vassar was a frequent visitor to her apartment in the Observatory and talked with her and her father. She came to know him exceedingly well and at his death quietly mourned his passing. She retired in 1888 and died the following year.

c. Benjamin Moran (1820-1876) was born in Chester, Pa. Though his family was of moderate circumstances, he was given a good education. After working for a printing firm, he left to tour England and Wales. He wrote a series of short sketches of his travels which were later published but were of no particular merit. In 1853, he secured employment in England as a clerk at the American legation in London when James Buchanan was minister to the Court of St. James. After a succession of appointments, he eventually became assistant secretary to the embassy in 1857 and secretary in 1864. It was during this period that he met Jewett who was touring the British Isles and Europe for Vassar College in 1862.

d. A study of the *Alumnae Biographical Register Issue,* Bulletin of Vassar College, Poughkeepsie, N.Y. 1939, is rewarding to anyone interested in what graduates of the college accomplished. It has been valuable in determining what alumnae of early classes did after finishing their studies. There is, however, no record that Mary Frances Hoyt (Moses) of the class of 1880 had the highest score on the first examination given under the Civil Service Act of 1883 and that she was appointed to a $900-a-year clerkship in the Treasury Department at Washington, D.C. See the *Smithsonian Magazine,* July 1977, 8:90.

e. On 1 September 1860, Vassar wrote the following letter to Ira Harris who later was chosen a member of the first board of trustees of the college:

Dear Sir Refering to a late conversation between you and my friend Prof. M.P. Jewett on the subject of my proposed "Vassar College" I would be happy to have you appoint an *hour* and *day* when it would be most convenient to meet us at your office to confer with you in relation to matters touching that portion of my *will* conveying grants &c &c.

Here is evidence that Jewett was not exaggerating his role in advising Vassar as to the disposition of his estate to benefit the college. Actions such as these troubled the Poughkeepsie advisers and led to their distrust of Jewett's influence over Vassar and of his attempts to work behind the scenes.

f. These four men, Cornelius DuBois, Cyrus Swan, Charles Swift, and Matthew Vassar Jr., together with the founder were to be the members of the first executive committee of the college. They all advised Vassar in some capacity or other for many years. Cornelius DuBois was the president of the First National Bank; Charles Swift was the adviser to the founder's nephews, Matthew Jr. and John Guy Vassar; Cyrus Swan had all of Vassar's confidence after many years as his friend and legal adviser. All of them were the founder's nominees. Jewett was not too happy about the choice of Matthew Jr. and Charles Swift for membership on so important a committee, but he hoped that Cornelius DuBois and Cyrus Swan might have some effect in reducing their influence.

g. Lossing wrote of this matter, "These labors resulted in the draft of a bill by Mr. Swan, who, during all the years of inquiry and discussion of the subject of Mr. Vassar's beneficent projects, had been one of his most friendly counselors". B.J. Lossing, *Vassar College and Its Founder,* Poughkeepsie, 1876, p. 86. Jewett drafted most of the document; Swan, as a lawyer, put the provisions in legal form.

h. Professor Samuel S. Sherman was Jewett's successor as president of Judson Institute in Marion, Alabama. He served there from 1854 to 1859 when he resigned to go to Milwaukee, Wisconsin. Jewett corresponded with Sherman most of the period from 1860 to 1865 and later joined him in a successful business enterprise in Milwaukee. On 27 February 1861, shortly after the first meeting of the trustees, Jewett wrote to Sherman clearly indicating that he should have the chair in natural history at Vassar College, if he wished the post. Nothing came of it, however. Perhaps Sherman was not interested.

i. The Honorable William Kelly, a charter member of the board of trustees of Vassar College and its first chairman, was a wealthy gentleman-farmer and politician of Dutchess County. He cultivated over eight hundred acres of his estate in Rhinebeck, N.Y. As a neighbor of Vassar, he could very well have been the founder's choice for chairman of the board. What particular characteristics he possessed that led to this nomination and his final election is not recorded. Perhaps his availability, his prominence in the community, and his willingness to serve were all in his favor. He seemed to make a good chairman and held the members of the board together in those first difficult years.

j. Vassar was very proud of his portrait painted by Charles Elliott. It was completed before a place was ready for it in the college, so it was hung in the Vassar residence on Main Street. For a short period, it was on display in the Baptist church. John Guy Vassar's letters of his travels were published in 1861 under the title, *Twenty Years Around the World*. According to the *New York Daily Tribune* of 25 January 1862, John Guy Vassar was "a traveler who for the past twenty years, has been almost uninterruptedly on voyage—who has visited more countries and traveled over more surface than any man who ever existed—not excepting Baron Humboldt or Bayard Taylor.

Chapter II

a. It was fortunate that the Rev. Howard Malcolm was in Poughkeepsie at the time of the breaking of ground ceremonies, for he was no ordinary preacher. His presence gave something special to this solemn occasion. Dr. Malcolm had attended Dickinson College in Pennsylvania and later the Princeton Theological Seminary. He was ordained a Baptist clergyman in 1820. His experience as a visitor to Baptist missions in India, Burma, and China, and as the author of a number of important works, made him a prominent member of the Baptist clergy. At the time of his visit to Poughkeepsie, he had resigned the presidency of Lewisburg University (now Bucknell) in Pennsylvania to permit him to devote full time to his scholarly pursuits and to facilitate his work as a writer and editor. He had moved to Philadelphia where he had become identified with a variety of public interests.

b. Edward Livingston Youmans (1821-1887) was another of those fascinating gentlemen that the founder seemed to attract. He was born of Quaker and Puritan ancestors in a small village near Albany, N.Y. His interest in things scientific began quite early in his life, but he was frustrated by his exceedingly poor eyesight. He had opthalmia, and early poor treatment of the disease almost completely destroyed his sight. In spite of the disease and its effects on his early education, he persisted in his study of science and assembled material for a class-book in chemistry. It was a standard text which went through two editions. By the time he met Vassar, his sight had improved to such an extent that he was able to go about alone. In the two decades between 1850 and 1870, he became a popular lecturer in science. His interests led him to the discovery of Herbert Spencer's *Principles of Psychology* and he became a disciple of Spencer and promoted the sale of his publications in the United States. He continued to write on scientific subjects and eventually established the *Popular Science Monthly,* which later became the *Scientific Monthly.* Youmans held the degree of Doctor of Medicine conferred upon him by the University of Vermont.

184

c. William F. Poole (1821-1894) was an excellent choice as adviser on the problem of the library of the young college. As a junior at Yale College, he assisted in the famous library of the Brothers of Unity there and became its librarian the next year. This experience led to a career as librarian and library consultant. From the library of the Boston Mercantile Association, he went to the Boston Athenaeum where he had already had earlier experience. It was during his years at the Athenaeum and shortly thereafter that he used his extensive knowledge of bibliographical affairs to advise in the setting up of several famous collections. He left the Athenaeum to go to the United States Naval Academy where he organized the library. He went on to Cincinnati and from there he joined the staff of the Newberry Library of Chicago in 1874. His work is very well known. Aside from his publications in this field, he wrote rather widely on a variety of historical subjects. His papers and articles in history led to his election to the presidency of the American History Association in 1888.

d. Robert S. Fisher, the first professor on the Vassar faculty, was appointed to the chair of chemistry in 1862. He asked the trustees for funds to enable him to go to Europe for further training and to study and to purchase scientific equipment for the laboratory at Vassar. He never taught at the college for he resigned in 1864 just before the college opened.

e. By 1862, George Peabody was a wealthy, well-known, and respected American who had lived for many years in London. For all his wealth, he lived simply but still moved with ease in the society of the British capital. His presence was sought after in just such an affair as that described by Vassar. His father was a poor farmer and was unable to afford much in the way of education for his son. He began his career at the age of eleven apprenticed to a grocer in a small Massachusetts town. After a variety of experiences, he became associated with Higgins and Peabody of Baltimore and soon became the senior partner. This association led to frequent visits abroad where he finally settled permanently in London. It was there that he amassed a large fortune. Seven years before his death, his name was associated with many philanthropic ventures—the Peabody Institute in Baltimore, the Peabody Museum of Natural History and Science at Yale, and the Peabody Museum of Archaeology and Ethnology at Harvard. He was honored in many ways in England, not the least of which was an honorary degree conferred upon him by Oxford University. His seated statue in bronze, dedicated by the Prince of Wales in 1862, stands behind the Royal Exchange in London. This statue was given in recognition of the vast sums that he gave for the building of working men's dwellings in London. No wonder that Vassar was impressed by Jewett's report of the dinner.

f. Vassar set forth his ideas about nonsectarianism quite clearly to Mrs. Hale. He wrote to her on 23 March 1864 as follows:

> ...with regard to the Chaplaincy & Chair of Moral philosophy &c^a Dr J. wanted these filled with Baptists, but while I was a Baptist by birth, my father and mother Baptists by profession, have attended Baptist Church for over 60 years, was a Baptist in principle, built a Baptist Edifice in 1840 in this city at my own cost of $25000 and gave to the Society and from that time down to this very hour have contributed annually 3 to 500$ per year for the Support of a Baptist minister &c^a, yet I hold all *Christians alike* and thus wish to carry out the principle that all who truly love the Lord Jesus Christ and do his Will are *Brethern*, outward forms of Religion are but aids,. . .eternal life begins & ends *within* the *heart* and not the *head* we must be born again.
> So much for my Sectarianism.

g. For the last few years of her life, Mrs. Vassar was so ill that she was confined to her room. Because she was unwell, Miss Amanda Germond was hired as a house-keeper. From the correspondence of the early 1860s, it would appear that she also assumed the duties of an official hostess and was of great service to Mr. Vassar. Apparently, she had his confidence and was aware of much that was happening during those years. In the *Origin* (1879), Jewett accused Miss Germond of being among those who opposed him.

h. Dr. Nathan Bishop (1808-1880) was born in Vermont, N.Y., of New England stock. In 1822, as a student at Hamilton Academy (N.Y.) he taught several courses. He eventually completed his studies at Brown University and graduated in 1817. The five years spent there as a student were taken up with work which was necessary to finance him. A few years after graduation from Brown, he was appointed superintendent of the public schools of Providence, R.I. He built up a fine school system there and in 1851 resigned to accept a like post in Boston. In the late 1850s, he resigned this position and went to New York where he soon became involved in many independent projects. Bishop's prominence in the field of education began and was enhanced by the part he played in the reorganization of the curriculum of Brown University under the direction of Dr. Francis Wayland, president of that institution from 1827 to 1855. Bishop was a charter member of the Vassar board of trustees and was appointed chairman of the executive committee in 1865. He served on the board until his death.

i. The letter reproduced below was written by Truman J. Backus and gives the views of someone who knew Vassar slightly. Backus was the professor of rhetoric and English at Vassar College from 1867 to 1883, when he left to accept the presidency of Packer Collegiate Institute at Brooklyn, N.Y. He could not have helped knowing Vassar during his first year of residence at the college though he made no reference to the fact in his letter. The copy of the letter which he enclosed with his, was undoubtedly Vassar's communication with Kelly, chairman of the board—the letter which has been dealt with in this section. The text is as follows:

The Packer Collegiate Institute,
Brooklyn, N.Y. Nov. 26th 1888.

My dear President Taylor:

Among Mr. Wights papers, now in my hands, there is a letter from Mr. Matthew Vassar, the Founder, to the Honorable William Kelly, a copy of which is sent to you herewith.

The episode in the history of the College to which that letter refers, was reported to me by the late President Jewett. His view of the attitude of the Founder towards him, and of the influences which were active in his removal are quite inconsistent with the Founder's statement in this most interesting letter.

I have been informed that President Jewett left an autobiographical sketch in manuscript, whose publication would show that unworthy motives were operative in his removal from the Presidency of the College. But, now, that Mr. Vassar's letter has been read by Doctor Jewett's literary executor, I think it unlikely that the Doctor's view of the episode will be published.

It has seemed to me that the original letter should be in the hands of the College, and I have, perhaps with too much urgency, expressed my opinion to Mr. Wight. He is not ready to act upon the suggestion and chooses, for the present, to keep the original letter in his valuable collection of autographs. I have, however, secured his approval to my sending a copy of the letter to you, for deposit in the archives of the College.

186

You will agree with me that the letter was not written by an imbecile old man, who was compelled to remove a trusted official at the dictates of his ignorant and passionate nephews. That was President Jewett's inaccurate view of the case. . . .
With sincere congratulations and with all good wishes
I am fraternally yours,
Truman J. Backus

j. At the special meeting of the board of trustees called on 29 April 1864, Vassar's 72nd birthday, nineteen of the twenty-nine trustees were present to consider Jewett's letter of resignation. They were Vassar, William Kelly, the chairman, Anderson, John Thompson, Charles W. Swift, E. Lyman Magoon, S.M. Buckingham, Nathan Bishop, M. Vassar Jr., Benson J. Lossing, E.G. Robinson, S.S. Constant, William Hague, Rufus Babcock, Cyrus Swan, A.L. Allen, Cornelius DuBois, Sherman Sheldon, and J.G. Dougherty.

Chapter III

a. Rebecca Lawrence Lowrie, Vassar College '13, read a paper at the Fortnightly Club of Chicago in 1962. This paper, entitled "The Lady and the Brewer," took a similar view as that given here. It was much shorter and dealt primarily with the change of title from Vassar Female College to Vassar College. Lowrie gave a concise and informative résumé of Mrs. Hale's career; of her marriage to David Hale and their life together until his death five years later; of Mrs. Hale's poems, particularly "Mary had a little lamb"; of her connection with the *Ladies Magazine,* the first publication devoted exclusively to women's interests; and, then, of the beginning and success that she had as editor of *Godey's Lady's Book.* There is much in this short paper portraying Mrs. Hale's general philosophy and her ideas of woman's sphere. Lowrie's treatment of the Vassar College-*Godey's Lady's Book* connection concerned itself only with the intense and successful campaign to change the name of the college. The paper has great charm.
b. Of Vassar's letters to Mrs. Hale quoted here, six are from the Lamport Collection which is in the Francis Fitz Randolph Rare Book Room of the Lockwood Library at Vassar College. Many of Vassar's papers and much of his correspondence were sold or destroyed by the executor of his will. His Copy Book (Letter Book) survived. It and the Lamport Collection of six letters constitute thirty-two letters of Vassar to Mrs. Hale. He generally acknowledged the receipt of letters from his correspondent and, in that case, there should have been a like number from Mrs. Hale to Vassar. Of these, only six are in the archives. A few of her letters to Milo P. Jewett and John H. Raymond survive. There are as well two or three letters to other members of the board of trustees written between the years 1861 and 1867.
c. Mrs. Hale apparently thought that her son, Horatio, was competent to speak and write on the subject of college organization. Strangely enough, he had no experience in the field of education other than that he had had as a student at Harvard College in 1814. His attention was given largely to the study of ethnology. When he entered Harvard, he had already published the paper, *Remarks on the Language of St. Johns or Wlastukweek Indians with a Penobscot Vocabulary.* On graduation, he used every device to promote his knowledge in this his chosen field. He had a splendid opportunity to study the distribution of languages while on a voyage around the world with Captain Charles Wilkes. After his marriage in 1854, he was admitted to the bar and by 1856, he had established a law practice in Canada. He continued his

187

interest in ethnology and published occasional papers in the field. He was a meticulous researcher and contributed much to the development of the science of language.

d. Anna Dickinson (1842-1932) had a great reception as a lecturer in the nineteenth century. She carried her beliefs in the rights of people before large and enthusiastic audiences. Her parents were Quakers and so the rights of the individual were constantly brought to her attention as she was growing up. Very early in her life, she took up the cause of antislavery. Her first experience as a public speaker was made in a Friend's meeting where the subject of women's rights was being discussed. She became the outspoken advocate of many causes.

Chapter IV

a. Jewett wrote in his *Origin* (1879): "The dimensions given of all these rooms were ample for health and comfort, but the architect in his drawings forgot to provide closets which I had directed him to introduce into every sleeping Apartment. When I pointed out this omission Mr Renwick told Mr Vassar that closets could easily be taken out of the rooms and still leave them large enough for all necessary purposes. I remonstrated. . .but Mr Renwick insisted urging that delay would ensue. . .and Mr Vassar yielded the point—a concession which he lived deeply to deplore. Of course there is no foundation for the Story that the building was erected without a single closet within its walls, and when Mr Vassars attention was called to the fact he said, 'never mind, the Girls can drive nails into their rooms and hang their gowns on them'. "

b. The wall space of the library room was just sufficient to accommodate 10,000 volumes. The floor space, 1050 square feet, was woefully inadequate to meet the needs of 300 students and some 30-odd faculty members. No more than 30 persons could use the library at any one time with any comfort.

c. A catalogue of 4,000 books was prepared by Jewett and Vassar. The nature of this catalogue and the character of the books listed in it cannot be known for no copy of it remains in Special Collections. Furthermore by 1863, a catalogue that would serve as a basis for the selection of books for the next decade seemed necessary. William F. Poole, librarian at the Boston Athenaeum was asked to prepare such a catalogue. This he did, apparently making provision for purchases over the next few years. This catalogue, too, has mysteriously disappeared. A letter of Vassar indicated that it had been turned over to Babcock, a member of the committee on the library. That is the last reference to its whereabouts. Attempts to find it in other library collections have failed.

d. A report of the committee on the library of 30 June 1863, included the following statement: "Of the sum, $600 were expended in London securing sets of the *London Quarterly, & Edinburgh Review, Blackwood's The Gentleman's Magazine, &* other standard works at unprecedented low prices". About 400 volumes were purchased by Jewett at this time, costing about twenty-five cents a volume.

e. Here is the longer passage from which the sentence in the text was extracted:

> Dr. Elias Magoon stands out vividly in my portrait gallery. Dear, kind, eccentric man! He looked, and we all thought him in his enthusiasm, mildly crazy, but we came to appreciate him and delight in his ardor. The college bought from him his whole private art collection of pictures, folios, books, armor, etc., to stock the Vassar gallery. The books—chiefly editions de luxe—were later transferred to the library proper, and it made the librarian sore at heart to discover how much Dr. Magoon had apparently read, pencil in hand, and how much patient work in eradication must result in consequence, impossible to

accomplish wholly, as traces today testify.

Dr. Magoon was a lover and student of nature as well as art. He was a frequent visitor at the college in the spring, coming from his Philadelphia home "just to get up at five o'clock in the morning for a tramp over Sunset Hill or around the lake to hear and see the birds." My table in the dining room was near that of the Faculty, and it was a pleasure to see him come into breakfast with face aglow from his walk, and to mark the interest and brightness he carried with him.

Now and then he gave us a talk in chapel. The frequent eight o'clock lecture was not quite so welcome always as it should have been, and when one evening at prayers it was announced that Dr. Magoon would talk on art at the usual hour, there were many reluctant feet hitherward. As we entered, he was already on the platform behind the desk, on which rested a huge bouquet of wax flowers. Of course attention was arrested, and as the last comer was seated he leaned over the flowers and gazing in mock admiration began, "Now ain't that pooty?" A great wave of laughter went over the room, and if any one present had feared to be bored and grudged the hour from other duties, she forgot it all in the charm and delight of what followed this queer introduction. A hint of the true and beautiful in art, shown by contrast with ugliness that all could recognize, gave many of us our first wonderful lessen then and there.

Dr. Magoon and Miss Mitchell were warm friends in spite of difference in religious belief and opinions. She liked his unconventionalism and independence. They used to have great discussions and he took very meekly her ratings for not being "more progressive". "But do me the justice to say I try", he would retort, and if he had occasion to write a note to her was fond of signing himself "your ever growing E.L.M.".—Wood, Frances A. *Earliest Years at Vassar,* Vassar College Press, N.Y. 1909, pp. 62-64.

f. Magoon made gifts to Bates College, Lowell Theological Seminary, the Metropolitan Museum of Art, the Philadelphia School of Design for Women, the Broad Street Church of Philadelphia, and the University of Rochester.

g. See ch. I, note 10. This colorful portrait of the founder hung in Rockefeller Hall on the Vassar campus until a few years ago. It was seriously damaged by vandals but was satisfactorily restored. It now hangs in the Vassar College Art Gallery.

h. Several letters written by Vassar to Emma Church, dating from the late autumn of 1862 and continuing through June 1864, remain. These are mostly about the copies she was making for the art gallery. Benson J. Lossing in his *Vassar College and Its Founder* attributed only two in the list of copies to Church. These were *The Incredulity of St. Thomas* after Guercino and *The Blessed Mother* after Dolci. The third, the Raphael *Madonna* was listed but not attributed to her. This *Madonna,* the "Foligno," was hung back of the organ in the chapel. The wooden engraving of the interior of the chapel in *Vassar College and Its Founder,* p. 126, shows its position there.

i. As a matter of fact, Vassar was really quite perturbed about the price Church had put on the copy of the Raphael masterpiece. In one letter to her somewhat later in the negotiations, he made it clear that he found the charges excessive. "I have been in the hope", he wrote, "that you could see your way clear to forward the Foligno for a sum less than you so far named. The first price and the difference of Exchange made a very large bill before the picture is in hand. But I must leave it with you". (Vassar to Church, 18 May 1864.) Church did not lower the price. It is of some interest that she visited the college in December 1865. Two notations in Vassar's diary, one on 5 December and the other on 6 December of that year, remarked on her two-day visit to Poughkeepsie and her meeting with John Guy Vassar and Mrs. Hannah Lyman, the principal. She was suggested as a possible candidate for the professorship in art. Apparently, nothing came of it.

j. Vassar wrote to Magoon on 28 November 1863, "We just received another letter from Miss Toffey informing us that the Catalogue of prints are sold for $9,000. So it was well you did not go [to Cambridge]".

k. This last paragraph echoes a thought Mrs. Hale expressed in the *Lady's Book.* She put it in this fashion: "Man was to subdue the earth and reign over it. Woman by her moral virtues, was to subdue man, and, by the aid of the Holy Spirit, imbue him with faith in her promised seed." (See *Godey's Lady's Book,* 70:553.)

l. Vassar's understanding of the contract was that he was to purchase the complete collection for $20,000. At the same time, it must be pointed out that Magoon had the well-being of the college at heart.

m. In the Vassar College Special Collections there are several letters written to Magoon by John Ruskin. They are concerned with the purchase of four small sketches by J.M.W. Turner, the English landscape artist. At the time, these pictures were valued at about $250 apiece. Magoon eventually acquired all four and they were among the several paintings, water colors, and sketches sold to the founder in 1864. These letters are interesting for they give an idea of the respect that Ruskin came to feel for Magoon as the correspondence progressed. Jean T. Fotheringham wrote an article about these letters which appeared in *The Vassar Journal of Undergraduate Studies,* 1:231 (1926). The interesting paper suggests an idea of Magoon's method of collecting and also shows that Magoon did make valuable contacts in England through whom he secured advice and who would act for him in securing works of art. Magoon never saw Ruskin, for the only time he called upon him in 1854, the gentleman was on the Continent. A manservant with whom Magoon talked at the time of his visit gave him a sketch by Ruskin. Magoon's possession of this sketch led to the correspondence which began in 1855 and continued until 1858.

n. This may be one of the reasons for selling the collection, but the correspondence during these months gave evidence that Magoon was planning to sell his collection to the college through Vassar. After the sale, he began all over again, acquiring a library and works of art. His letters to Anderson support this contention.

o. All of the work of placing the art collection in the gallery was not done in the summer of 1864. Vassar's diary as late as November of that year made a note that "Magoon's Ford & another man this morning [came] to hang pictures in the College"; a day later, "Met Mr Ford & Ware, finishing hanging pictures this noon."

p. Magoon's original offer referred to a collection of art objects and a library on art which was to exemplify *Christianity, Illustrated by its Monuments.* The new proposal, *Transition from Art to Literature,* was an idea typical of Magoon. There did not seem to be much doubt that he assumed the books which could uphold this thesis were not a part of the original sale. Since no complete inventory had been prepared prior to the initial sale and since the contract without such an inventory was subject to any interpretation, the problem was serious. Magoon meant well and Vassar recognized this but his understanding of the original contract was that the first sale included the books which Magoon proposed to sell to illustrate the *Transition from Art to Literature,* and he meant to hold Magoon to the contract as he understood it.

Afterword

a. At this same time, the membership of the executive committee was increased from five to seven. Kelly and Buckingham were appointed to serve so that the committee was composed of Bishop, as chairman, with Buckingham, Kelly, Swan, Swift, DuBois and Matthew Vassar Jr. as members.

b. Vassar wrote a note to the secretary of the students on 29 April 1866, the day after the first Founder's Day. It speaks for itself.

> To Miss Mary L. Gilbert, Cor. Sec. of the students of V.F.C.
> My dear Madam
> Words are impotent to express my feelings at the doings at your College to honor my Birthday yesterday—to say that I was highly pleased would be a meagre reply—In truth I now learn that the heart finds things which the power of language *cannot* express, and these things occurred yesterday—Please to accept my thanks for your kindness—The scene of which will never, no never, be obliterated from my Memory.
> > I remain Dear Miss G.
> > > Yours truly &c. &c
> > > > Matthew Vassar.

SOURCES

Abbreviations

AL Archives of Adriance Library, Poughkeepsie, New York
DCL Archives of Dartmouth College Library, Hanover, New Hampshire
URL Archives of University of Rochester Library, Rochester, New York
VCA Archives of Special Collections, Francis Fitz Randolph Rare Book Room, Lockwood Library, Vassar College, Poughkeepsie, New York
ts typescript

Introduction

1. Benson J. Lossing, *Vassar College and Its Founder* (New York: C.A. Alvord, 1867), 2-3.
2. Oliver S. Tonks, "Mr. Vassar's Portraits, a history of twenty known likenesses," *Vassar Quarterly* 24 (December 1938): 5-6.
3. Lossing, *Vassar College and Its Founder*, 55.
4. Vassar to Youmans, 8 March 1861, *Matthew Vassar's Letter Book* (VCA), 1.
5. John H. Raymond, *Biographical Sketch of Matthew Vassar, the Founder of Vassar College,* in *Vassar College Documentary History,* 1:785.
6. Edmund Platt, *History of Poughkeepsie, 1683-1905,* 56,102.
7. Vassar to Allibone, 26 March 1862, *Matthew Vassar's Letter Book* (VCA), 30.

Chapter I

1. Elizabeth Hazelton Haight, ed., *The Autobiography and Letters of Matthew Vassar* (New York: Oxford University Press, 1916), 33.
2. Milo P. Jewett, *Origin of Vassar College* (1879) (VCA), 7.
3. Ibid.,2.
4. *Minutes of the Board of Trustees of Vassar College* (VCA), 26 February 1861, 1:7.
5. Frances Swan et al, eds. *Communications to the Board of Trustees of Vassar College by its Founder* (New York, 1886), 17, 18.
6. Jewett, *Origin* (1879), 4.
7. Vassar to Anderson, 2 July and 10 July 1856, (URL).
8.-12. Jewett, *Origin* (1879), 6,7,8.
13. Helen Wright, *Sweeper in the Sky, The Life of Maria Mitchell,* (Nantucket: Nantucket Press, 1949), 181.
14. Sarah A. Wallace and Frances E. Gillespie, eds., *The Journal of Benjamin Moran, 1857-1865,* (Chicago: Univ. of Chicago Press, 1948), 2:982,983.
15. Jewett, *Origin* (1862) (DCL), 2-4.
16. Jewett to Vassar, undated letter c. November 1856 (DCL), 1.
17. Ibid.
18. Ibid.
19. *Alumnae Biographical Register Issue,* Bulletin of Vassar College (Poughkeepsie, New York, 1939). See also n. d.
20. Vassar to Allibone, 26 March 1862, *Letter Book* (VCA), 30.
21. Jewett, *Origin* (1879), 35.
22. Ibid., 20-21.
23. Jewett, *Origin* (1862) (DCL), 8.

24. John Guy Vassar, *Twenty Years Around the World* (New York: G.W. Carleton and Co., 1861).
25. Rosalie Thorne Mackenna, *A Study of the Architecture of the Main Building and the Landscaping of Vassar College, 1860-1870* (Master's thesis, 1949) (VCA).
26. Vassar to Jewett, 29 December 1856, B.J. Lossing Papers (VCA).
27. Jewett to Vassar, 31 December 1856, (DCL), 1-2.
28. Ibid., 20.
29. Jewett, *Origin* (1879), 36-37.
30. Ibid., 41.
31. Milo P. Jewett, *Hints in regard to the proper location of a College for Young Ladies,* 29 April 1859 (DCL).
32. Matthew Vassar Jr., 23 March 1859, *Diary* (AL).
33. Jewett, *Origin* (1879), 58-59
34. Matthew Vassar Jr., 6 February 1860, *Diary* (AL).
35. Ibid., 9 March 1860.
36. Ibid., 13 March 1860.
37. Jewett, *Origin* (1879), 42-43.
38. Jewett to Vassar, 11 March 1860, *Origin* (1879), 44.
39. Matthew Vassar Jr, 23 April 1860, *Diary.*
40. Ibid., 30 August 1860.
41. *Poughkeepsie Telegraph,* 20 March 1860. In *Scrapbook, the Annals of Vassar,* 1.
42. Vassar to Anderson, 24 March 1860 (URL).
43. *An Act of Incorporation of Vassar Female College, Section 7, Minutes of the Vassar Board of Trustees* (VCA), 1:4.
44. Jewett to Sherman, 28 January 1861 (DCL).
45. *New York Times,* (?) January 1861, *Scrapbook* 1:3.
46. Jewett to Sherman, 21 September 1860, (DCL).
47. Ibid., undated, c. October 1860.
48. *Minutes,* op. cit., 26 February 1861, 1:11.
49. Vassar to Jewett, 29 November 1860, *Origin* (1879), 60-61.
50. Jewett to Anderson, 26 March 1861 (URL).

Chapter II

1. Vassar to Anderson, 7 May 1861, *Letter Book,* 3.
2. Vassar to Kelly, 13 May 1861, *Letter Book,* 4.
3. Matthew Vassar Jr., 3 June 1861, *Diary* (AL).
4. *Daily Press,* Poughkeepsie, New York, 5 June 1861.
5. *Poughkeepsie Daily Eagle,* 5 June 1861.
6. Vassar to the Rev. Dr. Howard Malcolm, 16 May 1862, *Letter Book,* 38.
7. *Minutes of the Board of Trustees of Vassar College,* 25 June 1861, 1:25.
8. Vassar to E.L. Youmans, 31 August 1861, *Letter Book,* 8-9.
9. Vassar to E.L. Youmans, 3 September 1861, *Letter Book,* 9.
10. Vassar to E.L. Youmans, 11 October 1861, *Letter Book,* 10-11.
11. *Poughkeepsie Eagle,* Poughkeepsie, New York, 30 September 1861, 1:21.
12. Jewett to Sherman, 27 February 1861 (DCL).
13. Jewett to Sherman, undated (late 1861) (DCL).
14. *Minutes,* 25 February 1862, 1:28.
15. Jewett to Sherman, 27 February 1861 (DCL).
16. *Minutes,* 25 February 1861, 1:8. See n. d.

17. Vassar to Jewett, 15 February 1862, *Letter Book,* 23.
18. Jewett, *Origin* (1879), 78.
19. Matthew Vassar Jr., 25 February 1862, *Diary* (AL).
20. Vassar to Rev. E.J. Goodspeed, 23 July 1862, *Matthew Vassar's Letters* (ts) 3:229 (VCA).
21. Milo P. Jewett, *The President's Visit to Europe* (New York: C.A. Alvord, 1863), 5.
22. *Minutes,* 25 February 1862, 1:30.
23. Jewett, *Origin* (1879), 81.
24. *Minutes,* 30 June 1861, 1:34.
25. Jewett, *The President's Visit,* 16.
26. Jewett, *Origin* (1879), 78-80.
27. Jewett to Anderson, 27 August 1861 (URL).
28. Horace Mann, *Report of an Educational Tour of Germany, Parts of Great Britain and Ireland,* in *7th Annual Report of Horace Mann* (London, 1846). Also, Calvin Ellis Stowe, *Report of Public Instruction in Europe made to the 36th General Assembly of the State of Ohio* (Boston: Stowe, Dutton and Wentworth, 1838).
29. Vassar to Babcock, 31 October 1861, *Letter Book,* 12-13.
30. Jewett to Vassar, 31 May 1862 (DCL).
31. *Minutes,* 24 June 1862, 1:33.
32. Jewett, *Origin* (1879), 129-30.
33. Vassar to Babcock, 9 May 1863, *Letter Book,* 64-65.
34. Vassar to Babcock, 12 May 1863, *Letter Book,* 65.
35. Vassar to Babcock, 30 May 1863, *Letter Book,* 66-67.
36. Vassar to Babcock, 2 June 1863, *Letter Book,* 67-68.
37. Jewett, *Origin* (1879), 128-131.
38. Vassar, *Diary,* 31 October 1863.
39. Ibid., 15 December 1863.
40. Jewett, *Origin* (1879), 82.
41. Frances W. Swan, *Communications to the Board of Trustees of Vassar College by its Founder* (New York, 1886), 20.
42. Jewett to Sherman, 11 April 1859 (DCL).
43. Charles A. Raymond to Cyrus Swan, 21 January 1864, (VCA), 2-3.
44. Vassar to Raymond, 6 February 1864, *Letter Book,* 90.
45. Ibid., 30 July 1862, *Letter Book,* 42-44.
46. Raymond to Vassar, 6 August 1862 (VCA).
47. Raymond to Vassar, 9 August 1862 (VCA).
48. Raymond to Vassar, 28 August 1862 (VCA).
49. Raymond to Vassar, 22 September 1862 (VCA).
50. Vassar to Raymond, 2 October 1862, *Letter Book,* 50-52.
51. Vassar to Raymond, 25 October 1862, *Letter Book,* 55.
52. Raymond to Vassar, 25 November 1862 (VCA), 2-3.
53. Raymond to Vassar, 6 February 1863.
54. Vassar to Anderson, 19 January 1864, *Letter Book,* 83.
55. Moses C. Tyler, "Vassar Female College," *The New Englander,* 21(1862):7.
56. Raymond to Vassar, 12 December 1862 (VCA).
57. Raymond to Vassar, 13 March 1863 (VCA), 1:2-5.
58. Raymond to Vassar, 24 May 1862 (VCA), 2-3.
59. Vassar to Raymond, 5 June 1863, *Letter Book,* 68-69.
60. Raymond to Vassar, 13 August 1863, (VCA).
61. Vassar to Raymond, 2 September 1863, *Letter Book,* 70-71.
62. Raymond to Swan, 21 January 1864 (VCA), 2-3,4,7.
63. Raymond to Swan, 17 February 1864 (VCA), 4.
64. Ibid.,5.

65. Jewett to Sherman, 10 March 1864 (DCL).
66. Francis Wayland, *Thoughts on the Present Collegiate System in the United States* (Boston, Massachusetts, 1842).
67. *Minutes,* 30 June 1863, 1:35.
68. Jewett to Vassar, November 1863 (VCA).
69. Jewett to Vassar, November 1863 (DCL).
70. Vassar to Jewett, 24 October 1863, *Letters* (ts), 3:306.
71. Matthew Vassar Jr., *Diary,* 15 December 1863 (AL).
72. Vassar to Magoon, 5 January 1864, *Letters* (ts), 3:324.
73. Jewett to Anderson, 8 January 1864 (URL).
74. Jewett to Anderson, 9 January 1864 (URL).
75. Vassar to Anderson, 19 January 1864, *Letter Book,* 83-84.
76. Vassar to Anderson, 28 January 1864, *Letter Book,* 86.
77. *Minutes,* 23 February 1864, 1:41.
78. *Minutes,* 23 February 1864, 1:42.
79. Jewett, *Origin* (1879), 134-147.
80. Vassar to Jewett, 2 March 1864, *Letters* (ts) 4:352-355.
81. Jewett to Bishop, 8 March 1864 (VCA).
82. Bishop to Jewett, 14 March 1864 (VCA).
83. Jewett to Bishop, 17 March 1864 (VCA).
84. Vassar to Kelly, 24 March 1864, *Letters* (ts) 4:346-350.
85. Ibid., 348-349.
86. Ibid., 349.
87. Vassar to Jewett, 9 March 1864 (VCA).
88. Vassar to Jewett, 22 March 1864 (VCA).
89. Jewett to Kelly, 16 April 1864 (VCA).
90. Jewett to Bishop, 23 April 1864 (VCA).
91. Jewett, *Origin* (1879), 143.
92. *Minutes,* 29 April 1864, 1:50-51.
93. Jewett to Sherman, 26 April 1864 (DCL).
94. Jewett to Sherman, 25 August 1864 (DCL).
95. Matthew Vassar Jr., *Diary,* 29 February 1864; 1 March 1864; 5 April 1864 (AL).
96. Vassar to his nephews, 5 March 1864, *Letters* (ts), 1:1-2.

Chapter III

1. Helen Wright, *Sweeper in the Sky, the Life of Maria Mitchell* (Nantucket: Nantucket Press, 1949).
2. *Godey's Lady's Book and Magazine* (Philadelphia), 67 (1863):276.
3. Ibid.
4. *Vanity Fair,* 3 (1861):82.
5. Mrs. Hale to Vassar, 30 April 1860 (VCA).
6. Vassar to Mrs. Hale, 8 May 1860, *Letter Book,* 1.
7. *Godey's Lady's Book,* 63 (1861):347.
8. Vassar to Mrs. Hale, 13 November 1861, *Letter Book,* 13.
9. Vassar to Mrs. Hale, 26 February 1864, *Letter Book,* 93.
10. Vassar to Babcock, 23 October 1861, *Letter Book,* 11.
11. Vassar to Carrie F. Stowe, 29 November 1861, *Letters* (ts) 2:169.
12. Vassar to Mrs. Hale, 7 January 1865, *Letter Book,* 117-118.
13. Mrs. Hale to Vassar, 21 January 1865 (VCA).
14. *Godey's Lady's Book,* 71 (1865):264-5.

15. Frances Swan, *Communications to the Board of Trustees of Vassar College by its Founder,* 13 April 1865, 32.
16. Vassar to Mrs. Hale, 6 March 1865, *Letter Book,* 120-121.
17. Mrs. Hale to Vassar, undated (VCA).
18. *Minutes,* 13 April 1865, 1:60.
19. Vassar to Mrs. Hale, 4 December 1865 (VCA).
20. *Godey's Lady's Book,* 70 (1865):278.
21. Ibid., 278.
22. *Godey's Lady's Book,* 51 (1856):468.
23. Ibid.
24. *Godey's Lady's Book,* 53 (1856):79-80.
25. Ibid., 79.
26. *Godey's Lady's Book,* 55 (1857):177-78.
27. *Godey's Lady's Book,* 66 (1863):396-97.
28. *Godey's Lady's Book,* 68 (1864):488-89.
29. *Godey's Lady's Book,* 70 (1865):279-80.
30. Ibid., 553-54.
31. Ibid., 553.
32. Vassar to Gregory, 6 November 1863, *Letter Book,* 71.
33. Mrs. Hale to Jewett, 17 February 1864 (VCA).
34. Vassar to Mrs. Hale, 26 February 1864, *Letter Book,* 92.
35. *Godey's Lady's Book,* 68 (1864):577.
36. Mrs. Hale to John H. Raymond, 6 June 1864 (VCA).
37. Mrs. Hale to John H. Raymond, 24 February 1865 (VCA).
38. Mrs. Hale to Vassar, 30 March 1865 (VCA).
39. Frances Swan, *Communications to the Board of Trustees of Vassar College by its Founder,* 13 April 1865, 37.
40. Vassar to Mrs. Hale, 7 June 1865 (VCA).
41. Vassar to Mrs. Hale, 6 July 1865, *Letter Book,* 122-23.
42. Vassar to Mrs. Hale, 29 January 1866, *Letters* (ts), 4:450.
43. Mrs. Hale to Lossing, 26 August 1865 (VCA).
44. Mrs. Hale to Anderson, 14 June 1866 (VCA).
45. Frances Swan, *Communications,* 28 June 1866, 42-43.
46. Vassar to Mrs. Hale, 27 June 1866 (VCA).
47. *Godey's Lady's Book,* 74 (1867):374.
48. *Report of the Committee on Faculty and Studies,* 25 June 1861 (VCA).
49. Frances Swan, *Communications,* 30 June 1863, 13.
50. *Minutes,* 30 June 1865, 1:13.
51. Vassar to Mrs. Hale, 25 January 1864, *Letter Book,* 85.
52. Mrs. Hale to Jewett, 17 February 1864 (VCA).
53. Ibid.
54. Ibid.
55. Mrs. Hale to Jewett, 20 February 1864.
56. *Godey's Lady's Book,* 68 (1864):577.
57. Ibid., 199-200.
58. Frances Swan, *Communications,* 23 February 1864, 23-25.
59. *Minutes,* 23 February 1864, 1:40.
60. *Godey's Lady's Book,* 68 (1864):577.
61. *Godey's Lady's Book,* 75 (1872):488.
62. Vassar to Mrs. Hale, 23 March 1864 (VCA).
63. Vassar to Babcock, 9 May 1863, *Letter Book,* 65.
64. Frances Swan, *Communications,* 25 June 1867, 46.
65. *Godey's Lady's Book,* 70 (1865):95.

66. Cornelia Raymond, ed., *The Life and Letters of John Howard Raymond* (New York: Fords, Howard, and Hulbert, 1881), 527.
67. Mrs. Hale to Raymond, 7 June 1865.
68. *Prospectus of the Vassar Female College* (Poughkeepsie, New York:1865), 27.
69. *Godey's Lady's Book*, 72 (1866):278-279.
70. Frances Swan, *Communications*, 25 June 1867, 46.
71. Ibid., 54.
72. Vassar to Mrs. Hale, 22 March 1867 (VCA).
73. *Godey's Lady's Book*, 75 (1867):354-55.
74. Vassar to Powell, 28 April 1866, *Letters* (ts), 4:531.

Chapter IV

1. Benson J. Lossing, *Vassar College and its Founder* (New York: C.A. Alvord, 1867), 131.
2. Jewett, *Origin* (1879), 41.
3. Vassar to Jewett, 29 December 1856 (Benson J. Lossing Papers, VCA).
4. *Documentary History of Vassar College*, 30 June 1863, 25-6.
5. *First Annual Catalogue of the Officers and Students of the Vassar Female College*, 1865-66 (New York, 1866), 21.
6. Magoon to Vassar, 19 January 1861 (VCA).
7. Magoon to Anderson, 14 July 1845 (URL).
8. Ibid., 1845.
9. *Report of the Committee on the Art Gallery to the Trustees of Vassar Female College*, 28 June 1864 (VCA), 3.
10. Cornelia Raymond, *A Course of Reading*, *VQ,*19 (1934):104-5. See n. e.
11. James Wynn, *Private Libraries of New York* (New York, 1860), 299-300.
12. Magoon to Anderson, 2 April 1883 (URL).
13. *Minutes*, 26 February 1864, 1:21.
14. Vassar to Swan, 25 June 1861, *Letters* (ts), 2:150.
15. C.A. Raymond to Vassar, 24 July 1863 (VCA).
16. Vassar to Emma Church, 21 November 1862, *Letter Book*, 58.
17. *Minutes of the Executive Committee of Vassar Female College*, 25 May 1863, 1:122.
18. Ibid., 30 November 1863, 156.
19. Ibid., 14 December 1864, 158.
20. Vassar to Church, 15 December 1863, *Letter Book*, 74-75.
21. Vassar to Toffey, 17 November 1863, *Letter Book*, 72.
22. Vassar to Magoon, 23 November 1861, *Letter Book*, 72-73.
23. Ibid., 28 November 1863, 74.
24. Ibid., 22 December 1863, 76.
25. Ibid., 30 December 1863, 78.
26. Ibid., 5 January 1864, 79.
27. Matthew Vassar, *Diary*, 13 January 1864.
28. Vassar to Magoon, 15 January 1864, *Letter Book*, 80.
29. *Minutes of the Executive Committee of Vassar Female College*, 23 February 1864, 1:44.
30. *Report of Committee on the Art Gallery to the Board of Trustees of Vassar Female College*, 28 June 1864, (VCA), 8.
31. Ibid., 14-15.
32. Ibid., 20.

33. Magoon to Vassar, 16 July 1864.
34. Matthew Vassar, *Diary,* 15 June 1864.
35. Magoon to Vassar, 30 May 1864.
36. Ibid., 4 June 1864.
37. Vassar to Magoon, 8 June 1864, *Letter Book,* 103.
38. Vassar to Church, 9 June 1864, *Letter Book,* 106.
39. *Report of Committee on the Art Gallery,* 53.
40. Vassar to Magoon, 19 August 1864.
41. Magoon to Vassar, 4 August 1864.
42. Vassar to Magoon, 19 August 1864, *Letters* (ts), 4:401.
43. Magoon to Vassar, undated, 1864 (VCA).
44. Vassar to Magoon, 30 September 1864, *Letter Book,* 110.
45. Magoon to Vassar, 1 October 1864 (VCA).
46. Ibid., 4 October 1864.
47. Vassar to Magoon, 6 October 1864, *Letter Book* (VCA), 111-112.
48. Magoon to Vassar, 7 October 1864 (VCA).
49. Vassar to Magoon, 10 October 1864, *Letter Book,* 112-113.
50. Magoon to Vassar, 14 October 1864 (VCA).

Afterword

1. Vassar to Bishop, 17 June 1865, *Letter Book* (VCA), 171-2.
2. Frances A. Wood, *Earliest Years at Vassar* (Poughkeepsie, 1909), 15.
3. Mary Harriott Norris, *The Golden Age at Vassar* (Poughkeepsie, 1915), 139-140.
4. Vassar to Mrs. Hale, 25 August 1866, *Letters* (ts) 4:467.
5. Vassar to Swan, 10 April 1866, (VCA).
6. Matthew Vassar, *Diary,* 15 May 1868.
7. *Minutes of the Board of Trustees of Vassar College,* 1:89-90.
8. Frances Swan, *Communications,* 48-49.
9. Helen Wright, *Sweeper in the Sky, The Life of Maria Mitchell* (Nantucket: Nantucket Press, 1949), 181.

APPENDIX 1
Books in Matthew Vassar's Library

Many of the books from Matthew Vassar's collection can still be consulted in the Francis Fitz Randolph Rare Book Room of the Lockwood Library, Vassar College. Below is a representative list of the variety of titles.

Abbott, Jacob. *A History of King Charles the First of England.* New York, 1848.
_____. *Fireside Piety, or, the Duties and Enjoyments of Family Religion.* New York, 1834.
Adlum, John. *A Memoir on the Cultivation of the Vine in America, and the Best Mode of Making Wine.* Washington, 1828.
Beadle, Delos W. *The American Lawyer and Business-Man's Formbook.* New York, 1855.
Beecher, Henry Ward. *New Star Papers: or, Views and Experiences of Religious Subjects.* New York, 1859.
Belsham, Thomas. *A Summary View of the Evidence and Practical Importance of the Christian Revelation.* London, 1809.
Bement, Caleb N. *The American Poulterer's Companion.* New York, 1856.
Bingham, Hiram. *A Residence of Twenty-One Years in the Sandwich Islands.* New York, 1847.
Bissot, Robert. *The History of the Reign of George III.* 3 vols. New York, 1822.
Black, Adam and Charles. *Black's Picturesque Tourist and Road-book of England and Wales.* Edinburgh, 1844.
Bloomfield, Robert. *The Poems of Robert Bloomfield.* New York, 1821.
Bridgeman, Thomas. *The Young Gardener's Assistant.* New York, 1844.
Buckle, Henry. *Essays.* New York, 1863.
Burns, Robert. *Poems.* 4 vols. Philadelphia, 1801.
Burr, Fearing. *The Field and Garden Vegetables of America.* Boston, 1865.
Bush, George. *Anastasios or the Doctrine of the Resurrection of the Body.* New York, 1846.
Butler, Samuel. *Hudibras.* Baltimore, 1812.
Cervantes, Migues de. *The History and Adventures of the Renowned Don Quixote.* (Trans. T. Smollett.) 4 vols. New York, 1814-15.
Chalmers, Thomas. *The Application of Christianity to the Commercial and Ordinary Affairs of Life.* New York, 1821.
Chambers, Robert. *Vestiges of the Natural History of Creation.* New York, 1846.
Cheetham, James. *The Life of Thomas Paine.* New York, 1809.
Christmas, Henry. *Echoes of the Universe from the World of Matter and The World of the Spirit.* Philadelphia, 1850.
Cleaveland, Henry. *Village and Farm Cottages.* New York, 1856.
Cochrane, James. *Protestant's Manual, consisting of sermons and tracts selected from the works of the best English divines.* Edinburgh, 1839.
Coghlan, Francis. *Hand-book for Central Europe, or Guide for Tourists.* London, 1845.
_____. *Hand-book for Italy.* London, 1845.
Cole, S.W. *The American Fruit Book.* Boston, 1849.
Colenso, John W. *The Pentateuch and Book of Joshua Critically Examined.* New York, 1863.
Coleridge, Samuel Taylor. *The Complete Works.* Ed. Professor Shedd. New York, 1860.

Coles, George. *Memoir of Miss Catharine Reynolds.* New York, 1848.

Coppée, Henry. *Academic Fallacies.* Philadelphia, 1859.

_____. *Grant and His Campaigns.* New York, 1866.

Cowper, William. *Poems.* 3 vols. New York, 1814.

Crabb, George. *English Synonymes with copious illustrations and explanations.* New York, 1832.

Curran, John Philpot. *Speeches.* 2 vols. New York, 1811.

Davidson, G.M. *A Traveller's Guide through the Middle and Northern States and Provinces of Canada.* Saratoga Springs, 1837.

Davis, Andrew J. *The Great Harmonia.* 3 vols. Boston, 1851.

Doddridge, Philip. *The Rise and Progress of Religion in the Soul.* Northampton, 1804.

Dodge, Mary A. *A New Atmosphere.* Boston, 1865.

Downing, Andrew J. *Architecture of Country Houses.* New York, 1850.

_____. *Cottage Residences: or a Series of Designs for Rural Cottages and Cottage Villas and Their Gardens.* New York, 1852.

_____. *A Treatise on the Theory and Practice of Landscape Gardening Adapted to North America with a View to the Improvement of Country Residences.* New York, 1844.

Draper, John W. *Human Physiology, Statical and Dynamical.* New York, 1859.

Duyckinck, Evert A. *National Portrait Gallery of Eminent Americans.* 2 vols. New York, 1861-64.

Durbin, John P. *Observations in Europe Principally in France and Great Britain.* 2 vols. New York, 1844.

Dwight, Timothy. *Sermons.* 2 vols. New York, 1828.

Dwyer, John H. *An Essay on Elocution.* Albany, 1847.

Edwards, Jonathan. *A Careful and Strict Inquiry into the Modern Prevailing Notions of the Freedom of the Will.* Albany, 1804.

Ewbank, Thomas. *A Descriptive and Historical Account of Hydraulic and Other Machines for Raising Water.* New York, 1851.

Fessenden, T.G. *The New American Gardener Giving Practical Directions in the Culture of Fruits and Vegetables.* Boston, 1828.

Fleetwood, John. *The Life of Our Blessed Lord and Saviour, Jesus Christ.* Philadelphia, 1822.

Fuller, J.G. *Conversations between Two Laymen on Strict and Mixed Communion.* Boston, 1811.

Fuller, Richard and Francis Wayland. *Domestic Slavery Considered as a Scriptural Institution.* New York, 1845.

de Gasparin, Agénor. *America before Europe: Principles and Interest.* New York, 1862.

Gibbon, Edward. *History of the Decline and Fall of the Roman Empire.* 6 vols. New York, 1822.

Gillispie, W.M. *Rome as Seen by a New Yorker.* London, 1845.

Goldsmith, Oliver. *Poems and also the Minstrel, or, the Progress of Genius by James Beattie.* New York, 1820.

Goodhue, J.A. *The Crucible, or Tests of a Regenerate State.* Boston, 1860.

Guild, Reuben A. *A History of Brown University with illustrative documents.* Providence, 1867.

Gunn, Alexander. *Memoirs of the Rev. John H. Livingston, D.D.* New York, 1829.

de Gurowski, Adam. *Russia As It Is.* New York, 1854.

Hammond, Jabez D. *The History of Political Parties in the State of New York.* 2 vols. Albany, 1842.

Hartley, David. *Of the Truth of Christian Religion.* Boston, 1808.

Harvey, James. *Meditations and Contemplations together with the Life of the Author.* New York, 1822.

Hicks, Elias. *The Quaker, being a series of sermons by members of the Society of Friends.* Philadelphia. 1830.

Howitt, William. *History of Priestcraft in All Ages and Nations.* New York, 1857.

Hume, David. *The History of England from the Invasion of Julius Caesar to the Revolution in 1688.* 9 vols. Philadelphia, 1821.

Hunt, F. *Letters about the Hudson River and Its Vicinity.* New York, 1863.

Hunt, Robert. *The Poetry of Science; or, Studies of the Physical Phenomena of Nature.* New York, 1850.

Huntington, Frederic D. *Sermons for People.* Boston, 1864.

Irving, Washington. *A History of New York from the Beginning of the World to the End of the Dutch Dynasty.* 2 vols. Philadelphia, 1819.

Jay, William. *Morning Exercises for the Closet for Every Day of the Year.* Baltimore, 1834.

Johnson, Louisa. *Every Lady Her Own Flower Gardener.* Charleston, 1843.

Jones, Henry. *Principles of Interpreting the Prophecies, briefly illustrated and applied.* New York, 1837.

Jones, William. *History of the Christian Church from the Birth of the Christ to the Eighteenth Century.* 2 vols. New York, 1824.

Kane, E.L. *Arctic Explorations: the Second Grinnell Expedition in Search of Sir John Franklin.* 2 vols. Philadelphia, 1856.

Kemble, Frances. *Journal of Frances Ann Butler.* Philadelphia, 1815.

Knowles, James D. *Memoir of Ann H. Judson, Missionary to Burma.* Boston, 1829.

Lapham, I.A. *A Geographical and Topographical Description of Wisconsin.* Wisconsin, 1844.

Law, William. *Call to Christians: showing the necessity of a devout and holy life.* Philadelphia, 1851.

LeSage, Alain. *Adventures of Gil Blas of Santillane.* Trans., T. Smollett. 3 vols. New York, 1824.

Leuchars, Robert B. *A Practical Treatise on the Construction, Heating and Ventilation of Hot-Houses.* Boston, 1851.

Lossing, Benson J. *Seventeen Hundred and Seventy-Six; or the War of Independence.* New York, 1847.

Loudon, J.C. *An Encyclopaedia of Cottage, Farm, and Villa Architecture and Furniture.* London, 1852.

Macauley, Thomas. *The History of England from the Accession of James II.* 2 vols. New York, 1849.

Malcolm, Howard. *Travels in South-eastern Asia.* 2 vols. Boston, 1839.

Marshall, John. *The Life of Washington.* 5 vols. Philadelphia, 1804.

Mathews, J.M. *The Bible and Men of Learning.* New York, 1855.

McCosh, James. *The Method of the Divine Government, Physical and Moral.* New York, 1851.

McIlvaine, Charles P. *Evidences of Christianity in Their External, or Historical Division.* Philadelphia, 1859.

Merle d'Aubigne, Jean H. *History of the Great Reformation of the Sixteenth Century in Germany and Switzerland, etc.* 4 vols. New York, 1846.

Michelet, Jules. *Life of Martin Luther gathered from his own writings.* Trans. G.H. Smith. New York, 1859.

201

Mills, Abraham. *The Literature and Literary Men of Great Britain and Ireland.* 2 vols. New York, 1851.

Milton, John. *Works of, with a Life of the Author.* 2 vols. Philadelphia, 1821.

Miner, T.B. *The American Bee-keeper's Manual.* New York, 1849.

Mitchell, S.A. *An Accompaniment to Mitchell's Reference and Distance Map of the United States.* Philadelphia, 1834.

Mooney, Thomas. *A History of Ireland.* 2 vols. Boston, 1846.

Moore, George. *Health, Disease, and Remedy.* New York, 1850.

Morris, J.H. *Memoirs of the Life and Writings of Rev. Andrew Fuller.* Boston, 1830.

Mosheim, John L. *An Ecclesiastical History, Ancient and Modern, from the birth of Christ to the beginning of the present century.* 4 vols. New York, 1821.

Murphy, William D. *Biographical Sketches of the State Officers and Members of the Legislature of the State of New York in 1862 and'63.* Albany, 1863.

Newman, John Henry. *An Essay on the Development of Christian Doctrine.* New York, n.d.

O'Meara, Barry. *Napoleon in Exile.* 2 vols. Boston, 1823.

Paine, Thomas. *Political Writings.* 2 vols. New York, 1830.

Pitkin, Timothy. *A Political and Civil History of the United States of America.* 2 vols. New Haven, 1828.

Pollock, K. *The Course of Time.* Boston, 1829.

Quimby, M. *Mysteries of Bee Keeping Explained.* New York, 1858.

Ramsey, David. *Life of George Washington.* Boston, 1811.

Ramsey, William. *The Drunkard's Doom.* Philadelphia, 1845.

Raymond, David. *Thoughts on Political Economy.* Baltimore, 1820.

Renan, Earnest. *Life of Jesus.* Trans. by Charles E. Wilbour. New York, 1864.

Richardson, Albert D. *The Secret Service; the Field, the Dungeon, and the Escape.* Cincinnati, 1865.

Robertson, Hume. *Life of Napoleon Bonaparte, Emperor of France, and King of Italy.* Philadelphia, 1808.

Sedgwick, Catherine M. *Letters from Abroad to Kindred at Home.* 2 vols. New York, 1842.

Shakespeare, William. *Dramatic Works.* 10 vols. New York, 1842.

Sidney, Algernon. *Discourses on Government.* 3 vols. New York, 1805.

Sinding, Paul. *History of Scandinavia.* New York, 1858.

Smith, Adam. *Wealth of Nations, An Inquiry into the Nature and Causes of.* 3 vols. Philadelphia, 1796.

Smollett, Tobias G. *The History of England from the Revolution in 1688 to the Death of George II.* 2 vols. Philadelphia, 1822.

Snowe, Joseph. *The Rhine.* 2 vols. Frankfort, 1840.

Sparks, Jared. *The Life of George Washington.* Boston, 1839.

──────────. *Letters on the Ministry, Ritual, and Doctrine of the Protestant Episcopal Church.* Baltimore, 1820.

Spencer, Herbert. *Education: Intellectual, Moral and Physical.* New York, 1861.

Spurgeon, Charles H. *Sermons.* New York, 1857.

Sterne, Laurence. *Works.* 6 vols. New York, 1813.

Strong, James. *The Gospel History, a New Harmony and Exposition of Christian Scripture.* New York, 1852.

Tanner, H.S. *American Traveller or Tourists' and Emigrants' Guide through the United States.* New York, 1852.

Thomas, E.S. *Reminiscences of the Last Sixty-five Years, Commencing with the Battle of Lexington.* 2 vols. Hartford, 1840.

Thomason, Thomas. *A System of Chemistry.* 4 vols. Philadelphia, 1818.

Townshend, C.H. *Facts in Mesmerism with Reasons for the Dispassionate Inquiry into It.* New York, 1841.

Tripp, Alonzo. *Crest from the Ocean World.* New York, 1841.

Trollope, Anthony. *The West Indies and the Spanish Main.* New York, 1860.

Vaux, Calvert. *Villas and Cottages.* New York, 1857.

Walker, John. *Elements of Elocution.* Boston, 1810.

Wayland, Francis. *A Memoir of the Life and Labors of the Rev. Adoniram Judson, D.D.* 2 vols. Boston, 1853.

Welby, Horace. *Mysteries of Life, Death, and Futurity.* New York, 1863.

Youatt, William. *The Horse.* Philadelphia, 1844.

Youmans, Edward L. *Handbook of Household Science, a popular account of heat, light, air, ailment and cleansing in their scientific principles and domestic applications.* New York, 1860.

APPENDIX 2

Letters to Taylor about Jewett

Letters to James Monroe Taylor, president of Vassar College (1886-1913) written in response to his interest in Milo P. Jewett, which arose out of his preparation of his book, *Before Vassar Opened,* (Houghton and Mifflin Co., 1914.) They are the impressions of Jewett's friends written nearly twenty-five years after his death. (Papers of Milo P. Jewett, Box 1, Folder 6, Special Collections, Vassar College.)

From the Rev. A.K. Parker, D.D., recorder of the University of Chicago:

Friday, Nov. 23, 1912

My dear James,
    Now that I am at liberty to answer your inquiries I find that your letter is not at hand, but I can recall I think its chief points.
    Mrs. Matthew Vassar, I believe, was never at all in sympathy with the College. Certainly, it owes nothing whatever to her counsels or cooperation. In fact, the good lady was a tartar. In my boyhood I used to hear all sorts of stories of her eccentricities in conversations between my father and Matthew Vassar Jr. It was always good fun when the talk turned upon "Aunt Catharine." Her queerness took the form oftenest I suspect of absurd and unexpected parsimonies to the discomfort of her husband.
    I am inclined to agree with you that the story of Miss Booth's influence is an invention of Mr. Lossing. Mary Lyon at Holyoke had perhaps more influence indirectly by her example. The story told a thousand times relates that Matthew Vassar in his first and only visit to London discovered Guys Hospital, founded by a remote ancestor (you remember John *Guy* Vassar) and this discovery suggested that he also should found a hospital. Later the project took the form of a school for indigent females. The pupils were to learn to wash and sew and cook and incidentaly do the house work. Of course the three Rs and perhaps Algebra and even Latin were to be taught. Of this in general I think there can be no question. Dr. Jewett comes in here and it is to Dr. Jewett who has never had his due appreciation that we owe the Vassar College of today. As the successor of Miss Booth he of course came into intimate acquaintance with Mr. Vassar and was able to stretch the brewer's mind to the admission of the conception of a college for women. You say you have Jewett correspondence. It must be worth examination & [I] should like to know whether it bears out my youthful impressions of Milo P. Jewett as a man of ideas, sagacity.

From Dr. S.S. Sherman:

1433 North State Street
Chicago, March 5th 1913.

J.M. Taylor D.D.L.L.D.
President of Vassar College.
Dear Dr. Taylor—
    In reply to your letter of Feb. 28th, I will say that I never had any connection with Vassar College, and was but slightly acquainted with Mr. Vassar. My acquaintance with Dr. Jewett began in 1839 when he accepted the Principalship of the Judson Female Institute of Marion, Ala. We became intimate personal friends; and I finally succeeded him as Principal of the Judson Insti-

tute. On his removal to Poughkeepsie, our correspondence was frequent and I was made familiar with his acquaintance with Mr. Vassar and with many of the preliminary steps to the founding of Vassar College. Once, on passing through Poughkeepsie, I visited Dr. Jewett and he took me to call on Mr. Vassar. After some talk about the College Mr. Vassar took us to see the grounds he had selected for the buildings of Vassar College; and this is the only interview I ever had with Mr. Vassar.

I am sorry that I can not respond more fully to the objects of your letter.

Yours respectfully,

S.S. Sherman, M.D.

Dictated

Three letters from Nathan E. Wood to James Monroe Taylor. Wood made clear his relationship to this history in these letters:

> First Baptist Church
> Massachusetts Avenue
> Arlington, Mass.
> November 13, 1912

My Dear Dr. Taylor—

You are both right and wrong in your recollections about Dr. Jewett. He confided in me his whole story by word of mouth and we agreed that a written copy of the events which led up to the founding of Vassar should be left both with Dr Edward Bright and in the Vassar Library and that another copy should be deposited in the safe of his business firm. This last copy was to be within my control, if I ever needed it to vindicate his memory. Years ago I told you the whole story and how his deposition from the Presidency came about through a confidential letter which he had written to Dr William Hague and in which he expressed himself rather strongly about Mr Vassar, his ignorance, vanity and pigheadedness, although I do not know that these exact words were used—Mr V. was very difficult to get on with in all the details of founding the College, especially in educational matters of which he was profoundly ignorant.—This confidential letter was carried in the top of Dr Hague's silk hat and Dr H.set his hat down in the late Mr Swan's office in Poughkeepsie—while Dr H was out . . . Mr S., who was an ally of the Vassar nephews who were opposed to their uncle's gift for a woman's college, read the letter and reported the contents to Mr Vassar, with the natural result that an explosion followed. Dr. Jewett was deposed only a little while before the College was opened for instruction. Hence, Dr Raymond was called (by some people) the first President of Vassar. This injustice has more recently been righted and Dr Jewett has been given his rightful place. At the 25th Anniversary, I had an earnest talk with Dr Lossing before he read his historical paper, and at my suggestion and with his own hearty concurrence after I had recalled to his memory the facts concerning Dr Jewett, he wrote in the paragraph in his address the statements concerning Dr. Jewett's presidency. I did not leave the paper of Dr Jewett with you, I simply called your attention to the fact that there were three copies of the paper in existence and that one of them was in the possession of your college. I suggested that you would find much of interest in the paper—It is in these ways that you have associated me with that paper. Refreshing my memory, I recall that Dr J. in his letter to Dr. Hague called Mr V "a pigheaded old fool" because of his obstructive methods—I think that it was this phrase which Mr. Swan kindly repeated to Mr Vassar. Upon such small matters, great events turn. Because Dr H. left his hat in Mr Swan's office, Dr Jewett's hopes were dashed to the earth—I have written more garrulously than I meant to. I am glad to hear from you again and

rejoice always in your success and usefulness—Always sincerely yours
Nathan E. Wood

Nathan E. Wood to James Monroe Taylor:

Nov. 25—1912.
My dear Dr Taylor
    Dr Jewett was one of the most refined and cultivated Christian gentlemen whom I have ever known. I have never met *his equal* for the utter charm of his felicitous English speech in private conversation—I used to leave his house with a kind of intoxication or as one in a lively dream. I did know him well, and when in the beginning of my public life spent many hours and even days in his company. When I was at the head of the Wayland Institution in Beaver Dam, Wisconsin, whenever I was in Milwaukee, I always made my home with him. He was my chief ally in rescuing that defunct institution and raising it from the dead. His mind was perfectly clear and his memory very exact even to minute details. He often referred to the determined efforts, constantly repeated, of the Vassar brothers to break his own influence over Matthew Vassar and so to divert the gift of his fortune from the founding of the College for Women. He never spoke in malice or heat, always quietly and in perfect Christian kindliness of them, but he left the impression on my mind that they did everything in their power *to prevent Vassar College.* Dr. Jewett's spirit was catholic, genial, kindly, Christian. My memory of him after all these years, during which I have met many men, is that of one of the loveliest Christian gentlemen, whom I have known. He was no weakling. Nothing that I ever saw of him would suggest even that he could write the irritable note to Dr. Hague. He was a man of such admirable poise and so equitable a temper that I should have been slow to believe in the reality of the note if he had not himself told me of it—He must have been tried beyond endurance. He was surely the ideal gentleman . . .
    With warmest regards
      I am always yours
      Nathan E. Wood.

Nathan E. Wood to James Monroe Taylor.

Nov. 30, 1912
My dear Dr. Taylor,
    You are right in supposing that Dr. Jewett originated the idea of a woman's College in the mind of Mr Vassar. Dr Jewett again and again told me the difficulty in turning Mr Vassar from the idea of a hospital to the idea of a college. Mr V. had his *mind set* on a hospital and the nephews encouraged him in it probably with the idea that it would cost less of his fortune. I still recall vividly the description of Dr J's adroit way of introducing Mr V. in the college. For example, he described to Mr Vassar again and again, how Mr V. would drive up the broad avenue in his barouche and be met with crowds of beautiful young ladies who would cover him with roses and lavish thanks on him as their wonderful benefactor. This picture was presented to Mr V. until it had laid hold of his imagination. I believe that some such thing was actually done to him afterward. I think that no man ever worked more skillfully to enlist a man in a great enterprise. I am sending you the memorial volume—It is the only copy which I had, but it ought to be in your library—You have my best wishes in your undertaking. I have read with great interest the articles which you sent me.
    With warmest regards
      Nathan E. Wood

INDEX

Allen, A.L., trustee, 187
Allibone, S. Austin, 23
Alumnae Biographical Register Issue, 183
Anderson, Martin B., trustee, 17, 23, 30, 33, 41, 45, 48, 56, 76, 90, 91, 92-3, 99, 109, 125, 148, 152, 177, 187; biographical note, 182
Avery Hall, 179 illus.
Avery, Alida, M.D., 76, 77 illus., 135

Babcock, The Rev. Rufus, 8, 9, 14, 57, 61-7, 93, 100, 161, 177, 182, 187, 188; biographical note, 181
Backus, Truman J., 131 illus., 186-7
Baptist Church of Poughkeepsie, 5, 184
Bishop, Nathan, trustee, 85, 99, 100-02, 105, 107, 108, 125, 152, 175, 187, 191; biographical note, 186; member executive committee, 173
Booth, Lydia, 14, 15, 18
Brewery, 4 illus.
Buckingham, Stephen M., trustee, 107, 173, 187, 191

Chambers, Robert, 8
Chambers, William, 8, 23
Church, Emma, 153, 189; *Foligno Madonna*, 151 illus., 155, 157, 163; prices of reproductions, 154, 189
Civil War, 45, 116
Constant, S.S., trustee, 187
Cottage Hill Seminary, 14, 17, 21, 38

Davis, Andrew Jackson, 9
Dickinson, Anna, 141; biographical note, 188
Dougherty, J.G., trustee, 187
Downing, Andrew Jackson, 9; biographical note, 182
DuBois, Cornelius, trustee, 23, 33, 45, 47, 92, 187, 191; member of executive committee, 183

Elliott, Charles Loring, 1, 41; Vassar portrait, frontispiece; 152, 184

Farrar, Charles, 90, 131 illus.
Fisher, Robert S., 185
Foord (?), 164, 190
Founder's Day, 175, 191

Gate House, 88, 141, 144, 174 illus.
Germond, Amanda, 83; biographical note, 186
Godey's Lady's Book, 38, 112, 114, 120, 129, 130, 132, 135, 187, 190; "Editors' Table," 112, 116, 120, 126, 129, 139
Goodspeed, The Rev. E.J., 53
"Grand Enterprise," 3, 29, 31, 45, 112, 140
Guy, Sir Thomas, 16, 17, 25

Hague, The Rev. William, trustee, 97, 99, 108, 187
Hale, Horatio (son of SJH), 130, 132-3; biographical note, 187-8
Hale, Sarah Josepha, 38, 112, 113, 140, 187, 190; advice on calendar, 118-9; advice on uniform dress, 117-8; crusade against "female," 120-8; crusade for "domestic economy," 138; crusade for women professors, 129-30; ideas on educated women, 120, 132; interest in Vassar College, 112, 114, 115 illus., Raymond's description of, 139; salaries of women professors, 132, 135
Harper's Weekly, 44
Harris, Ira, trustee, 38, 183
Hinkel, Charles, 131 illus.
Hoyt, Mary Frances '80, 183
Hudson River Railroad, 5, 181

Jewett, The Rev. Milo P., 17, 20 illus., 48, 66, 90, 91-4, 112, 115, 124, 129-30, 138, 146, 158, 183, 186, 187; biography, 14-5; recommendation of Emma Church, 154; relations with Babcock, 57-67; relations with C. Raymond, 68, 78, 82, 84; relations with MV, 16-39, 41-2, 86-7, 96-105; *Report of Committee on Faculty and Studies*, 81; Resignation, 57, 99-108, 125, 187; suspicions about MV Jr., 24, 41, 86, 90; trip to Europe, 51-5, 85, 129; trip to New England, 50, 129
Judson Female Academy, 15

Kelly, William, trustee, 38, 48, 100-4, 191; biographical note, 184; trustee chairman, 39, 46, 96, 105, 177, 186, 187

207